W.S.

Amontillado

...lgartener   *Krug*   *St. Julien*
...iesling   *1937*   *1940*
1937

Stokes Port

Prunier Brandy

Coin...

Bénéd...

...1 Downing Street,
... Potsdam.
...rd. July, 1945.

30.   Mr. Pu...
31.   Mr. Ra...
32.   Mr. Re...
33.   Sir Nai...
34.   Sir Fra...
35.   Mr. Taylo...
36.   Mr. Linto...
37.   Mr. ...

N CHURCHILL
BRITAIN

☆ ☆ ☆

...D STATES

...UGUSTA
...ND
...9, 1941

List of ...
i.e. 12 Members
41 ...
5 Outs...

58

1.   Lord Ampthill
2.   **Lord** Carrington
3.   Lord Clive
4.   Lord FitzAlan
5.   Lord Lawrence
6.   Lord Lloyd
7.   Lord Middleton
8.   Lord Mount Temple
9.   Lord Phillimore
   Lord Rankeillour
   Lord ...more

THE
CHARTWELL

60

A HAPPY NEW YEAR

WINE LIST | Water | Port | plain water | Zon | Wassin | Apes | Water | Bed water Boil.

Dec. 30th.
mutton Roth
Roast Chick
onions
Entremets
Cheese.

With Best wishes for
... New Year's
Eve ... year.

DINNER WITH

CHURCHILL

DINNER WITH
CHURCHILL

POLICY-MAKING
AT THE DINNER TABLE

---•◦◦◦◦•---

CITA STELZER

First published in 2011 by
Short Books
3A Exmouth House
Pine Street, EC1R 0JH

Copyright ©
Cita Stelzer 2011

A CIP catalogue record for this book
is available from the British Library.

ISBN 978-1-907595-42-4

Printed in Great Britain by Clays Ltd, Bungay, Suffolk

Jacket design by Two Associates Ltd
Typeset by Nicky Barneby @ Barneby Ltd

For Irwin,
for everything

❧ CONTENTS ❧

INTRODUCTION

On 27 October 1953 a Labour MP asked Winston Churchill during Prime Minister's Questions whether he would "indicate if he will take the precaution of consulting the consuming public before he decides to abolish the Food Ministry?" Churchill replied, to gales of laughter, "On the whole, I have always found myself on the side of the consumer." It was true; Churchill always was a great consumer when it came to food, but also when it came to drink and cigars. As this well written, meticulously researched and beautifully illustrated book shows, Churchill's appetites were enormous, and not least his appetite for life.

Nobody could be better qualified to have written this book than Cita Stelzer, an assured political and society hostess around whose own dinner tables on both sides of the Atlantic well-informed conversation sparkles, but it is nonetheless astonishing that the subject of Churchill's dinner diplomacy has not been written about before. For as the author authoritatively proves in her first chapter, Churchill used mealtimes – and primarily dinners – almost as political weapons.

Dinner parties provided the ideal opportunity for Churchill to establish a personal dominance that allowed him to get his way so often that Stelzer's scholarship counts as groundbreaking in identifying the phenomenon. His great gifts of conviviality, intelligence, humour, memory, anecdotal ability, wit, hospitality and – not least – alcoholic hard-headheadness, all helped him to charm and ultimately to persuade all but his most intellectually prosaic of guests. The fact that his daily afternoon nap meant that he rarely flagged even into the early hours of morning helped a good deal too, especially when surrounded in wartime by busy men who could not indulge in the same luxury.

Yet as Stelzer acutely observes, the social etiquette of dinner parties also provided an opportunity to discuss great matters of state with powerful decision-makers in an environment where there were no agendas, civil servants, stenographers or private secretaries to formalise things. Conversation could be directed towards the most important issues of the day without the impedimenta of official records, committee minutes or any of the other barriers to open expression that so often tend to inhibit free exchanges of view.

When Churchill went to war he fought with every weapon in his formidable personal arsenal, and Stelzer brilliantly shows how one of these was undoubtedly the dinner party.

During the course of a life devoted to persuasion, Churchill employed argument, eloquence, anger (both real and feigned), occasional threats, charm and even sometimes tears, but here we also see his deployment of the dinner party as a means of getting his way. How much better his methods than those of Hitler and Stalin ...

Now that we already have biographies of Churchill's grandmother, his bodyguard and his (wholly obscure) constituency association chairman, it is high time that we have one of his stomach. It helps that good food and drink and cigars mattered to Churchill, and that he had a late-Victorian aristocrat's taste for the best in all three. Stelzer's meticulous research proves conclusively that if he had not been the greatest world statesman of the twentieth century – perhaps of any century – he would have made a very fine sommelier or maitre d'hôtel at the Savoy or the Ritz hotels.

However, this book is not simply a paean to all things Churchillian: Stelzer also acknowledges the great man's chronic unpunctuality at mealtimes, the fact that he would practise his seemingly impromptu aperçus, and of course the way that he was able to supplement the rationing rules that made life difficult for so many of his countrymen for six long years of war (and several more of peace too). Yet if, as Napoleon said, an army marches on its stomach, Winston Churchill certainly marched to victory in the Second World War on *his* stomach, and no one in their right mind would begrudge him a mouthful of Beef Wellington or a drop of 1870 brandy as he did so.

One area in which Stelzer's scholarship makes an invaluable contribution to the protection of Churchill's reputation lies in her demolition of the arguments of those who accuse him of chronic alcoholism. Adolf Hitler was obsessed by

Churchill's drinking, describing him on various occasions as an "insane drunkard", a "garrulous drunkard" and as "whisky-happy". Similar accusations were regularly made by Dr. Goebbels' propaganda machine, and have since been made by the revisionist historians John Charmley and Clive Ponting and the former historian David Irving. In a sense, Churchill helped his enemies enormously in this, because of the great number of jokes he made himself about his own drinking, never for a moment considering it something which he needed to apologise for or explain. Stelzer's explosion of the myth, and her careful estimation of the true level of Churchill's drinking, is wholly convincing, and will hopefully set the record straight for good. Churchill enjoyed his drink, but had a constitution that could easily take it.

Stelzer's discovery and publishing of many never-before-seen photographs of people* and places connected with Churchill and his dinners is another useful contribution to our understanding of the period, the result of her diligent research in private and public archives and her acquaintance-ship with so many people – now sadly a dwindling band – who knew and worked with the great man. At breakfasts, luncheons, picnics and dinners Churchill never conformed to the Regency rules regarding the banning of politics as a proper conversational topic over meals. Instead, he would turn mealtimes into information-exchange seminars, inter-national summits, intelligence-gathering operations, gossip-fests, speech-practice sessions and even semi-theatrical per-formances. It must have been thrilling to have been present.

The visitors' book at Chartwell is testament to the way

---

*Photos of Churchill "with food and drink are extremely uncommon" writes Warren F. Kimball, *Finest Hour*, The Alcohol Quotient, p 31* in which Churchill would invite top experts in their fields to brief him during his "wilderness years" of the 1930s, almost always during mealtimes. His questing mind is just as evident in Stelzer's wartime and post-war pages. When Churchill travelled – which he did an astonishing amount during the Second World War, despite the obvious and terrifying dangers involved – he defeated the ravages of jet-lag by obeying the dictates of his hunger, and living not on Greenwich Mean Time, Eastern Standard Time or the date-line time where he was, but instead on what he dubbed his "tummy-time", eating and sleeping when his stomach told him to. It was part of his special genius that he was able to harness even his intestines to the service of his country, and to ally his own alimentary canal to the cause of victory over barbarism.

On reading this delightful and fascinating book, we are reminded that an evening dining with Winston Churchill must have been one of the most memorable and enjoyable occasions one could have hoped for, almost whatever mood he was in. (Even the black ones rarely lasted that long.) In recapturing so many of them so acutely, and placing them all in their proper historical context – complete with scores of menus – Cita Stelzer has rendered Churchillian scholarship a signal service. Bon appetit!

Andrew Roberts

PROLOGUE

───────⬦───────

This is a book about an extraordinary man deploying an extraordinary method of representing his nation's interests and, in his view, those of the English-speaking peoples. Winston Churchill was one of those rare men who made history, most notably in his decision in 1940 that Britain would not strike a deal with Hitler but would fight on.

Churchill's definitive biographer, Sir Martin Gilbert, and others have chronicled the techniques used by Churchill to develop and persuade others to accept his strategic vision for fighting the war. This book focuses on just one: his use of dinner parties and meals to accomplish what he believed

Downing Street dining room

could not always be accomplished in the more formal setting of a conference room.

It is a story of both successes and failures: success in persuading the President of the United States after Pearl Harbor to adopt a "Europe first" strategy despite the fact that America had been attacked not by Germany but by Japan, and that public opinion favoured retaliation across the Pacific rather than the Atlantic; failure in his inability to persuade another American president to meet with the Soviet Union's leaders in an effort to resolve differences that resulted in the Cold War.

Churchill had no illusions about the limits of personal diplomacy. As he told the House of Commons:

It certainly would be most foolish to imagine that there is any chance of making straightaway a general settlement of all the cruel problems that exist in the East as well as the West ... by personal meetings, however friendly.[1]

Churchill was also well aware that his success depended not only on the detailed planning that went into his dinner parties, or on his ability to make a case for his strategy of the moment. It depended, also, on facts on the ground. In late December 1941, when he visited Franklin Roosevelt for an extended round of informal and formal meetings, British troops were carrying the burden of the fight against Hitler, while the United States, so soon after Pearl Harbor, had yet to deploy a single soldier in Europe. But in the final phases of the war, by the time of the meetings of the Allies in Yalta and Potsdam, the Soviet Union and the United States were clearly the dominant powers, and there was little Churchill could do to affect the future of Europe. When he met with President Dwight Eisenhower and his implacable Secretary of State, John Foster Dulles, in 1953 in Bermuda, Britain was as close to financial ruin as any nation could be, struggling to sustain its contribution to the battle against communism and the maintenance of world order.

Sadly, it is also the case that the man who became Prime Minister in May 1940 at the age of 65, and had seen his nation through the most desperate period in its history, was by the time he attempted to appeal to President Eisenhower no longer as acute as he had been a decade earlier. The physical strain of wartime leadership as Churchill practised it – hands-on control of all details, numerous gruelling trips – the inevitable effects of age and the diminished condition of Britain combined to reduce the effectiveness of such persuasive powers as Churchill clearly retained.

Any reasonable assessment of Winston Churchill's dinner-table diplomacy must conclude that he won more than he lost. At numerous dinners at the White House he did help to persuade the Americans to throw their massive industrial and military power against Hitler, leaving Japan for later. He did use the occasion of a private meeting with Joseph Stalin to suggest a division of spheres of influence in Europe which saved Greece from communism. He accepted that he could not persuade Stalin to cede what his armies had conquered in Eastern Europe, but then again, neither could Franklin Roosevelt nor Harry S Truman. And he could not persuade Eisenhower, after Stalin's death, to seek a settlement with the Soviets, or at least to see if one might be within the reach of the West. Even so, his personal diplomacy, deployed en route to Fulton, Missouri in 1946, combined with Truman's secret information eventually contributed to Truman's willingness to adopt policies that reflected Churchill's definition of the post-war geopolitical situation after the Iron Curtain descended on Europe.

It is clear that Churchill used the informal setting of dinner parties to enhance his efforts to shape the future of Europe and the post-war world. The eminent military historian Carlo D'Este sums up Churchill's efforts:

> Not a single moment of his day was ever wasted. When not sleeping he was working, and whether over a meal or traveling someplace, he utilized every waking moment to the fullest.[2]

It occurred to me that it might be interesting to look into the details of the many dinners that Churchill organised and attended. His curiosity led him to want to know, first-hand, what his negotiating partners were like; his self-confidence led him to believe that face-to-face meetings, the less formal the better, were the perfect occasions in which to deploy his skills. And his fame enabled him to bring together the best, brightest and most important players of his day.

Where better to get to know an ally or opponent, where better to display his charm and breadth of knowledge than at a dinner table? Where better could Churchill rally political supporters, and plan strategy and tactics, than at a working dinner?

In the spring of 1935, Churchill, who was then "in the wilderness", having been out of ministerial office for six years, planned a dinner for those, like himself, who opposed the contentious India Bill then making its way through Parliament. Fifty-five MPs and Lords attended. One thank-you letter to Churchill pointed out that the dinner, held a week before the forthcoming vote, had helped "not only to steady the troops for next week but to form a rallying point for our Conservative and Imperial thought".[3] Churchill paid the £125 11 shillings and 6 pence bill from Claridge's personally.

After losing this legislative battle, Churchill resorted to dinner-table diplomacy to make the best of a losing hand. He invited one of Gandhi's supporters, G.D. Birla, to lunch at Chartwell, his beloved country house, "as a gesture of reconciliation", greeting him in the garden in a workman's apron and sitting down to lunch, very informally, without removing the apron. Birla was charmed, reporting back to Gandhi that it "had been one of my most pleasant experiences in Britain".[4]

At his dinners and lunches Churchill sought to convey information as well as to receive it and, in the case of the King, to discharge his obligation as the King's First Minister.

1915

List of Guests for 31st May at Claridges.

i.e. 12 Members of House of Lords.
     41 "   "   Commons.
      5 Outside supporters.

     58

1.   Lord Ampthill
2.   Lord Carrington
3.   Lord Clive
4.   Lord FitzAlan
5.   Lord Lawrence
6.   Lord Lloyd
7.   Lord Middleton
8.   Lord Mount Temple
9.   Lord Phillimore
10. Lord Rankeillour
11. Lord Rothermere
12. Lord Salisbury.

1.   Sir William Allen
2.   Sir William Alexander
3.   Mr.Shackleton Bailey
4.   Mr.Beaumont
5.   Mr.Bracken
6.   Mr.Erskine Bolst
7.   Mr.Hall Caine
8.   Mr.Churchill
9.   Sir Cyril Cobb
10. Sir Reginald Craddock
11. General Critchley
12. Sir A.Boyd Carpenter
13. Mr.Donner
14. Mr.Emmott
15. Mr.Fuller
16. Sir Patrick Ford
17. Colonel Gretton
18. Mr.Howard Gritten
19. Mr.Hartland
20. Captain Hunter
21. Sir George Jones
22. Mr.Lawrence Kimball
23. Sir Alfred Knox
24. Mr.Lennox-Boyd
25. Mr. Levy
26. Commander Marsden
27. Sir John Mellor
28. Mr.Nunn
29. Sir Henry Page-Croft

30. Mr.Furbrick
31. Mr.Raikes
32. Mr. Romer
33. Sir Nairne Sandeman
34. Sir Frank Sanderson
35. Mr.Taylor
36. Mr.Linton Thorp
37. Mr.Templeton
38. Mr.Touche
39. Sir William Wayland
40. Mr.H.G.Williams
41. Mr. Wragg

3rd June 19 35.

The Rt. Hon. Winston Churchill, M.P.,
Chartwell, Westerham, Kent.

Dr. to Claridge's Hotel
NEW CLARIDGE'S HOTEL L'D
BROOK STREET, LONDON, W. I.

1935.

STATEMENT

May 31st	55 Dinners @ 42/6	116	17	6
	2 Bots. Whisky @ 20/-	2		
	1 Bot. Brandy	1	5	
	26/2 Lager @ 1/6	1	19	
	8 Syphons @ 1/6		12	
	3 Perrier @ 2/-		6	
	1 Bot. Liebfraumilch Auslese 1921		14	
		1	18	

Receipt No. 9946   Room No.

NEW CLARIDGE'S HOTEL LTD.
London, W.1

Received with thanks from
The Rt. Hon. Winston Churchill
the sum of

£125 - 11 - 6

Cashier's Signature

125 | 11 | 6

Digesting the
India Bill

Churchill established a regular lunch, called his Tuesdays, to report all the details in the progress of the war to King George at Buckingham Palace. The first such lunch was on 10 June 1940, exactly a month after he became Prime Minister. Churchill shared with the King the results of the Enigma intelligence he made known to very few people, and the military details of the war and discussed military and staff appointments with his sovereign. The lunches were private, just the two men – no servants – serving themselves, buffet-style from a sideboard.

During the war, the Prime Minister also invited the King to Downing Street for dinners in the basement dining room, introducing him to British and American military personnel, and to members of the Coalition Cabinet. At Churchill's suggestion, these dinners are commemorated on an impressively large plaque still set into the wall in the Downing Street basement, now used to house the secretarial staff:

In this room during the Second World War his Majesty the King was graciously pleased to dine on fourteen occasions with the Prime Minister Mr. Churchill, the Deputy Prime Minister Mr. Attlee and some of their principal colleagues in the National Government and various high commanders of the British and United States forces. On two of these occasions the company was forced to withdraw into the neighbouring shelter by the air bombardment of the enemy.

The menu at a small lunch there on 6 March 1941 was: "Fish patty, tournedos with mushrooms on top and braised celery and chipped potatoes, peaches and cheese to follow. The drinks were sherry before lunch, a light white wine

A reinforced dining room fit for a king

(probably French) during lunch and port and brandy afterwards as well as coffee. Saccharin as well as sugar was on the
coffee tray".[5]

Churchill's relationship with the King deepened as the war
went on and they enjoyed each other's company. At one lunch
in 1943, the King surprised the Prime Minister by serving him
a special French wine from 1941, but would not reveal how
he was able to obtain a bottle from what was then behind
enemy lines.[6] Mrs. Churchill remembered that at one lunch
with the King and Queen, the Prime Minster had "tried to
interfere with the menu" but she was able to stop him and
recalled that the lunch turned out very well indeed.[7]

Churchill often said he felt more comfortable with some-

Churchill seemed to like Tuesdays for his regularly scheduled meals: when he was reappointed First Lord of the Admiralty, in 1939, he instituted another one of his Tuesdays, dinner at Admiralty House for some fourteen Cabinet colleagues and others, breaking "the ice by a Swedish milk punch".[8] And, later in the war, he had regular Tuesday lunches with General Eisenhower at which Irish stew was always served.

one with whom he had broken bread, and not necessarily at dinner. Even a tea break would serve his purpose. Early in his career, when Minister of Munitions, Churchill had to deal with a serious strike in a munitions factory. Striking workers had been deported from their homes in Glasgow. Churchill agreed to meet one of the strikers and suggested, according to the returned deportee: "'Let's have a cup of tea and a bit of cake together.' What a difference so small a thing can make! We debated over the teacups".[9] The issue was resolved to the mutual satisfaction of both parties.

Of course, for really serious dealings, dinner was the preferred venue. "If only I could dine with Stalin once a week, there would be no trouble at all,"[10] Churchill told Field Marshal Montgomery during a picnic lunch on the Normandy beaches a few days after D-Day, one of several informal picnics that Churchill held with his military commanders.

A few months later, just after D-Day, the Prime Minister asked Field Marshal Montgomery if he could visit the front, promising: "We shall bring some sandwiches with us."[11] Early in the war, Major General Montgomery had been invited to lunch on the Prime Minister's train but replied

Strategy al fresco

testily to Churchill: "The right place for an A.D.C. to lunch is in a ditch, off sandwiches."[12] But Churchill insisted and the General lunched on the train.

Churchill had definite views on sandwiches, insisting that "the bread must be wafer-thin, nothing more than a vehicle to convey the filling to the stomach", as he munched happily on some cold beef sandwiches he had brought with him.[13] Because of Churchill's sometimes troublesome indigestion, Dr. Hunt, his gastroenterologist, had, in 1936, recommended eating sandwiches before going to bed, a suggestion to which Churchill agreed.[14]

So here is a tale of some dinners – and other meals – at which Churchill changed history, and others at which he failed to do so. Dr. Leon Kass wisely sums up:

So too with friendship, whose beginnings are made possible by dinner, the shared meal itself grounds our being together. Amiability and friendliness are required and shared around the table. But it is the community of stories and conversation that is the true communion. Fellow diners get to know each other's minds and hearts, even though no one is explicitly baring his soul or trafficking in personal matters. We are drawn to those whose tastes and tales we find admirable and charming. We arrange to dine with them again on another occasion.[15]

SECTION 1

CHAPTER I

The Importance of Dinners

—————⌖—————

"As Churchill's life unfolds, it becomes an unending succession of meals with bigwigs."[1]

"Food in diplomacy can be a lubricant."[2]

Dinner parties were an important means by which Churchill rewarded friends, won over rivals and gathered information on all subjects, from diplomatic secrets to social gossip. He also hugely enjoyed them. His meals had the advantage over most other more formally scheduled encounters of being easily extended, even into the early hours of the morning, the time of day when Churchill would gather strength while others were flagging. His daughter, Mary, reports that "mealtimes tended to prolong themselves far into the afternoon or evening", with luncheons lasting until half past three or even four o'clock, and dinners going on "endlessly" after the ladies had withdrawn, to the increasing annoyance of her hostess-mother.[3]

After Churchill became Prime Minister in May 1940, these extended dinners were more than ever an important part of the day's work. At Chequers, the country house used by British prime ministers, a typical Churchillian evening during the war would run:

> From eight-thirty until nine we had drinks with Mrs. Churchill and perhaps one or two of the daughters were there. Then we went into dinner. Dinner was from nine until just after ten. Then the ladies left the room and the most amusing part of the evening started as Winston held forth in his own inimitable manner until about ten-thirty to ten forty-five. Then we would go up and join the ladies ... and marched up to the library where he ran a cinema film. About half past midnight we'd come down for a nightcap with the ladies. Finally at about 12:45 or 1 a.m. we'd go up to the main room where we used to meet. We would sit down and he would say, "Now, down to business". And then he worked there until two, or three or four in the morning.
>
> Other guests were "Sometimes a chief of staff ... sometimes a Cabinet minister, sometimes a visiting foreigner".[4]

From his earliest days Churchill was able to captivate his dinner companions. Violet Bonham Carter, the daughter of H.H. Asquith, later a Liberal Prime Minister, dined with the leading figures of the day. In 1906 the nineteen-year-old found herself seated next to the 31-year-old Churchill and was:

> spellbound ... I was transfixed, transported into a new

16

element … There was nothing false, inflated, artificial in his eloquence. It was his natural idiom. His world was built and fashioned in heroic lines. He spoke its language.[5]

John Maynard Keynes, a man not easily impressed with the eloquence and intelligence of others, wrote to his mother in September 1940, contrasting Churchill with a First World War Prime Minister, David Lloyd George:

Last night I went to my Other Club and was put next to Winston, so I had some two or three hours' conversation with him and listening to him. I found him in absolutely perfect condition, extremely well, serene, full of normal human feelings and completely un-inflated. Perhaps this moment is the height of his power and glory, but I have never seen anyone less infected with dictatorial airs or hubris. There was not the faintest trace of the insolence which LL.G., for example, so quickly acquired.[6]

The Other Club, a dining club, was founded in 1911 by Winston Churchill and his very good friend, F.E. Smith, a member of the Conservative Party at a time when Churchill was a Liberal, to accommodate the men they deemed worthy of joining. The Pinafore Room at the Savoy was the location then as it is today. Churchill always sat in the middle of one of the longer sides of the table. Membership was limited to 50 but would include not fewer than 24, and its only purpose was "to dine" on alternate Thursdays, at 8:15 punctually, when Parliament was in session. Members' names were secret (and are to this day), but the club rules are not. There were to be no

The Pinafore Room: home of the Other Club

speeches. The last rule reads: "Nothing in the rules or intercourse of the Club shall interfere with the rancour or asperity of party politics."[7]

The architect Basil Ionides, a member of the famous Victorian art-collecting family, was commissioned to sculpt a black cat. The statue would be used to fill out the table in case the diners numbered the awkward 13. This lucky cat, named Kaspar, was to have a napkin tied around his neck, and be served as if he were a regular diner, with the usual champagnes and wines and appropriate silverware.

One day Kaspar disappeared. He had been stolen in a prank but was later found to be resting comfortably somewhere in Lincolnshire. Other sources say he was found in Hong Kong. No matter. Although all conversations are secret at The Other Club, it is known that the Prime Minister was glad to have his Kaspar cat back at the table.[8]

Harold Macmillan, many years later to be Prime Minister, recalled the dinner meetings with Churchill, then Chancellor of the Exchequer, and young Conservative backbenchers in the late 1920s:

All the rest of us would sit around, sometimes late into the night, smoking, drinking, and arguing and of course listening. The flow of Churchill's rhetoric once it got under way was irresistible. Nevertheless, he quite happily allowed rival themes to be put forward.[9]

One guest, at a family lunch, reported that the Prime Minister "gave a short lecture on the various invaders of Russia, especially Charles XII".[10] Churchill undoubtedly inherited and absorbed from his mother, Lady Randolph Churchill, his skills as a brilliant conversationalist and dinner-party organiser. His mother organised a dinner party so that Winston could meet Ivor Novello whose song "Keep the Home Fires Burning" Churchill admired.[11] She, like her son, planned dinners to include both good conversation and beautiful surroundings.

Churchill also displayed his talent for the theatrical, using the dinner table and its settings as props. James Lees-Milne, the noted diarist, dined at Chartwell in 1928 and remembered that:

One evening we remained at that round table till after midnight. The table cloth had long ago been removed. Mr.

Churchill spent a blissful two hours demonstrating with decanters and wine glasses how the Battle of Jutland was fought. It was a thrilling experience. He got worked up like a schoolboy, making barking noises in imitation of gunfire and blowing cigar smoke across the battle scene in imitation of gun smoke.[12]

Churchill's interest in recreating battlefield tactics extended to the American Civil War. One biographer noted that Churchill "using salt shakers, cutlery, and brandy goblets … can re-enact any battle in that war, from Bull Run to Five Forks".[13]

The greatest tribute to Churchill's ability to enthrall in company comes from as renowned a conversationalist as Franklin Roosevelt, the man whom the historian Andrew Roberts describes as being, like Churchill, "stratospherically self-confident".[14] On the occasion of a dinner for Churchill, the Canadian Prime Minister Mackenzie King, and others during Churchill's December 1941 visit to the White House, the President "willingly turned the show over to Star Boarder Winston Churchill, leaned back and listened to the leader of another fighting people carry the conversational ball".[15]

But Churchill was interested in more than merely the exercise of his rhetoric and the airing of his ideas at the dinner table: he was perpetually in search of information, and used lunches and dinners to pick the brains not only of political allies and opponents, but also of specialists and academics, including many not necessarily in tune with his own views.

During the First World War, when Churchill was Minister of Munitions, his office on the Western Front was at Chateau Verchocq in north-west France. In August 1918 he was there with his brother Jack, Sir Maurice Bonham Carter and several political and military figures. Churchill's pilot, Lieutenant Gilbert Hall, reports:

> In the evening we all assembled in the dining room for a meal … At that first meal Mr. Churchill sat at the head of the table and acted as host. Food was not too plentiful in the fourth year of the war and the first course was a plain and wholesome Shepherd's pie. Mr. Churchill, with characteristic brio, referred to it as "minced meat under a glorious cloud of mashed potatoes", and it tasted all the better for that.[16]

Churchill energetically quizzed the group on a wide range of topics, including how to get tanks, "the new surprise weapon", across rivers, and attitudes on the home front towards the progress of the war.[17] More than ten years later, Churchill played host to Harold Laski, called by his biographers "everyone's favourite socialist … the enduring conscience of the British left",[18] among a company that included an admiral, several other naval officers and a young civil servant. Churchill had an opportunity to note how well (or poorly) the naval men handled a debate Laski initiated on "the meaning of maritime rights"; and to learn from the civil servant something about Radclyffe Hall, the author of the just-published lesbian novel, *The Well of Loneliness*.[19] R. A. Butler ("Rab"), President of the Board of Education during the war years, contended that dinner parties were a good source of information which he could not get sitting in his office. "Wives talk …".[20]

Joseph E. Davies, when serving as American Ambassador to the Soviet Union, dined with the Churchills in their London apartment in May 1937 and recorded in his diary:

He plied me with questions ... He ... wants to know the facts ... He asked about the strength of the Soviet industry and the army ... He impressed me as a great man.[21]

At these lunches and dinners, Churchill acquired and improved relationships that would stand him in good stead at some later point in his career. Even the dinner he organised at Claridge's in 1932 to celebrate his son Randolph's "coming of age" included what one guest described in his note of thanks as "Men who have made history and others who will no doubt figure equally prominently in the future".[22] Another commented: "It will be a very long time – if ever – before I find myself in a gathering of people such as these ..."[23] The bill from Claridge's came to £135 16 shillings and 8 pence*. The dinner was on 16 June, the hotel billed Churchill on 17 June and was paid promptly on 22 June.[24]

Churchill also used dinner parties to advance his financial interests. In 1929 he visited the media mogul William Randolph Hearst, who arranged a lunch for 200 guests at the MGM bungalow of his mistress, Marion Davies, in Churchill's honour and a lunch for 60 at the exclusive Montmartre Restaurant in Los Angeles.[25] This resulted in several remunerative journalistic assignments.

Financial wizard Bernie Baruch, whose advice Churchill often sought about money matters, and who later became an important adviser to President Roosevelt, was another important dinner companion. When Baruch visited Britain in 1933, Churchill organised a dinner in his honour at Claridge's – dress to be white tie and tails – carefully choosing between the two "specimen" menus offered and selecting as

---

*Close to £7,000 in today's money.

17th. June *1932* (21)

The Rt. Hon Winston Churchill, M.P.,

D.ʳ to Claridge's Hotel.
NEW CLARIDGE'S HOTEL LTᴰ

BROOK STREET, LONDON, W.1.

1932.

STATEMENT

Hotel Account		9	1	8
Dinner "		126	15	
		£ 135	16	8

THE CHARTWELL TRUST (stamp)

Receipt.№ **13039**   Room.№. *lay*

NEW CLARIDGE'S HOTEL LTD.

London, w. 1. 22 - 6 - 1932 .

RECEIVED *with thanks from*

The Rt Hon Winston Churchill M.P.

the sum of One hundred + thirty five

£ 135 - 16 - 8

M.P 16/8

Cashier's Signature H Beard

THE CHARTWELL TRUST (stamp)

Randolph's 21st birthday, 1932

accompaniment his favourite Pol Roger, of which six magnums were consumed by Churchill, Baruch and their eighteen guests.[26] He also asked Baruch for sufficient advance notice so that he could be certain to gather an interesting group. "As much trouble should go to considering the guests" as considering the food at dinner parties, agreed Woodrow Wyatt, Labour Member of Parliament elected in 1945 (later Lord Wyatt).[27]

Churchill was sensitive to the needs of his guests, in this case Baruch's need for privacy. So when *The New York Times* requested permission to photograph the guests on the night, Churchill refused.[28]

In the early 1930s, Churchill wrote a letter to *The Times* protesting at the habit that was then developing of taking photographs at banquets while people were eating. He felt strongly that this was an intrusion, and that photographs should be taken only at the start of the formal proceedings.[29]

Protecting his guests' privacy was just one example of Churchill's careful discharge of his duties as host. One guest described him as a "meticulous host. He would watch everyone all the time to see whether or not they wanted anything".[30] Another commented:

> It is a marvel how much time he gives to his guests … He is an exceedingly kind and generous host, providing unlimited champagne, cigars and brandy.[31]

And still another, Anthony Montague Browne, described Churchill "as a generous and entertaining host and dinners with him always fun and gastronomically agreeable".[32]

Joan Bright, who throughout the Second World War organised overseas travel for Churchill and the Chiefs of

Do not confuse his meticulous attention to details for dinner parties with any culinary skills, his claims to the contrary notwithstanding. Once, when Chartwell was closed, and Mrs. Churchill told him it would be impossible to spend the weekend there because there was no one to cook for him, he replied: "I shall cook for myself. I can boil an egg. I've seen it done."[33] Brave talk. Lady Williams told me that Churchill "certainly never, to my knowledge, looked at a grill or could boil a kettle". Churchill was interested in dining not in cooking. And this despite his determination to acquire other practical skills like bricklaying.

Staff, said he had lovely manners.[34]

Churchill was certainly aware that his talents were shown to best advantage on a carefully set stage. In 1929 he wrote to his wife from Santa Barbara, California, where he had been visiting Hearst:

I am v. glad you are taking Venetia's [Montagu] house for the session. Do not hesitate to engage one or two extra servants. Now that we are in opposition we must gather colleagues and MPs together a little at luncheon & dinner. Also I have now a few business people who are of importance. We ought to be able to have luncheons of 8–10 often & dinners of the same size about twice a week. You shd have a staff equal to this.[35]

In 1922 Churchill had bought Chartwell, a country house in the county of Kent, within easy driving distance of London. It required a considerable amount of renovation, which he supervised, and some of which he carried out "with the same meticulous obsession he gave to his speeches".[36]

Churchill's favourite stage: the dining room at Chartwell

Dining at Chartwell, 1928

Perhaps aware of the effect of the low ceiling in the dining room, to which he paid particular attention, Churchill specified floor-length windows and doors on three sides of the almost-square room to give it an open feeling. He directed to his wife a Dissertation on Dining Room Chairs:

> The Dining Room chair has certain marked requisites. First, it should be comfortable and give support to the body when sitting up straight; it should certainly have arms which are an enormous comfort when sitting at meals ... One does not want the Dining Room chair spreading itself, or its legs, or its arms as if it were a plant ... this enables the chairs to be put close together if need be, which is often more sociable ...[37]

The fun goes on. His wife answered that she had "digested his Dissertation".

Today, under the care of the National Trust, Chartwell remains much as it was during Churchill's time, with white-flowered chintz on comfortable armchairs around a great round table in the dining room: round to ease conversation and create a sense of equality, no opposing sides, nor corners, no one below the salt.

Two months before Churchill left for the Potsdam Conference and before the 1945 election, his cousin, Clare Sheridan, needing money, wrote to him offering to sell him her mother's set of Napoleon's special china. Clare's mother was Lady Randolph's sister, Clara. Clare thought the Prime Minister ought to have the china "on account of its family association ... Before the Tuilleries [sic] were burnt [1871], the Commune sold at auction the contents! And our dear grandmother Jerome was there, bless her, and bid on the Tuilleries [sic] lawns for the china".[38]

Thomas Goode appraised the china and Clare attached the listing for Churchill's consideration. Always considerate of family, Churchill sent her a cheque for more than the amount requested. The large set (38 dinner plates!) is white Sèvres china, gold-rimmed, with a large gold N below a crown – "the same monogram on chiffre as that of the first Napoleon".[39] I am told that Churchill used this china at Chartwell, where it is on display today.

Attention to detail remained the order of the day at Chartwell even after its completion. For a garden party on Saturday 21 July 1934, the marquee was to be lined in olive green and lemon,[40] and to accommodate some 250 guests, "all sitting at one time" according to the caterer's notes. The menu was predictably lavish, and equally predictably, the musical selections reflected Churchill's preference for Gilbert and Sullivan – selections from HMS *Pinafore*, *The Gondoliers*, and *Iolanthe*. And a bit of Clementine caution – insurance against rain, with the pay-out a function of the amount of rainfall: reportedly 30% of the insured amount for .5 inches of rain, up to 100% if .15 inches fell. It did not rain. [41]

Nothing was more important to Churchill than the seating arrangements at his dinners, as we shall see when describing the Big Three dinners in Teheran, Yalta and Potsdam. He personally undertook this chore, which other politicians usually left to diplomatic wives or officials, reflecting yet another lesson learned from his mother, the widely acclaimed society hostess. She carefully seated strangers and, often, people who were not friendly, next to each other at her

MENU.

Indian and China Tea
Brown and White Bread and Butter

Sandwiches de Volaille, Jambon,Tomate,
Foie Gras, Oeufs et Cressonnette, Napolitaine
Caviar, Saumon Fume
Cucumber

Canapes Royale
Petits Pains Bechamel
Petits Pains Fourres

Eclairs, Millefeuille, Glace Fingers
Chocolate Leaves, Petits Fours Glaces

Savoys, Madeleines, Genevas
Royal Hearts, Champagne Fingers

Raspberries or Strawberries and cream

Orangeade   Lemonade
Hot Coffee   Iced Coffee

Strawberry and Vanilla cream ices
Wafers

----ooo----

*Chartwell garden party and
Mrs. Churchill's prudence*

Mrs. Churchill

Gunters telephoned about your insuring against rain
for the Garden party, and gave the following particulars:-

If .5 of an inch of rain falls, the insurance company will
                                  pay 30% of the amount for
                                  which you insure.
If .10 "   "   "   "   "   60%
If .15 "   "   "   "   "   100%

If you wish to insure for 12 hours you pay 20% of the value
                                   you want insured
       "   "   9   "   15%
       "   "   6   "   10%
       "   "   "   6%

The rain is measured from the nearest official place.

Westwood
Pumping Station
Limpsfield Chart 87.

dinner parties, calling them the "dinner of deadly enemies".[42] Churchill said of his mother that "In my interest she left no wire unpulled, no stone unturned and no cutlet uncooked."[43] As a young man, he once sent her a letter of New Year's wishes, with a sketch of her holding a menu.

President Eisenhower, interviewed years later, remarked on the great attention Churchill paid to correct placement at dinners. He said Churchill always put him on his right at the table, explaining: "anybody who held a commission from two countries outranked anyone who had a commission from one". Only once did this change. Churchill rang him to explain that he would have to sit on his left as

My old friend Field Marshal Smuts is to dinner with us this evening. Won't you give up your place on my right and take a place on my left?[44]

Detailed attention extended to costs. Churchill quite regularly questioned bills received from Claridge's and the Savoy,[45] but was always careful to reward staff at such venues, for example adding £3 to the bills for his dinner for Baruch and again for a dinner for sixteen at Claridge's on 30 January 1935, for which the manager thanked Churchill profusely.[46]

In one letter, Churchill thanks the Savoy Hotel manager for sending back his opera hat which he had left at the hotel. He then complains that the charge included a full bottle of port, whereas only one half was consumed, and requests the details on the charges for cigars and cigarettes.[47] The manager responds fully, giving details of the expenses: no cigarettes were consumed and the bill was adjusted, but the eight cigars, two of which were taken away by Churchill's son, are listed and named.

11th September 1937

Dear Sir,

I am desired by Mr. Churchill to thank you for your letter of September the 6th, and to say he is not prepared to pay for more than half the bottle of port, and he will give a gratuity of 10/-.   I therefore enclose Mr. Churchill's cheque for £8.19. 0.

Yours faithfully,

Private Secretary

Restaurant Manager,
The Savoy Hotel.

*Best to look over
the bills*

3rd November 1934

Dear Sir,

Mr. Churchill is surprised at the amount of this bill which works out at nearly £ 3 a head. The dinners which the Other Club hold at the Savoy every fortnight or so cost 21/-, irrespective of course of the membership fee each year. and they are in every way equal in quality to that provided by Claridges on the 30th. Oysters are invariably supplied in the season and probably a larger consumption of wine and spirits per head also. Mr. Churchill thinks that for a single dinner of this kind £ 2 or £ 2.5.0 a head inclusive of everything would have left ample profit to the hotel. Mr. Churchill will of course send you a cheque for the amount of your bill, but if your charges range upon this scale, he will not be able to come again to Claridges. He will regret this as he likes the apartments and had hoped to give more dinners there.

Yours faithfully,

Private Secretary.

The Manager,
Claridges Hotel.

The missing port is explained:

Martinez Port was as usual charged for by the bottle out of which five glasses were consumed. The remainder, that is to say more than half the bottle, is being kept at the bar for Mr. Churchill's use next time we are honoured with his patronage.[48]

The letter then specifies that:

Two Half Cider Cups were ordered and served. As to the Whiskey, when the bottle was returned to the bar it was found that nine measures had been consumed. The 7/6d Liqueurs is for the Brandy which Mr. A. Eden had.[49]

Note that at these functions the whisky bottles were left on the table for guests to serve themselves.

Churchill's fondness for combining dining and business extended to picnics. Some of the picnics he organised during the Second World War were hastily convened conferences with his field commanders to discuss tactics and strategy – one in the sands at Tripoli in 1943 and another one "somewhere in north-west Europe". Concerned as always for the morale of his troops as well as the British public, Churchill had tea with Royal Air Force pilots and with army gunners.

At another picnic, during a campaign tour, he was accompanied by his daughter, Sarah. Still others, later in life, were jolly affairs including large numbers of friends and associates.

Churchill had his own idiosyncratic picnic customs: some snippets of verse were to be recited only at picnics, and there

Churchill and British generals, Alan Brooke, Montgomery and Ismay, plus Randolph, picnic in the desert, Tripoli, 1943

Churchill and American generals Eisenhower and Patton, picnic lunch in northwestern Europe

Tea with RAF pilots, September 1941

*Picnic on the hustings, Churchill's daughter, Sarah, pouring tea,
June 1945*

Lady Diana Cooper, in her memoirs, described a 1944 picnic with Churchill in the North African desert in some detail "... we laid out our delicatessen, the cocktail was shaken up, rugs and cushions distributed, tables and buffets appeared as by a genie's order ... he is immediately seated on a comfortable chair ... a pillow put on his lap to act as a table, book-rest etc. A rather alarming succession of whiskies and brandies go down, with every time a facetious preliminary joke with Edward, an American ex-barman."[50]

Picnic at Marrakesh 1944

Her husband, Duff Cooper, summarises the seven picnics in a two-week stay in Marrakesh as comprising "large amounts of food and drink". It seemed to him "a curious form of entertainment".[51]

As late as 1948, when Churchill was 74, one of his secretaries reports that at a picnic in Morocco the fare included "a whacking great slab of ice (to keep the white wine cool), a box of cold luncheon ... consisting of poached eggs and ham in aspic jelly (2), two slices of cold beef, half a cold chicken, potato salad, bread, butter, 2 apricot or strawberry tarts, cheese, orange, tangerine and lots of wine and brandy".[52] A reasonable repast after a hard morning at the easel.

was singing while "drinking old Indian Army toasts" at the end of every picnic.[53]

No matter the circumstances – whether in the dining room at Chartwell or on a picnic chair in the desert – Churchill's profound belief in the importance of face-to-face meetings, and his unshakeable confidence in his ability to get his own way in such intimate encounters, never wavered. It is summed up in a telegraph to Roosevelt, sent shortly before he headed to Moscow in October 1944: "I feel certain that personal contact is essential."[54]

Churchill thought such personal contact, preferably at dinner, important not only with allies, but also with enemies. He planned to bring the Greek Civil War to an end by inviting the Communist Greeks to the negotiating table with the Greek Archbishop, Damaskinos, in Athens at Christmas 1944. There Churchill reversed his earlier vow not to shake hands with the three ELAS representatives, and afterwards told Lord Moran that he "felt that if the three Communists could be got to dine with us all difficulties would vanish".[55]

On board HMS *Ajax*, off the coast of Athens, where Churchill, Eden and others were staying (for their own protection) during the Christmas 1944 meetings, a temporary valet, who usually cared for Commanders-in-Chief, was assigned to Churchill. He complained to his

36

Admiral that Churchill "breakfasts at nine-thirty in the morning off a wing of chicken and a bottle of white wine … "[56] Perhaps an accurate report, perhaps not.

Churchill could not always convert his dominance of the dinner table into dominance of events. Conversational skills and conviviality were no match for facts on the ground, as he was well aware, or for the need of other leaders to pursue the interests of their own nations, as they perceived them.

Three of Churchill's diplomatic defeats – the losses that most affected the shape of the post-war world – came at dinner tables at Yalta (1945), Bermuda (1953) and in Washington (1954), the latter when he was 80. On each of these occasions, an American president failed to succumb to Churchill's immense personal charm and intellect.

At Yalta, Roosevelt used the Big Three dinners to make it clear to Stalin that Churchill was no longer to be regarded as consequential a player as he had been and they now were. In Bermuda in 1953 and again in Washington in 1954, when he once again lived at the White House, Churchill was unable to persuade President Eisenhower, or his Secretary of State, John Foster Dulles, to agree to a summit meeting with the Soviets. This was particularly galling, since Eisenhower arguably owed his career and the wartime reputation that eventually landed him in the White House to Churchill, who had even amended the US edition of his history of the Second World War to delete anything unfavourable to Eisenhower. Churchill, fearful of the consequences of a continuation of the Cold War, was convinced that the Anglo-American Allies should meet with the new Soviet leaders to try to end or ease the tensions before they led to a nuclear war.

Despite the opportunity presented by dinners in balmy Bermuda, and a three-night stay in his familiar haunt, the White House, Churchill was defeated in his quest for trilateral talks by the intransigence of John Foster Dulles and Eisenhower's view that "under this dress" – the dress of post-Stalin Russia – the Soviet Union was "still the same old girl" – a "woman of the streets".[57] Of little use to the outraged Churchill was Eisenhower's assessment of the wartime leader's place in history: "He comes closest to fulfilling the requirement of greatness of any individual that I have met in my lifetime."[58]

The defeat at Bermuda must be viewed in the light of John Foster Dulles' implacable opposition to any negotiations with the Soviet Union and in the context of what Churchill's special brand of personal, dinner-table diplomacy had accomplished in the past. One of the leading military historians of our time, Eliot Cohen, puts it best:

> Churchill's conduct of the diplomacy of war reveals an extraordinary blend of techniques and approaches ... The cohesiveness of the Grand Alliance stands out as a remarkable feat. Churchill's personal control of those relations – through extensive correspondence and frequent overseas trips for private meetings and the large conferences that dominated the strategy of war – accounts for much of the success.[59]

Churchill, a star player on the world's stage for more than 50 years, looking back on his time spent at dinner tables, could be confident that those meals involved a lot more than excellent food, good champagne and robust cigars. One achievement – if one were needed – the establishment of the special relationship with Roosevelt that was so crucial to defeating Nazi Germany, clearly outweighs any subsequent setbacks.

CHAPTER 2

Meeting off Newfoundland
August 1941

———————⬡———————

"It is fun to be in the same century with you."[1]
President Roosevelt to Prime Minister Churchill

When Churchill became Prime Minister in May 1940, he was powerfully aware that his best chance – probably his only chance – of not losing the war was to persuade the United States to come in on Britain's side. But America in May 1940 was in no mood to have its sons fight again in foreign wars, and, in the election in November of that year, President Roosevelt promised he would never send Americans on such a mission.

Churchill also knew of a considerable reservoir of anti-British feeling among two important voting blocs in the United States, the Irish- and German-Americans.

Many Irish-Americans were "instinctively anti-British"[2] and opposed, with a harsh hatred, British rule in Northern Ireland. Joseph Kennedy, a leader of Boston's Irish community and the American Ambassador to the Court of St. James's*, sent the President several emphatic reports claiming that Britain could not possibly defeat Hitler. And 20,000 German-Americans rallied at Madison Square Garden in New York in February 1939, in opposition to Roosevelt's increasing criticism of Hitler's foreign policy.

All this made it urgent, in Churchill's view, that he meet face to face with Roosevelt. The two had been corresponding on a regular basis for several years but Churchill felt correspondence was no substitute for a face-to-face meeting. Harry Hopkins, the President's closest adviser, had told Churchill on his crucial visit to Britain in January 1941 that the President was also eager for such a meeting.[3] The Prime Minister intended to explain Britain's situation, persuade Roosevelt to help, belatedly, with the loan – better still, the gift – of destroyers, and pave the way for America's entry into the war as soon as the President felt it would be politically possible for him to take such a step. Churchill believed, as he wrote to the President, a conference between them "would proclaim an ever closer association and would cause our enemies concern, make Japan ponder, and cheer our friends".[4]

Most heartening to Churchill was Hopkins' news that Roosevelt favoured a meeting. Personally welcome, too, were the gifts Hopkins brought with him from America: "ham, cheese, cigars etc. for the P.M.",[5] the first of many food parcels the Churchills were to receive from the Roosevelts. In Washington, planning for the meeting was top secret: the

---

*The official title of the US Ambassador to the United Kingdom.

Washington press corps was told that the President was going fishing off the Maine coast on board the USS *Potomac*, his presidential yacht. He was then transferred to the USS *Augusta* on the morning of 5 August to sail to Newfoundland.

In London, the Prime Minister's plans were also top secret. Colville writes in his diary: "The PM disappeared to Chequers and I shall not see him for a fortnight as he is very shortly off on a historic journey (Operation Riviera!)."[6] On 3 August, Colville notes, Churchill took the train "north with a retinue Cardinal Wolsey might have envied".[7]

The Foreign Office diplomat, Sir Alexander Cadogan, records in his diary that, on board the Prime Minister's

The Prime Minister's railway dining car

private train, he and Churchill had a "V. good lunch – tomato soup, sirloin of beef (in unlimited quantities and quite excellent), delicious raspberry and currant tart".[8] On 4 August, Churchill boarded the *Prince of Wales*, at Scapa Flow, the deepwater harbour of the Atlantic fleet in the Orkney Islands off Scotland's far north-eastern coast.

The North Atlantic seas were rougher than usual, and the destroyer escorts were alert to U-boats, whose presence in the area had been confirmed. An erratic course was taken in an attempt to evade the enemy. Churchill, however, was not worried and enjoyed the trip. His mind was on the work to be done to prepare for the meeting with Roosevelt. But he had also planned his leisure time, bringing along his favourite films. On the first night out, he and his staff watched *That Hamilton Woman* (about Lord Nelson's mistress, a story of British defiance in the Napoleonic Wars, appropriate for a wartime sea voyage), and *Pimpernel Smith*, a 1941 remake of the 1934 movie, *Scarlet Pimpernel*, based on Baroness Orczy's swashbuckling novel about a dashing hero who saved French aristocrats from the revolutionary guillotine. In the updated version, Leslie Howard (who also produced) smuggles Nazi victims out of Germany.

Churchill read what he cites as "Captain Hornblower R.N." by C.S. Forester, and cabled his Minister of State for the Middle East, Oliver Lyttelton, who had recommended it: "Hornblower Admirable". This created a minor flurry amongst senior officers on board as to what possible military or naval operation had the code name "Hornblower". Throughout the trip, the Prime Minister clearly enjoyed himself, even though the crew were continually anxious about the U-boat threat.

Planning for meals had been meticulous: the ovens of

the *Prince of Wales* could bake 1,500 loaves of white bread; and to its distinguished passengers its galley challenged "comparison with the kitchens of The Ritz".[9] Provisions aboard were "ceiling-high", including chocolates and cigarettes. Cadogan, whose diaries contain more comments on food than do those of any of his contemporaries, tells us: "We took on a cargo of grouse in Scotland, and we have some very nice beef. Masses of butter and sugar".[10] The grouse, a Churchill favourite[11], were available because, it seems, the grouse season was opened earlier than usual to allow shooting to supplement rationed foods. The butter and sugar were especially appreciated since they had been rationed since January 1940.

On 6 August, Cadogan again records a memorable meal. The ship was in mid-Atlantic, in dense fog, awaiting a new flotilla of destroyers that had set out from Iceland to guard the convoy. Harry Hopkins was on board one of the ships in the flotilla, hitching a ride home after his visit to Stalin. Hopkins had brought along

> a tub of admirable caviare, given him by Joe Stalin. That, with a good young grouse, made a very good dinner. As the PM said, it was very good to have such caviare, even though it meant fighting alongside the Soviets to get it.[12]

When Hopkins, who years earlier had had two-thirds of his stomach removed due to a cancer, prudently refused a second brandy, the Prime Minister said, "I hope that, as we approach the US, you are not going to become more temperate."[13] It was another instance of Churchill's contribution to the myth-making and humour about his drinking habits. Hopkins recorded Churchill's high spirits about his forthcoming meeting with the President: "You'd have thought he was being carried up to the heavens to meet God."[14]

On 9 August, the *Prince of Wales* sailed into Placentia Bay, Newfoundland. An eager Churchill and his staff then crossed by barge to the USS *Augusta*, where the Prime Minister handed the President a personal letter from King George VI, smiled, shook hands and lit his signature cigar. The President lit his cigarette and to Churchill's delight, invited him to remain aboard for a tour and a private lunch. That evening, the President invited the Prime Minister and his party to return for a formal dinner, at which broiled spring chicken, vegetable puree, spinach omelettes, candied sweet potatoes, hot rolls, currant jelly, mushroom gravy, tomato salad and cheeses were served. Dessert was a choice of ice-creams, cupcakes or cookies, or all three for the food-rationed British guests. "In place of liqueurs, they were offered coffee, tea, mints ..."[15] Surely wines were served, as the presidential party was not subject to a dry Navy rule, but they are not listed on any menus or mentioned in letters or diaries.

Churchill had spent many hours devising a Divine Service for the following day, Sunday, 10 August, to be celebrated on board the *Prince of Wales* with Roosevelt and crew members from both ships. Ever alert to possibilities that would enhance what came to be called the special relationship, the Prime Minister instructed members of his staff not to stand at attention during the church parade but to mingle freely and informally with their new American friends.

It was a very moving occasion. Churchill chose two hymns and asked the President to choose another. Churchill chose "O God Our Help in Ages Past" and "Onward, Christian Soldiers". The President chose his favourite, "Eternal Father, Strong to Save", the official US Navy hymn,

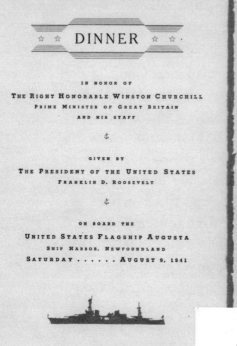

DINNER

IN HONOR OF

THE RIGHT HONORABLE WINSTON CHURCHILL
PRIME MINISTER OF GREAT BRITAIN
AND HIS STAFF

⚓

GIVEN BY

THE PRESIDENT OF THE UNITED STATES
FRANKLIN D. ROOSEVELT

⚓

ON BOARD THE

UNITED STATES FLAGSHIP AUGUSTA
SHIP HARBOR, NEWFOUNDLAND
SATURDAY . . . . . . AUGUST 9, 1941

President's dinner for the Prime Minister aboard the Augusta, 9 August 1941. Right: the guests.

Menu

ALMONDS
VEGETABLE PUREE
CELERY   OLIVES   CRACKERS

BROILED SPRING CHICKEN
BUTTERED SWEET PEAS
SPINACH OMELET
CANDIED SWEET POTATOES
MUSHROOM GRAVY
HOT ROLLS   CURRANT JELLY

SLICED TOMATO SALAD
ASSORTED CHEESE
CRACKERS

CHOCOLATE ICE CREAM
COOKIES   CUP CAKES
COFFEE   TEA   CREAM
CANDY   MINTS   GINGER
CIGARETTES
CIGARS

PRESENT

[signature: Franklin D. Roosevelt]

FRANKLIN D. ROOSEVELT,
    PRESIDENT OF THE UNITED STATES.

HONORABLE
    SUMNER WELLES,
    UNDER SECRETARY OF STATE.

ADMIRAL
    HAROLD R. STARK, U.S.N.,
    CHIEF OF NAVAL OPERATIONS.

GENERAL
    GEORGE C. MARSHALL, U.S.A.,
    CHIEF OF STAFF.

ADMIRAL
    ERNEST J. KING, U.S.N.,
    COMMANDER-IN-CHIEF,
    ATLANTIC FLEET.

MAJOR GENERAL,
    HENRY H. ARNOLD, U.S.A.,
    CHIEF OF AIR CORPS.

HONORABLE
    HARRY L. HOPKINS

HONORABLE
    AVERILL HARRIMAN

[signature: W. Averell Harriman]

[signature: Winston Churchill]

RIGHT HONORABLE WINSTON CHURCHILL,
    PRIME MINISTER OF GREAT BRITAIN.

HONORABLE
    SIR ALEXANDER G. M. CADOGAN,
    G.C.M.G.,
    PERMANENT UNDER SECRETARY OF
    STATE FOR FOREIGN AFFAIRS.

ADMIRAL OF THE FLEET
    SIR ALFRED D.P.R. POUND,
    G.C.B., G.C.V.O.,
    CHIEF OF THE NAVAL STAFF

GENERAL
    SIR JOHN G. DILL, K.C.B.,
    C.M.G., D.S.O.,
    CHIEF OF THE IMPERIAL
    GENERAL STAFF.

AIR CHIEF MARSHAL
    SIR WILFRID R. FREEMAN, K.C.B.,
    D.S.O., M.C.,
    VICE CHIEF OF THE AIR STAFF.

LORD CHERWELL

[signature: Cherwell.]

sometimes also sung on Royal Navy ships (and which was played at Roosevelt's funeral at Hyde Park, New York). British and American officers and seamen – some 250 men in all – stood together during the church service, which was jointly conducted by the chaplain from the *Prince of Wales* and the chaplain of the US Fleet.

The Prime Minister also spent some time deciding what to serve the President for lunch on such a momentous day. He wanted food that was "unusual, seasonable and definitely British ... decided to take grouse ... It was arranged that sufficient birds for the luncheon party, and an extra brace for the President, should be put on the train at Perth".[16] Duff Cooper had "bagged the grouse in Scotland; on the PM's orders, another dozen brace had been frozen and brought along as a gift for the president".[17]

H.V. Morton, a British journalist and best-selling travel writer, invited along on the trip by Brendan Bracken, then Minister of Information,[18] noted:

> It is typical of the Prime Minister that he should have remembered it was once the custom of the Lords of the Admiralty when they voyaged abroad to take with them a turtle, which they were entitled to draw from a naval establishment. This strange custom began when Britain, in order to watch Napoleon at St. Helena, took over Ascension Island and every warship on its way to England from Ascension Island brought a turtle home with it ... Mr. Churchill might have been hard put to it to discover a turtle in war-time London. Nevertheless he served turtle soup to the President. It so happened that Commander Thompson, who had heard Mr. Churchill wish for a turtle, was in a grocer's shop in Piccadilly and, noticing some bottles of turtle soup and find-

ing that neither coupons nor ration books were required for them, promptly bought them and took them back in triumph to No. 10.[19]

Churchill had great affection for animals. When First Lord of the Admiralty, in 1911, on first exploring HMS *Enchantress*, the Admiralty yacht, he found a "tank of turtles, to be turned into soup. He was much moved by their plight and ordered their immediate release".[20] That affection did not always prevail over Churchill's appetite.

During his visit to Williamsburg, Virginia, in March 1946, he apparently specifically requested Maryland diamondback terrapin. His hosts agreed that "the world's first citizen should have the world's first food if available" and so we must assume that Churchill's request was granted.[21]

One last word on turtle soup. To celebrate 50 years in the House of Commons, on 31 October 1950, the Conservative Party gave a dinner at the Savoy in Churchill's honour, with turtle soup a feature

"Each course traced his Parliamentary life from election in Oldham in 1900. Turtle soup au sherry d'Oldham, and other courses named after some of his constituencies. Fillets of Sole after the Cinque Port, Mushrooms Epping Forest, from his 1924-1945 electorate, followed. Partridge on toast with English sauce Clementine. Les petits pois d'un grand ami de la France."[22]

Thirty-two men sat down for lunch that Sunday to eat Hopkins' ever-present caviar, along with smoked salmon and roast grouse and the symbolic turtle soup. The menu

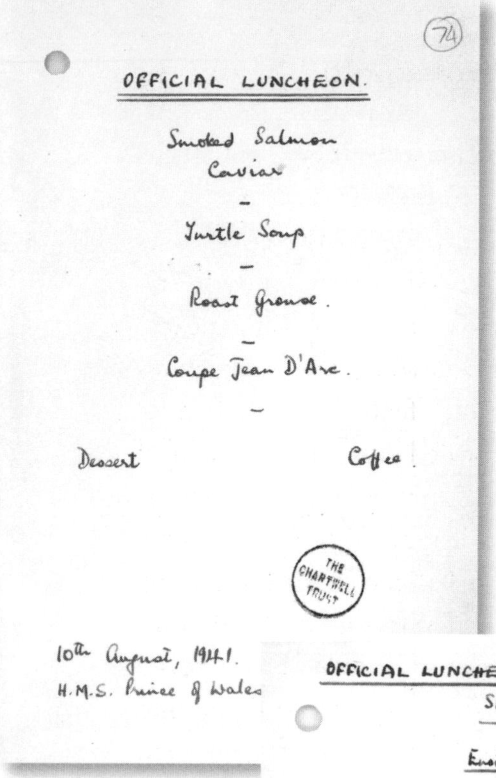

(74)

OFFICIAL LUNCHEON.

Smoked Salmon
Caviar
–
Turtle Soup
–
Roast Grouse.
–
Coupe Jean D'Arc.
–

Dessert Coffee.

THE CHARTWELL TRUST

10th August, 1941.
H.M.S. Prince of Wales

Churchill reciprocates, 10 August 1941

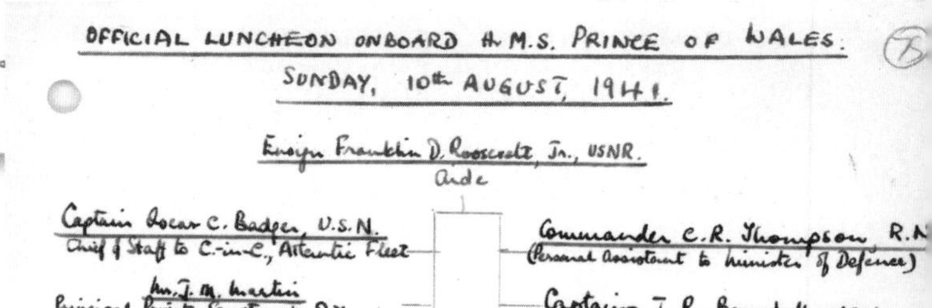

OFFICIAL LUNCHEON ONBOARD H.M.S. PRINCE OF WALES.
SUNDAY, 10th AUGUST, 1941.

(75)

Ensign Franklin D. Roosevelt, Jr., USNR.
Aide

Captain Oscar C. Badger, U.S.N. Chief of Staff to C.-in-C., Atlantic Fleet	Commander C.R. Thompson R.N. (Personal Assistant to Minister of Defence)
Mr. J. M. Martin Principal Private Secretary to P.M.	Captain J. R. Beardall, U.S.N. (Naval Aide to the President)
Major-General Edwin M. Watson, USA. Military Aide to the President.	Major-General Henry H. Arnold, USA. Chief of Air Corps
Surgeon-Commander F. B. Quinn, RN. Medical Officer, HMS Prince of Wales	Commander H.F. Lawson, RN. (Executive Officer, HMS Prince of Wales)
Rear-Admiral Ross T. McIntire MC. U.S.N. Surgeon-General of the Navy.	The Hon. Harry L. Hopkins Lease-Lend Administrator.
General Sir John Dill, C.I.G.S.	Air Chief Marshal Sir Wilfred R. Freeman Vice Chief of Air Staff.
Admiral Harold Stark, USN, Chief of Naval Operations	The Hon. Sumner Welles. Under-Secretary of State for Foreign Affairs of USA.
The PRIME MINISTER	Admiral of the Fleet Sir Dudley Pound First Sea Lord.
The PRESIDENT	General George C. Marshall, USA. Chief of Staff
Captain J. C. Leach, RN. Commanding Officer, HMS. Prince of Wales.	Sir Alexander Cadogan Permanent Under-Secretary of State, F.O.
Admiral Ernest J. King USN. C.-in-C., U.S. Atlantic Fleet.	The Hon. Averill Harriman Lease-Lend Expediter.
Professor Lord Cherwell Personal Assistant to Prime Minister	Pay Commander A.J. Wheeler, RN. Accountant Officer, HMS Prince of Wales
Major-General James H. Burns USA Executive to Assistant Secretary of War Lease-Lend executive	Rear-Admiral Richard K. Turner, USN Director of War Plans.
Lieutenant-Commander W.G. Agnew, RN Commanding Officer, HMCS Ripley	Commander (E) L.J. Goudy, R.N. Engineer Officer, Prince of Wales.
Captain Carleton H. Wright, USN, Commanding Officer, USS Augusta	Captain Elliot Roosevelt, USA (ACR) Aide.

Lieutenant-Commander A.G. Skipwith, RN.
First Lieutenant, HMS Prince of Wales.

THE CHARTWELL TRUST

was printed below the Prime Minister's cypher. No wines are listed.

Certainly there were differences between the conditions faced at home by American and British officers and sailors. One country had been at war for two years, the other at peace. Morton commented on the advertisements in the magazines he found on board the American ships featuring "almost eatable coloured photos of gigantic boiled hams, roast beef and other rationed food, to say nothing of rich, creamy puddings ..."[23] Another difference: by tradition, all US Navy ships are dry. British ships are not. This made British ships the popular place for meetings, especially around cocktail hour. The presidential party, fortunately, was not subject to the usual US Navy rules and Roosevelt's reputation among the British for mixing a martini with deadly Argentine vermouth[24] probably got its start at dinner on 9 August aboard the USS *Augusta*. The Americans quipped:

> The American Navy visits the British Navy in order to get drink, and the British Navy visits the American Navy in order to get something to eat.[25]

Roosevelt, sensitive to British privations, made a gesture of great courtesy and directed that every British seaman on the *Prince of Wales* and the other ships be given a gift box of American foods. Morton describes "a pyramid of something like one thousand five hundred cardboard cartons, which a chain of American sailors had soon stacked on our quarter-deck. Each box contained an orange, two apples, two hundred cigarettes, and half a pound of cheese, with a card saying it came from the President of the United States."

Churchill and the presidential gift boxes for every British seaman

On 10 August, Churchill boarded the USS *Augusta*, this time to dine in a smaller group with the President. The diary of Churchill's Principal Private Secretary, John Martin, records "a straightforward American meal of tomato soup, roast turkey with cranberry sauce and apple pie with cheese".[26] The dishes' lack of sophistication might have reassured the Prime Minister and his team that although they could not match the Americans in quantity, when it came to culinary skills, Britain retained its superiority.

While the leaders were meeting, both staffs continued their separate rounds of dinner-table diplomacy. On 10 August, Cadogan gave a dinner on the *Prince of Wales* for American generals, admirals and Sumner Welles, then Under-Secretary of State and one of the President's chief advisers. At Churchill's direction, and with Roosevelt's keen endorsement, these staff meetings, at all levels, would continue to the end of the war. They were the initial steps in a plan, brought to fruition during Churchill's stay in the White House in December 1941, to create a new Combined Chiefs of Staff Committee to prosecute the war.

These day-long sessions, the sharing of opinions and experiences, the informality created by the many lunches and dinner meetings, established an invaluable camaraderie between the British and the American military and political staffs, and their leaders. One sign of this developing friendship was a letter and package given by Harry Hopkins to John Martin, Churchill's Principal Private Secretary. The box contained a large supply of foods hard to find in wartime Britain. The accompanying letter, on White House stationery, reads:

> My dear Martin, if your conscience will permit, these are to
> be taken to London. If the niceties of the war would disturb,
> I suggest you give them to some other member of the party
> whose will to live well may be greater than yours.
>   Ever so cordially, Harry Hopkins[27]

The meetings resulted directly in the joint statement of Allied goals known as the Atlantic Charter. They also had two further important consequences: the military staffs took the first steps towards future cooperation in the execution of the war, and they established a pattern for what would become known as summit meetings – in Churchill's own words, almost a decade later, a "parley at the summit".[28]

No one says it better than Sir Martin Gilbert:

On these secret commitments and declarations the British

policy-makers and planners were to build their detailed prep-arations in the months to come, despite formidable obstacles of priority and production. For Churchill, it was the fact that he had established a personal relationship with the President, which constituted the main achievement of 'Riviera'"[29]

as this first summit was then code-named.

Three weeks later, back in London, the Prime Minister attended a lunch given by Ambassador Ivan Maisky at the Soviet embassy to mark their new-found comradeship. The two main planks of Churchill's Grand Alliance, the Soviet Union and the United States, were now in place.

Celebrating the Alliance

*Churchill and Soviet Ambassador Maisky's tête-à-tête: lunch at
the Soviet embassy, London, August 1941*

CHAPTER 3

Christmas in the White House
December 1941–January 1942

————————⟨◆⟩————————

"I would like to suggest delay." [1]

"Churchill hit the White House like a cyclone." [2]

Churchill never missed an opportunity to confer with key American policy-makers in his tireless effort to enlist the United States in Britain's struggle for survival. On the fateful evening of 7 December 1941, he was dining at Chequers with American Ambassador John "Gil" Winant; Averell Harriman (Roosevelt's Special Representative in the UK), and Harriman's daughter, Kathleen (whose birthday it was); Pamela Churchill, (the Prime Minister's daughter-in-law); his Principal Private Secretary, John Martin; and Commander "Tommy" Thompson, his ADC.

Churchill was in this distinguished company when Frank

Sawyers, his valet, entered the dining room with a small portable Emerson radio that Harriman had brought with him as a gift from Harry Hopkins.[3] The BBC news bulletin was reporting the devastating surprise Japanese attack on the US naval base at Pearl Harbor. Churchill immediately asked Winant to telephone Roosevelt for confirmation, and just as quickly decided to travel to Washington, both to offer support – "We are all in the same boat now,"[4] the President told the Prime Minister – and to promote his own strategy for prosecuting the war.

The following day, the Japanese attacked the British colony of Malaya and on 11 December, Germany declared war on the United States. Britain and the United States had become allies in what was clearly going to be a long war against two strong enemies, Germany and Japan. Because Roosevelt

Chequers dining room

was under substantial Pacific First pressure to avenge the attack on Pearl Harbor, Churchill feared that the war against Germany would be subordinated to an American war against Japan and that the Lend-Lease material would be diverted from Britain to that effort in the Far East.

As always, Churchill believed he could be most effective in a face-to-face meeting. Once ensconced in the White House, he would argue for the joint overall strategy – Europe First – he was convinced would win the war.

Arranging this meeting was no easy thing. Such an extended transatlantic visit needed the approval of both the King and the Cabinet, and an invitation from the President. Churchill had little difficulty obtaining the sovereign's approval. But the Cabinet was another matter.

The Foreign Secretary, Anthony Eden, then on his way to meet Stalin, joined his Cabinet colleagues in opposing Churchill's visit, arguing that Britain's Prime Minister and its Foreign Secretary should not be away from London and the House of Commons at the same time. But neither Eden nor the War Cabinet could dissuade the Prime Minister from his view that telegrams and phone calls were no substitute for personal contact. Oliver Harvey, Eden's Principal Private Secretary, noted in his diary:

> Really the PM is a lunatic: he gets in such a state of excitement that the wildest schemes seem reasonable. I hope to goodness we can defeat this one. AE believes the Cabinet and finally the King will restrain him, but the Cabinet are a poor lot for stopping anything.[5]

In Washington, enthusiasm for a Churchill visit was equally muted. Influential congressional supporters of

General Douglas MacArthur favoured a Japan-first strategy. Nor was the President's wife alone in Washington in viewing Churchill as an unreconstructed "old imperialist" trying to drag the United States into a war that would restore Britain's empire. The President, reluctant to receive the Prime Minister, enlisted the aid of the British Ambassador, Lord Halifax, to persuade Churchill to stay at home. Roosevelt told the Ambassador he was worried about Churchill's security, and suggested a meeting in Bermuda at a later date. Neither fears for his safety, nor the prospect of a meeting at some later – perhaps much later – date could dissuade Churchill from setting sail for America as soon as possible. The Prime Minister set aside the doubts of some of his Cabinet, confident that the potential effectiveness of his personal diplomacy would secure Britain's urgent national interest to give Hitler no respite in Europe. Churchill's greatest fear was that the Nazis would defeat the Soviet Union and then invade Britain.

The President's uncertainty about the visit from the Prime Minister was reflected in cables he, or perhaps members of his staff not eager to expose the President to the Prime Minister's persuasive powers, drafted for transmission to Churchill: "I would like to suggest delay ... full discussion would be more useful a few weeks hence ... I suggest we defer decision on your visit for [about] one week." In the event, the cables were not sent, and Churchill and Roosevelt spoke over a radio telephone link later that day. Churchill prevailed. The President finally cabled Churchill: "Delighted to have you here at White House."[6]

For security reasons conversations were never about grand strategy. Ruth Ive, who monitored and, when talk turned to sensitive areas, censored transatlantic calls between the President and the Prime Minister, noted that "Churchill would sometimes describe the excellent dinner he had just eaten to the somewhat surprised President".[7]

The invitation to stay at the White House certainly suited Churchill, as he wanted to spend as much personal time as possible with Roosevelt, with every opportunity to practise the dinner-table diplomacy in which he had such confidence. Far better than staying at the British Embassy or Blair House, the presidential guest house, where interruptions would be inevitable.

On 12 December, Churchill boarded his special train at London's Euston Station on his way to the Clyde. For security reasons, the story had been put out that Lord Beaverbrook was sailing, and that Churchill was at the train station merely to see him off. Beaverbrook "had his private saloon on the train, and had a dinner party there before the train started".[8] Churchill and his party then embarked on the battleship *Duke of York*, sister ship to the *Prince of Wales* on which he had sailed to meet Roosevelt the previous August. (The *Prince of Wales* had been sunk by the Japanese, north-east of Singapore, a few days earlier with the loss of many lives, including Admiral Tom Phillips, a friend of Churchill's.) While on board the *Duke of York*, Churchill telegraphed birthday wishes to Stalin, who was 63 on 21 December. Churchill had celebrated his 67th birthday three weeks earlier.

The transatlantic voyage took ten days. Churchill described it to his wife as "... unceasing gales ... No one is allowed on deck, and we have two men with broken arms and legs ... Being in a ship in such weather as this is like being in prison, with the extra chance of being drowned".[9] Commander Thompson described it also: "Of all the journeys which the Prime Minister was destined to make during the war few rivalled this first voyage to America for sheer discomfort."[10] Nevertheless, Beaverbrook joked that he "had never travelled in such a large submarine",[11] and Churchill wrote to his wife: "We make a friendly party at meal times, and everyone is now accustomed to the motion."[12]

Churchill's insistence on maintaining his usual habits was unaffected by the turbulence. At one point, the ever-present Sawyers rushed to the bridge to ask Captain Harcourt for help. "The Prime Minister doesn't like the ship's water, and I've run out of white wine."[13] Presumably, the Captain had extra wines aboard for just such emergencies.

Churchill, as usual, devoted himself to work, albeit following his eccentric daily habits. He told Clementine, in the same letter, of his routine:

I spend the greater part of the day in bed, getting up for lunch, going to bed immediately afterwards to sleep and then up again for dinner. I manage to get a great deal of sleep and have also done a great deal of work in my waking hours.[14]

The numerous memoranda Churchill wrote while on this sea voyage included: "Future Conduct of the War"; "US troops to Northern Ireland"; "Re-establish France as Great Power"; "The Pacific Front"; "Proposed strategy for 1943 and a possible landing in Europe".[15] He also read and considered Eden's reports from Moscow on his meetings with Stalin, and other staff reports from London – a full plate indeed. Also on Churchill's mind was preparing what he would say to the President.

On 22 December, Churchill, dressed as at Placentia Bay in a navy pea jacket and blue yachting cap, disembarked at Hampton Roads, at the lower end of the Chesapeake Bay. Insisting that there was not a minute to lose, he was flown up the Potomac to the new National Airport in the capital, where the President greeted him on the tarmac. Together, they drove to the White House. (The others on Churchill's staff were taken by private train to Washington, where they were served hard-boiled eggs, salad and fruit.[16]) Both politicians were aware of the perils they faced, aware of the symbolism of their meeting and eager to project confidence and determination – witness the President's jauntily angled Camel in his cigarette holder and the Prime Minister's ever-present cigar, which both well knew cartoonists had made a symbol of their imperturbability and steadfastness.

Churchill lived at the White House for the next three weeks. It was the first time in the long history of Anglo-American relations that a British prime minister had lived at the White House during wartime and probably – with the exception of Harry Hopkins – the only time that a non-family member, and a foreigner at that, was welcomed for such an extended period.

Both parties were alert to possible differences, concerned about what the other would think and, more worrying, might demand. Brigadier (later Sir) Leslie Hollis, who was with Churchill, wrote:

> The Anglo-American alliance was still untempered steel. The Americans were reeling under the disaster of Pearl Harbor, and possibly a little nervous that the war-tried British might try to tell them what to do. We, on the other hand, were anxious to show that we had no desire to act as

senior partners in the new-formed alliance, but as equals. We had no pattern to guide us ...[17]

At the White House, domestic planning was chaotic: because of the secrecy surrounding Churchill's transatlantic voyage, Roosevelt's wife, Eleanor, had not been told until the last minute that the Prime Minster would be her guest over Christmas, usually a family time. She was surprised – even angry – when her husband had asked her whom she had invited for Christmas dinner, as never before had he been interested in her guest lists. Early on the day of Churchill's arrival, the President told his wife and staff to arrange dinner for twenty that night, a dinner that would include the Prime Minister of Great Britain. An old friend of Eleanor, Mrs. Charles Hamlin, watched as Churchill arrived, and recalled that he "wore a knee-length double-breasted coat, buttoned high, in seaman fashion. He gripped a walking stick with an attached flashlight for the purpose of navigating London blackouts. He reminded me of a big English bulldog who had been taught to give his paw".[18] *Time* magazine said Churchill "swept in like a breath of fresh air, giving Washington new vigour, for he came as a new hero".[19]

There was some confusion as to sleeping arrangements. When Eleanor showed Churchill to the Lincoln Bedroom (not then as famous as it was to become during the Clintons' occupancy of the White House), he turned it down, claiming the bed did not suit him. Making himself at home from the start, Churchill then looked over the other available rooms. Alert as ever to opportunities, he chose a bedroom across the hall from Harry Hopkins' almost-permanent rooms, the Rose Room on the second floor, where Queen Elizabeth had slept on her 1939 visit with King George VI.

The Prime Minster had struck up a close relationship with Hopkins when the presidential adviser had visited Britain in January 1941, and intended to maintain it as a conduit to the President. With the strategically located bedroom secured (on New Year's Day the Prime Minister and the President would meet there for a key strategy discussion[20]), Churchill then obtained offices across the corridor from the President, so they could meet at any time. Churchill's travelling map room was set up in the Monroe Room, on the ground floor, by the valuable Captain Richard Pim who had run the Map Room since Churchill's arrival at the Admiralty in 1939. Roosevelt liked it so much he had his own Map Room set up in the White House as soon as Churchill left for home. The Prime Minister's Principal Private Secretary, John Martin, his naval ADC, Commander Thompson, two Scotland Yard detectives and Churchill's valet, Sawyers, were all assigned smaller rooms on the second floor. The other members of the Prime Minister's party, including Churchill's personal physician, Sir Charles Wilson, were billeted at the Mayflower Hotel.

Many years after the event, Alonzo Fields, the White House chief butler from 1931 to 1953, wrote a chatty memoir, *My 21 Years in the White House*. Fields records the secrecy, excitement and chaos of the Prime Minister's visit. On 22 December 1941, the day on which Churchill arrived at the White House, just after six p.m. Fields said he

> was preparing to leave for home when my phone rang. I was told that an important guest was expected at about 7:00 p.m. The number in his party would be anywhere from 25 to 40 people, and the name of the guest was off the record.[21]

No matter: Fields recognised Churchill immediately.

Fields goes on to describe the alcoholic beverages he served the British Prime Minister. He thus became partially responsible for some of the tales that have sprung up about the Prime Minister's drinking habits. According to Fields, on Churchill's first morning at the White House on 23 December, the Prime Minister summoned him to his bedroom and said:

"Now, Fields, we had a lovely dinner last night but I have a few orders for you. We want to leave here as friends, right? … I must have a tumbler of sherry in my room before breakfast, a couple of glasses of scotch and soda before lunch and French Champagne and 90 year old brandy before I go to sleep at night."[22]

Probably untrue. Fields later recounted another conversation he had with Churchill, who was in a joking mood:

He said, "Fields, I want to ask you something. I want to know if I can count on you." "Well, certainly Mr. Prime Minister, I will do whatever I can." He said: "In years hence when someone says was Winston Churchill a teetotaler; I want you to come to my defense." "Mr. Prime Minister, I will defend you to the last drop."[23]

Fields may not be the most reliable of reporters, either because of a fallible memory or a desire to add spice to his book and sell tickets for the subsequent dramatisation which toured the United States. Take the matter of breakfasts:

On his breakfast tray I was instructed to have something hot, something cold, two kinds of fresh fruit, a tumbler of orange juice and a pot of frightfully weak tea. For "something hot", he had eggs, bacon, or ham, and toast. For "something cold" he had two kinds of cold meats with English mustard and two kinds of fruit plus a tumbler of sherry. This was at breakfast.[24]

François Rysavy, White House chef at the time of Churchill's visits to FDR, has a different story to tell. He recalled serving the distinguished visitor "apples, pears and other fruits and a large pot of tea" for breakfast, which he says the Prime Minister consumed after his morning sherry.[25]

Then there is what in my view is the more reliable report, from Lady Williams (née Portal), who worked as Churchill's secretary from 1949 to 1955. She recalls that Churchill, after waking early, around seven or seven-thirty a.m., preferred a simple breakfast of orange juice, a boiled egg (a special daily treat since eggs were rationed in Britain to two per person per week), tea or sometimes coffee and a bit of fruit. He would then begin to work in bed. The sherry story has led to some of the misconceptions discussed in the chapter dealing with Churchill's preferences for certain kinds of alcoholic beverages. Lady Williams describes the whisky ordered by the Prime Minister with his breakfast as just a "tumbler of barely coloured whisky, heavily diluted with water, which was put by his bed and it would last all morning".[26] No Sherry. The Prime Minister would have been delighted if his daily White House breakfast tray included poached eggs every day, given rationing restrictions at home.

A detailed report by Harold Macmillan, subsequently Prime Minister himself, indicated that there were circumstances under which the Prime Minister preferred a more ample breakfast. In June 1951, as part of a campaign to demonstrate to his party that he was sufficiently vigorous to continue to lead it despite his age, Churchill participated in a 21-hour debate in the House of Commons, "crowned all by a remarkable breakfast, at 7:30 a.m., of eggs, bacon, sausages and coffee, followed by a large whisky and soda and a huge cigar. This latter feat commanded general admiration".[27]

Perhaps the best way to resolve these conflicting recollections and reports about the Churchillian breakfasts is to consult Churchill himself. On his last trip to the US as Prime Minister, in June 1954, aboard a BOAC flight, he had his son-in-law, Sir Christopher Soames, start to annotate a printed menu. Apparently finding that editing process tiresome or

BOAC breakfast menu, on flight to Washington, June 1954

The Churchills and Tango at Chartwell, *1933*,
by William Nicholson

complicated, Soames eventually started afresh and wrote
Churchill's preferred order on the reverse side. It specifies
almost exactly what Lady Williams, who was on the flight
with the Prime Minister, earlier described as Churchill's
favourite breakfast. Soames humorously writes "wash hands"
after the last words "whisky soda" and, finally, he writes
"cigar". Note that the washing of hands precedes handling
the sacred cigar, and that Churchill was permitted to smoke
a cigar aboard the flight. (This menu was auctioned off in
2009. The price anticipated by the auctioneers was £1,900
but so highly do Churchillians value such treasures that it
sold for £4,800.)

One thing is certain about Churchill's early-morning dining preferences: they included solitude. Even at the White House, where he was eager to maximise his time with the President, when it came to breakfast, Churchill would breakfast alone. His view was clear:

"My wife and I tried two or three times in the last forty years to have breakfast together, but it didn't work. Breakfast should be had in bed alone. Not downstairs after one has dressed." It is reported that Churchill's eyes twinkled as he reported this.[28]

Averell Harriman's private notes and memories of Churchill, written in 1962, tell of another and rather unusual breakfast. "We left (Baltimore) at midnight and got to (Botwold) at 8 o'clock by my watch, but noon local time. They served us scotch whisky and cold lobster for breakfast. Churchill seemed to thrive on it. I thought it a little rough."[29]

Neither the simplicity nor the privacy Churchill demanded of breakfast served as models for the lunches and dinners and he unquestionably noticed the difference between the management of the presidential household and his own residences in the UK. Mrs. Henrietta Nesbitt, principal White House housekeeper from 1933 until 1946, was in charge of all menus and foods, and of all servants, meal planning and purchases. She is generally acknowledged by all who were subjected to her foods and menu-planning to be the worst housekeeper in White House history. She had run a bakery-from-home in Hyde Park, New York. Mrs. Roosevelt, having taken a fancy to her home-made breads and pies, invited her to Washington in 1933 to be head housekeeper at the White House, and retained full confidence in Mrs. Nesbitt in spite of her lack of experience and the numerous missteps during her on-the-job learning, and in spite of the President's constant complaints about her cooking and her menu choices. Even the President of the United States was not master at his own table so long as his wife supported the White House cook. Mrs. Roosevelt, preferring the outside arena of policy to the management of the social aspects of life inside the White House, saw little need to modernise the White House kitchen, which was "like an old-fashioned German rathskeller with a great deal of ancient architectural charm". The icebox was lined in wood, Mrs. Nesbitt's predecessors had left no cookbooks, and there were only a few utensils. Fortunately for future researchers, Mrs. Nesbitt decided that when she left the White House she "was going to leave behind complete lists".[30] So we have detailed menus, with her notes, of every lunch and dinner – but not breakfast – served at the White House while the Prime Minister lived there.

Mrs. Nesbitt paints a picture of the British delegation:

Even Mr. Churchill looked poor-coloured and hungry, though he was heavy-set and, one could tell, had enjoyed good living. But they had pared to the bone over there, holding Hitler at bay, so I tried to feed them up while we had the chance. Every time the Churchill group came, it seemed we couldn't fill them up for days. Once we cooked for guests who didn't come, and offered it to some of the Englishmen who had just risen from the table, and they sat right down and ate the whole meal through, straight over again.[31]

Most of the thirteen dinners, and some of the lunches the President and the Prime Minister shared, began with the cocktail ceremony. Roosevelt was known for his robust and unusual cocktails – the proportions of his martinis were said to be "unfortunate".[32] Charles "Chip" Bohlen, one of Roosevelt's diplomats and his interpreter at Teheran, says the martinis were made with a "large quantity of vermouth, both sweet and dry, with a small amount of gin".[33] No mention of the infamous Argentine vermouth to which he had introduced his British guest at Placentia Bay.

The first White House dinner at which Churchill had an opportunity to deploy his combination of charm and draw on the careful planning he had done before and during his transatlantic voyage, was at a "semiformal" dinner on the day he arrived, 22 December 1941.[34] A note on the menu reads "17 people 8:30 Mrs. R."[35] Seventeen people settled down for dinner; one, the Prime Minister, also settled down to work. Guests that night included Cordell Hull, Secretary of State, and Under-Secretary of State Sumner Welles, both with wives; British Ambassador Lord Halifax and Lady Halifax; Beaverbrook, British Minister of Aircraft Production; Mrs. Bertie Hamlin, wife of the Assistant Secretary of the Treasury and an old Roosevelt friend; the President's wife and Harry Hopkins. Mrs. Hamlin recalls the President's champagne toast at the end of the dinner: "To The Common Cause". That surely was music to Churchill's ears.

The originally scheduled roast leg of lamb had been replaced at the last minute with broiled chicken. We can only suppose that the President's last-minute announcement that he would be joined by distinguished guests caused chaos in Mrs. Nesbitt's kitchen. Or perhaps the roast leg of lamb was deleted in favour of broiled chicken because there just wasn't enough lamb to feed seventeen people.

Neither this menu nor the other menus during the Churchill visit catered specifically to English tastes or to the preferences of the Prime Minister. Indeed, on the day following the first White House dinner, the lunch led off with a cream soup, much disliked by Churchill as we shall see in Chapter 10, in this instance cream of celery soup. The following courses – kedgeree and grilled tomatoes and raspberry Mary Anne – may have made Churchill long for some home cooking and for his favourite cook in Britain, Mrs. Landemare.

No matter. Churchill had come to do business, not to eat. His principal goal was to persuade the President that

The President loved sauerkraut and pigs' knuckles and had that dish served to Churchill, who politely asked what they were. When told, Churchill, on his best behaviour, only responded, according to Alonzo Fields, that they were "very good, but sort of slimy".[36]

The Prime Minister might have consumed the dish, but if so it would have been for no reason other than to please his host, on whose goodwill so much was riding.

Churchill was famously an animal lover, with special affection for those he knew personally. In his affectionate squiggles to Clementine he depicted himself as a pig. He refused to eat suckling pig as he had raised pigs at Chartwell and claimed to know them. During the First World War when food was in short supply, he refused to carve a goose from his farm at Lullenden, saying: "You'll have to carve it, Clemmie. He was my friend."[37]

the Germany First strategy he had enshrined in the series of memoranda written on the sea voyage to America – an "immense feat of intellectual effort and foresight", according to historian Andrew Roberts[38] – was in America's interests. So for him the Christmas festivities, no matter how welcome in themselves, were an interruption in the private time he felt he needed with Roosevelt. In the event, as later discussions revealed, Roosevelt had already decided that "Germany first" was the policy that would hasten victory in what had become a world war.[39] It was left to the Prime Minister to sell his plan for implementing that strategy – which proved no small chore given the competing claims on resources.

Meanwhile, with Christmas only two days away, the White House was decorated with evergreens, Christmas balls and wreaths. As in all houses full of children waiting for Christmas Day, the mood was excited and expectant, in part because of the Roosevelts' desire to convey calm and cheer only a few weeks after the Pearl Harbor disaster. It must have been doubly busy with messengers delivering gifts, journalists prying and the British military and political staffs with their red boxes needing the Prime Minister's attention: a "hugger-mugger"[40] atmosphere in which two powerful heads of state lived side by side, an unusual situation under almost any circumstances, and especially unusual when the two leaders were planning what would undoubtedly be a long war against two determined and mutual enemies.

As if that were not enough chaos, Churchill and Roosevelt held a press conference, American style, the Prime Minister wearing a polka-dot bow tie, striped trousers and a short black jacket, and responding to complaints from the press "boys" in the rear that he could not be seen by standing on a chair.

To add to the managerial problems, the reaction to Churchill's visit was electric: gifts, cards and letters to the Prime Minister poured in. Gifts were turned over to the British embassy, which catalogued them, showed them off to the press and sent out the requisite thank-you notes. One, a signed photo of the prizefighter and world champion Jack Dempsey, was perhaps sent because Dempsey had battered the much bigger Luis Angel Firpo into submission, and the sender was hoping Britain would similarly batter larger Germany. Among the oddest were a bag of lima beans with instructions for cooking; a copy of George Washington's will; a painting of the great seal of the State of Ohio;[41] and a six-foot tall V sign made of lilies.[42] More knowledgeable donors sent bottles of brandy and boxes and boxes of cigars that continued to be the gift of choice to Churchill from admirers throughout the war. More important than any gifts as tokens of the American public's growing affection for the Prime Minister was an invitation from Congress to address a Joint Session of Congress on the day after Christmas.

On the evening of 23 December, cocktails were followed by dinner at eight p.m., once again featuring typical 1940s American fare. That evening the menu was:

Noodle soup
Roast beef
Stuffed potatoes, broccoli
Orange & cress salad
Bavarian cream pie
Coffee

We can only assume that at some point Churchill managed to obtain a glass or two of champagne: although no champagnes or wines are listed on these detailed menus, they undoubtedly were available. (Today the White House menus list the wines served with each course.) In the days that followed, the President and Prime Minister typically stayed up talking, drinking brandy and smoking until two or three a.m. For the better part of three weeks, despite Eleanor Roosevelt's efforts, the late-night sessions continued. She was no more successful than Clementine Churchill in bringing such evenings to a close. "Mother would just fume," the President's son, Elliott, recorded, "and go in and out of the room making hints about bed, and still Churchill would sit there."[43]

On Christmas Eve, meetings between principals and their military and political staffs went on as usual amid the bustle typical of any large house the day before Christmas – in this case a house with two political giants living side by side.

At twilight, in weather warmer than usual for December, the President and the Prime Minister went onto the White House's South Portico balcony for the traditional ceremony of the lighting of the national Christmas tree. Somewhere between 20,000 and 30,000 people stood outside the White House singing carols and listening to Churchill say: "I cannot truthfully say that I feel far from home",[44] adding another building block to the special relationship he was constructing. Both the President's and Churchill's words were broadcast across the United States and overseas.

At dinner that night, an American guest, Percy Chubb, noted that the President was "buoyant" but Churchill "subdued". Always working, even at a Christmas Eve dinner, Churchill fretted about Britain's food supply and commented that the Americans were shipping too many powdered eggs to Britain, "the only thing you can make with them is Spotted Dick"[45], steamed suet pudding, served with custard, widely disliked, to boys at English boarding schools such as the one attended by a young Winston Churchill. FDR, needling, said: "Nonsense. You can do as much with a powdered egg as with a real egg." Chubb responded by asking "How could you fry a powdered egg?"[46]

On Christmas morning, the Prime Minister and the President, along with invited guests and their families, attended a special Divine Service, "surrounded by bevies of G-Men, armed with Tommy-guns and revolvers",[47] at the Foundry Methodist Church on 16th and P Streets in Washington. It was during that service that Churchill first heard the carol, "O Little Town of Bethlehem".

After the service, on to lunch. Once again, it began with the cream soup.

Cream of green pea soup
Broiled sweetbreads
Candied sweet potatoes
Peas and creamed onions
Chicory and cress salad
Ice-cream and cake

Fortunately, the Prime Minister was focused more on selling his war strategy than on what was put on his plate.

That Christmas night at the White House, at eight p.m., the President and Prime Minister sat down together for a traditional American Christmas dinner, 1941 style, in the State Dining Room, surrounded by some forty to fifty family members and friends, but oddly, no children, who apparently dined somewhere else. Churchill's physician noted that guests stood around in a circle while Mrs. Roosevelt went around shaking hands. Once again, dinner was American fare, with the soup mercifully clear:

Oysters on the half shell
Clear soup with sherry
Celery and assorted olives
Roast turkey with chestnut dressing
Deerfoot sausage (a well-known American brand)
Giblet gravy
Beans and cauliflower
Casserole of sweet potatoes
Grapefruit salad and cheese crescents
Plum pudding and hard sauce and ice-cream Cake

One of Mrs. Roosevelt's guests, Betty Hight, starry-eyed at the sumptuousness of that Christmas dinner and the richness of the setting, wrote to her family:

... we ate with gold cutlery ... from the Cleveland Administration. The plates had been designed by FDR and the horseshoe table with square corners had been decorated with huge bowls of red carnations ... with holly and ivy in between ... gold urns containing fruit were placed here and there.

Betty Hight mentions that a "sauterne wine" was served as well as champagne.[48] Churchill surely would have been sufficiently sensitive to the suffering of his countrymen to have compared the lush dinner with the thin fare available in Britain under the rationing programme in which he was so heavily involved, and under which the availability of vegetables often depended on the ability of each household to grow its own.

No charades, no Christmas crackers as in an English house, but an after-dinner showing of the film *Oliver Twist*. Churchill, with his mind on the importance of his speech to a Joint Session of Congress the next morning, uncharacteristically excused himself early to do his homework, a process that lasted until two in the morning. He knew that his first speech to America's elected representatives (there would be two more) was of critical importance for explaining the British position, and persuading the legislators who controlled the military's purse strings and could oppose any presidential strategy if they chose to do so. In the event, it was another triumph for the Prime Minister.

Sir Charles Wilson was with Churchill when he returned to the White House after the speech. Churchill thought it had gone well but was worried about something else: the reaction of some congressmen led him to fret that he was not in touch with Americans, other than the President. He knew that he would one day need the goodwill of top government officials. So he told Sir Charles he was planning a dinner at the British embassy for members of the Roosevelt administration, including Cordell Hull, then Secretary of State, and key congressmen.

That evening he confided an even greater worry to his physician. He told Sir Charles Wilson that he had been experiencing shortness of breath, dull pain down his left arm and pains in his chest, which he wanted to attribute to his excitement at the opportunity for intimate meetings with the President, saying: "It has all been very moving."[49] Sir Charles diagnosed "coronary insufficiency", for which the prescription would then have been complete bed rest for six weeks, but knowing Churchill would never have accepted, he made the decision not to tell him the truth.

Needing a few days' rest to recover from his heart attack, and according to Andrew Roberts, "keen not to overstay his welcome in Washington",[50] Churchill flew to Pompano Beach, Florida, to stay at the seaside villa owned by Edward Stettinius, then a presidential aide. Commander Thompson describes the meals:

> The President had sent down a staff from the White House to look after us, but apparently the cook had not been warned of the P.M.'s somewhat rigid preference for simple meals. He liked plain English cooking, and enjoyed roast beef or steak so much that, with rationing in force at home, he often saved half his portion at dinner-time and had it for breakfast next morning. I think he could have been perfectly happy to lunch off cold roast beef every day of his life, but our new cook felt he was on his mettle and on our first day there he provided an elaborately prepared clam chowder. [It was declined] and Mr. Churchill said firmly "If you haven't any clear soup, please bring me a plate of Bovril, double strength." As the butler had never heard of Bovril (which the P.M. pronounced Boe-vril), the request caused some consternation in the kitchen.[51]

Fortifying sunshine, some dips in the warm ocean, a return by train to the White House for a few final dinners, and back to Britain on a transatlantic flight, then considered very risky except by the American pilots. So successful had Churchill's table-top diplomacy been that General George Marshall later complained that Roosevelt "would communicate" only with Churchill on matters affecting the conduct of the war, leaving Marshall and others scrambling to find out what the two leaders had in mind.[52]

CHAPTER 4

Dinners in Moscow
August 1942

———— ❧ ————

"The food was filthy."[1]

"It was my duty to go."[2]

Churchill believed that his persuasive powers and personal charm would be effective not only with a well disposed ally like Roosevelt, but even with a far less congenial one like Joseph Stalin. Which is why he launched his usual first-phase tactic, one that had worked so well with Roosevelt: a personal letter-writing campaign. This began in June 1940, when he used the occasion of the appointment of Sir Stafford Cripps as British Ambassador to the Soviet Union to contact the Soviet leader directly.

Churchill had reason to regard this exercise of personal diplomacy a success: by July 1941 he and the Soviet leader were exchanging birthday greetings,[3] and Stalin immediately responded affirmatively to Churchill's request for a meeting.

Getting to Moscow required stopovers at Gibraltar, Cairo and Teheran for refuelling. As usual, Churchill turned these stops on an arduous journey to his advantage, finding time at Teheran for both his beloved baths and lunch with the Shah. In Teheran, amid an "atmosphere of deck chairs and whiskey and soda", Churchill escaped the "continuous hooting of the Persian motor cars"[4] and the heat by spending the night at the British summer legation high in the mountains above the capital. Not every Churchill whim was catered to. The Prime Minister's request that his bed at the legation in Teheran be dismantled, carted up to the cooler mountains and there reassembled, was refused. One of Churchill's wartime private secretaries, Leslie Rowan, and Commander Thompson spent the night in "a magnificent Persian tent in the garden" of the summer legation.[5]

Dinner at the legation featured turkey with all the trimmings.[6] A British bodyguard recalls the dessert served up by the kitchen staff. A large plate of fresh Persian peaches with the tops cut off were filled with melted chocolate and topped with whipped cream. Then the top was replaced "at a jaunty angle".[7]

On his arrival in Moscow on the evening of 12 August 1942, after the usual airport ceremony, Churchill promptly went to his villa eight miles outside Moscow. He was, as he put it "regaled in the dining room with every form of choice food and liquor, including caviar and vodka, but with many other dishes and wines from France and Germany, far beyond our mood or consuming powers".[8]

The 67-year-old Churchill, despite the long flight, insisted on an immediate appointment with Stalin – though he did take some time to bathe. He also took time to feed the goldfish at the villa Stalin had assigned him. Alexander Cadogan, the Foreign Office's permanent Under-Secretary, ever interested in food, noted there were excellent raspberries growing in the gardens of the villa.

Churchill had two reasons for anticipating a tough slog in Moscow. First was his long-standing and well-known hostility to Communism, Bolshevism, and all that the Stalin regime represented. He had made no secret of his desire to see the regime toppled in 1919, and had cooperated with efforts to overthrow it. But in 1942, as he put it, "If Hitler invaded hell, I would make at least a favourable reference to the devil in the House of Commons".[9] Stalin was to be wooed, but at dinner the Prime Minister would presumably dine with a rather long spoon.

His second reason for anticipating a difficult meeting was the news he was bringing to Stalin: there would be no second front in Europe in 1942 to ease the pressure on Soviet forces fighting on the Eastern front. Before the meeting, Churchill had written obliquely to the Soviet leader: "We could … survey the war together and take decisions hand-in-hand. I could then tell you plans we have made with President Roosevelt for offensive action in 1942."[10] That action was Operation Torch in North Africa, rather than the cross-Channel invasion that Stalin favoured.

So worried was Churchill about this visit that he had decided to take Averell Harriman, Roosevelt's emissary, with him. He had written to the President: "Would you be able to let Averell come with me? I feel that things would be easier if we all seemed to be together. I have a somewhat raw job."[11] Roosevelt promptly agreed.

The food laid out on his arrival at his dacha was not the only display of Stalin's hospitality. One aide recalls the breakfasts the Soviets provided: "caviar, cake, chocolates, preserved fruit, grapes, none of the normal breakfast dishes. Fortunately coffee and an omelette appeared and all was well. Leslie Rowan told me that when he asked for an egg and bacon, they produced four eggs and nine rashers of bacon – all very nice except that one remembers that the vast majority of the population are practically starving".[12] This may be why Churchill later described his quarters as being "prepared with totalitarian lavishness".[13]

Churchill set off for his first meeting with the man he called "the great Revolutionary Chief and profound Soviet Union statesman and warrior".[14] The meeting, not a dinner, lasted from seven to eleven p.m.

Although it began badly, as Churchill had anticipated, in the end, after Stalin reacted positively to tales of the British bombing of Germany, it ended on a sufficiently cordial note for Churchill to tell Sir Charles Wilson: "When I left we were good friends and shook hands cordially. I mean to forge a solid link with this man."[15]

That left Churchill to dine alone. "It was now after midnight, and the PM, who had had no dinner, proceeded to eat a huge meal. Presently, he put his half-finished cigar across the wine glass. He was plainly very weary."[16] It is unclear whether an entirely new feast had been prepared, replacing what had been set out earlier, as original records may have been destroyed by the Ninth Directorate of the KGB, which was then in charge of serving the elite.[17]

Discussions the following day proved fruitless. Churchill could pry no response from Stalin other than a repeated demand for a second front, prompting a disgruntled Churchill to announce to his staff that further meetings would be useless. He did, however, feel compelled to stay for Stalin's closing official banquet for his own staff and the British guests – some hundred in all – the following night.

The menu did not reflect any wartime food shortages in the hard-pressed Soviet Union.

HORS D'OEUVRES (Cold)

Caviar (soft). Caviar (pressed). Salmon. Sturgeon.
Garnished herrings. Dried herrings. Cold ham. Game
Mayonnaise. Duck. Soused sturgeon. Tomato salad. Salad
Payar. Cucumber. Tomatoes, radishes. Cheese.

HORS D'OEUVRES (Cold)

White mushrooms in sour cream. Forcemeat of game.
Egg-plant meunier.

DINNER

Creme de poularde

Consommé borsch

Sturgeon in champagne

Turkey chicken partridge

Potato purée

Suckling lamb with potatoes

Cucumber salad cauliflower

Asparagus

Ice-Cream fruit ices

Coffee liqueurs

Fruit petit fours roast almonds[18]

"The dinner dragged on," moaned Churchill's doctor, "the list of toasts – 25 of them – appeared interminable."[19] Churchill later told Sir Charles: "The food was filthy." As was the Prime Minister's changeable mood. Being assigned the place of honour on the Soviet leader's right was no compensation for the abuse to which Churchill felt he and his entourage were still being subjected. Unusually, Churchill wore his siren suit to this dinner instead of the traditional black tie that he often wore for such formal banquets.

At seven o'clock the next evening, after a day of staff meetings, Churchill went to see Stalin to say goodbye as he planned to leave Moscow early the following morning. The possibility that his ally would leave contemplating an open breach had its intended effect on Stalin, who quite unexpectedly invited Churchill to his Kremlin apartment for drinks. "I said that I was in principle always in favour of such a policy,"[20] responded Churchill.

Drinks became dinner, and what a dinner it was. This dinner was as close to the one-on-one, table-top diplomacy that Churchill preferred as anyone was ever likely to get in the Kremlin. It included interpreters, both A.H. Birse (stepping in at the last minute for Churchill) and Vladimir Pavlov (for Stalin), and, at Stalin's suggestion, Foreign Minister Vyacheslav Molotov. Even the serving staff was minimal: this apparently impromptu dinner was on a serve-yourself basis. Stalin brought in his daughter, Svetlana, to meet Churchill, and uncorked various bottles, "which began to make an imposing array."[21]

At first, Stalin ate very little. The Prime Minister reported that even after some three to four hours of talk – just the sort of substantive conversation that Churchill had always assumed would more likely produce results in the informal

New allies. With Stalin, Moscow, 14 August 1942

setting of a private dinner than in a meeting room – "there was no response from this hard-boiled egg of a man."[22]

Churchill later recalled:

> Dinner began simply with a few radishes, and grew into a banquet – a suckling pig, two chickens, beef, mutton, every kind of fish. There was enough to feed thirty people. Stalin spoilt a few dishes, a potato there, an oddment there. After four hours of sitting at the table, he suddenly began to make a hearty meal. He offered me the head of a pig, and when I refused, he himself tackled it with relish. With a knife he cleaned out the head, putting it into his mouth with his knife. He then cut pieces of flesh from the cheeks of the pig and ate them with his fingers … Of course we waited on ourselves.[23]

Perhaps any disgust on Churchill's part was tempered by his life-long fascination with the exotic, and undoubtedly by his sense of triumph at breaking through the frost that had characterised Soviet–UK relations. He cabled Clement Attlee, the Deputy Prime Minister, in London: "I have just had a long talk, with dinner lasting six hours, with Stalin and Molotov alone in his private apartment … We … parted on most cordial and friendly terms …"[24]

The Prime Minister returned to his villa at a quarter past three on the morning of 16 August, convinced his special brand of personal diplomacy, practised at a private dinner, had succeeded. We "ended friends,"[25] Churchill told Wilson as he left for a four-thirty flight to Teheran, and reported to the Cabinet, with a copy to President Roosevelt, that he had had "an agreeable conversation" with the Soviet leader. "I am definitely encouraged by my visit to Moscow."[26]

Once in Teheran, Churchill again rested in the British summer legation. Then on to Cairo, and, after recuperating from understandable fatigue, inspecting the troops, several meetings and a visit to Montgomery's forward position, back to London.

The meeting must be classified as a success, at least from Churchill's point of view. Stalin remained unhappy with the refusal of the US and Britain to create a second front, but did in the end respond positively to Churchill's detailed description of plans for Operation Torch by saying: "May God prosper this undertaking."[27]

On his way home, Churchill was happy to discover that the picnic basket that the Kremlin had packed for the flight was full of caviar and champagne. This more than made up for the ruckus on the flight into Moscow when Churchill demanded mustard for the ham sandwiches prepared for the flight by the British in Teheran. None was found and Churchill declared "... no gentleman eats ham sandwiches without mustard".[28]

Another mustard story: on his 1929 American tour, he had been invited to stay at the Virginia Governor's mansion. At one dinner, a favourite Virginia ham was served – but no mustard. When Churchill asked for some, the butler replied that there was none. The Governor's wife offered to have someone go down to the store and buy mustard, to which, much to her irritation, Churchill agreed.[29] Dinner was delayed.

CHAPTER 5

Adana
January 1943

―――――――⊙※⊙―――――――

*"We are grateful to the hospitality of the Turkish
government ... and also to the Director-General of
Gastronomy."*[1]

Ambassador Sir Hughe Knatchbull-Hugessen.

In January 1943, Churchill travelled to Turkey to "make
a new effort to have Turkey enter the war on our side".[2]
This meeting with President Ismet Inönü would be code-
named Operation Satrap. Not for the first time, and not for
the last, the Cabinet opposed the trip, although conceding:
"Your special trips have been recognised to be of the highest
importance."[3] That opposition notwithstanding, Churchill,
accompanied by a large staff that included Cadogan,
General Sir Alan Brooke, Chief of the Imperial General
Staff, and a bevy of top brass, flew to Adana, a city in southern Anatolia, close to the Mediterranean coast. In his newly

outfitted B-24 Liberator, equipped up front with side blister windows that could be opened to vent the inevitable cigar smoke,[4] Churchill could sit in the co-pilot's seat and puff away. The Prime Minister, always attentive to the details of these personal meetings, left his many military outfits behind as a sign of respect for Turkey's neutrality. On meeting President Inönü, Churchill handed him a letter reminding him that when he had been in Turkey in 1909, he had met "many of the brave men who laid the foundations of the modern Turkey", including Atatürk.[5]

From the airport at Adana, he was driven to a railway siding where an "extremely comfortable" special train waited,[6] complete with lunch. This then steamed a few miles to the Yenice station, fifteen miles outside of Adana, where it was coupled to the President's train, nicknamed by Churchill the enamel caterpillar.[7] All the houses along the train route had been whitewashed before the dignitaries passed by.

After lunch in the President's railway carriage, the meetings started, meetings made easier by the fact that President Inönü spoke English, but more difficult by the fact that he, his Prime Minister and his Foreign Minister were all a little deaf. The British party "shouted cheerfully" throughout.[8]

After a long meeting, dinner was served, consisting of Turkish cuisine that a contemporary observer characterises as "very curious … rich and varied … open to improvisation".[9]

Chicken soup was the starter, followed by a cheese pie with a flaky pastry, steak with side dishes, lettuce, and cauliflower in a white sauce. The dessert of chocolate pudding followed

> The railway station near Yenice is today a small museum with a plaque commemorating the railway meeting.

Yemek Listesi

31 / I / 1943

Öğle yemeği

T.C.D.D.

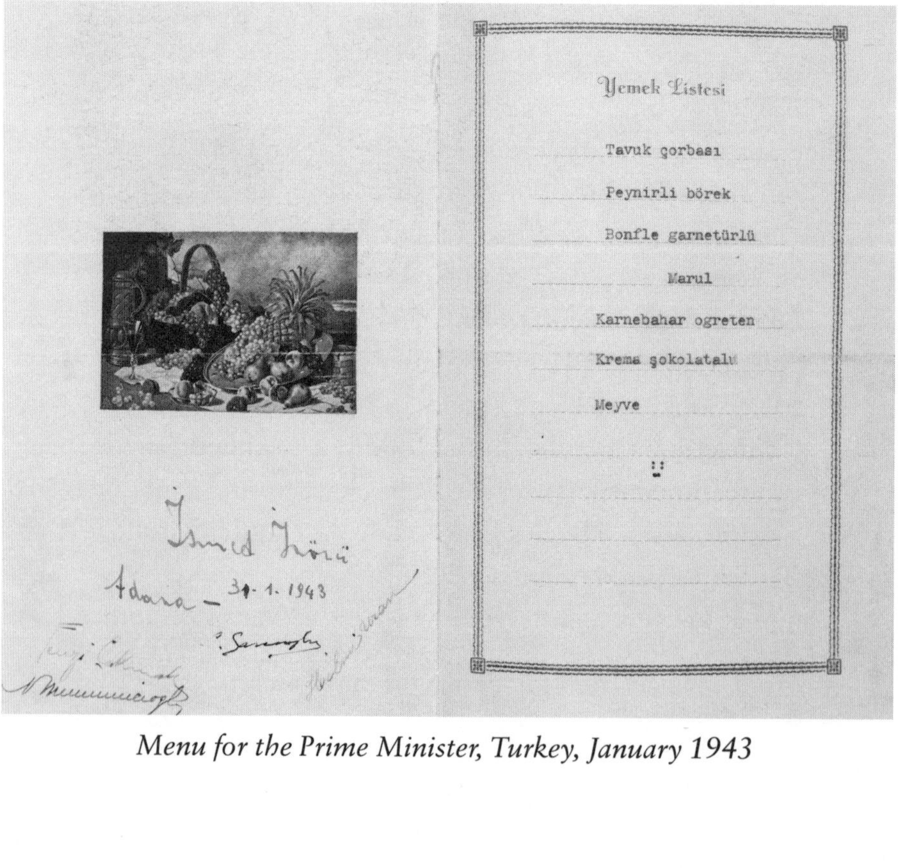

Yemek Listesi

Tavuk çorbası

Peynirli börek

Bonfile garnetürlü

Marul

Karnebahar ögreten

Krema çokolatalı

Meyve

::

İsmet İnönü

Adana — 30. 1. 1943

Menu for the Prime Minister, Turkey, January 1943

by fruit may not have been of interest to Churchill whose taste in desserts seem to have favoured ice cream.

If the President's train carriage was up to the standards of the diners built in Birmingham for Turkey's railways, it would have been built to accommodate "gleaming silver-ware ... spotless napery – even the double racks for hats and umbrellas".[10]

Dining with Turkish President Inönü in his private railway carriage, January 1943

The meeting was cordial, the food fine. General Sir Alan Brooke recorded in his diary:

The dinner party was a screaming success. Winston was quite at his best and had the whole party convulsed with laughter. In his astounding French, consisting of a combination of the most high flown French words mixed with

English words pronounced in French, he embarked on the most complicated stories, which would have been difficult to put across in English.[11]

Disconcerting, too, to the Turkish hosts must have been the sight of General Brooke indulging in a spot of impromptu birdwatching through the carriage windows. He thought he had spotted a pallid harrier but as he could not be sure, he continued to stare intermittently over the shoulder of his Turkish counterpart rather than concentrating on the discussions.

Agreement was reached on a variety of post-war issues, but the Prime Minister did not get what he came for. Although Turkey did agree to enter the war "when the circumstances are favourable"[12], as Churchill put it in his telegram to Attlee, it did not agree to join the Allies at that time.

CHAPTER 6

Teheran
November 1943

———— ◆ ————

*"Do you think you could bring me a little bit of butter
from that nice ship?"* [1]

"No more can be done here" [2]

Britain had been at war for four years before Churchill had an opportunity to meet simultaneously with his American and Soviet allies. So he gladly headed for Teheran and the first Big Three conference – there would be two more at Yalta and Potsdam – despite the fact that it meant still another arduous journey. As always, he arranged a series of very useful meetings along the way. To Malta, aboard one of his favourite ships, the HMS *Renown* for a meeting with the Chief of Staff Committee; to Cairo, via Alexandria, for a meeting with Roosevelt and the Combined Chiefs of Staff; and then a flight to Teheran.

In Malta Churchill found the food at the Governor's Palace not to his liking. He asked Lieutenant General Sir Hastings Ismay, his Military Secretary: "Do you think you could bring me a little bit of butter from that nice ship?" He complained that he only wanted "a cupful of hot water" for his bath "but could not get it".[3]

He did better in Cairo, where on 25 November, Thanksgiving Day for Americans, Roosevelt, also en route to Teheran, treated Churchill to a turkey dinner, carving the turkey himself.[4]

Churchill, who had been too ill to preside at Cabinet before setting off on his trip, arrived in Teheran with a bad sore throat, so bad that he was unable to speak or to have dinner with the President.[5] Instead, "he had dinner in bed like a sulky little boy ... practically no voice",[6] reading *Oliver Twist*.[7] Cadogan said that Churchill had strained his voice staying up late in Cairo arguing with the Americans and "then expressed surprise at having a sore throat".[8]

It must have been an easier flight as he was flying in his new Avro York aircraft newly fitted out, for the first time, with a "grill, fast heaters for drinks, and a toaster".[9]

The housing situation at Teheran was complicated by a battle between Churchill and Stalin for access to the President. The short version is that the Prime Minister's invitation to Roosevelt to stay at the British legation went unanswered, while Stalin's request that Roosevelt stay in the Soviet embassy's compound to foil an alleged assassination attempt (and facilitate bugging) carried the day, for two reasons. Roosevelt was eager to cement relations with an ally he had never before met, and the plenary sessions were to be held in the Soviet compound, a convenience for the wheelchair-bound President.

The British were able to be of service to the President in one particular. When the Americans, expecting the President to stay at their own compound, built ramps everywhere, they inadvertently blocked the entrance to the cellar of the house's official occupant, Louis G. Dreyfus. This serious problem was discovered only when Roosevelt asked for a whisky. Wisely, the Americans quickly sent out a request to the British legation and some eight cases of whisky appeared.[10] Another minor problem was that troops digging a protective trench in the British legation almost destroyed an important collection of Persian tulip bulbs collected and planted by the resident Oriental Secretary.[11]

Churchill, visions of a Big Two forming in his mind, was unhappy but helpless to prevent the rearrangement of living quarters in line with Stalin's, and very likely Roosevelt's, wishes, especially since Stalin was able "to give the impression he was the host" by arriving first, earlier than announced,[12] and greeting the arriving Roosevelt at the American legation, before his move into the Soviet compound.

Churchill's own base was at the British legation, built by the Indian Public Works Department. The British Minister was, by tradition, guarded there by "a small escort of Indian Cavalry for his personal protection".[13] Its gardens adjoined the Soviet embassy. Major Birse, Churchill's interpreter and an old Persia hand, noted men from Paiforce (Persian and Iraq Force) "... guarding the entrance gate and grounds. They were mainly men of the Buffs (as the Royal East Kent Regiment was known), and Indian troops".[14] John S.D. Eisenhower called them Sikhs.

On 28 November, the leaders met in the late afternoon, the same timing as at previous meetings, a schedule now traditional for summits, and certainly favoured by Churchill. The mornings were set aside for staff meetings to work on the briefings and communiqués to be presented to the leaders for discussion at the plenary sessions, all of which took place in the Soviet embassy. There were daily meetings of what has been called the Little Three: Hopkins, Molotov and Eden, as well as of the military staffs. The American delegation was small, according to Harriman, in order to emphasise the personal nature of the meetings.[15] The formation of cordial and even intimate relationships was facilitated, with four people for each of the three countries attending, one of whom was an interpreter. The President enlisted "Chip" Bohlen to interpret Stalin into English, a chore somewhat more demanding than mere translation. Churchill depended on Major Birse, who, in his memoirs, makes clear his distrust of Stalin but could not allow any of his own misgivings to colour his translations.

Each leader gave a dinner, another tradition established at earlier summits. The President was the host at his villa within the Soviet compound on the first evening, and he had pride of place as he was the only head of state present. A steak and baked-potato dinner[16] was cooked up by his private "indispensable Filipino mess men from Shangri-La"[17] (now called Camp David, the presidential country retreat), with cooking and serving equipment borrowed at the last minute from a nearby US military base. Stalin was the host on the next night, 29 November, a smaller and more intimate dinner but one with lasting effect. Widely reported were the taunts and barbs that Stalin threw at the Prime Minister, aided by the President. A bad night for Churchill.

Churchill planned his own gala dinner on 30 November, his 69th birthday, promising himself a "glittering, never-to-be forgotten" party at the British legation.[18] That morning, the Chiefs of Staff had thought about singing happy birthday to the Prime Minister in his bedroom "in the forenoon" but "decided it was beyond our capability".[19]

As always, Churchill fretted over every detail of the arrangements for his own dinner, wandering through the British legation dressed in a dinner jacket, waiting for his famous guests and puffing on a cigar,[20] his mind probably turning over how he wanted the dinner conversation to proceed and what the best outcome would be. Then Roosevelt arrived with his son, Elliott, and was wheeled up the improvised ramp onto the first floor of the British legation, surrounded by grim-faced Secret Service personnel. Roosevelt, who had not thought beforehand of an appropriate birthday gift, detailed Harriman to find one. The gift is described by one source as a twelfth-century Kashan bowl hastily purchased from the private collection of the Metropolitan Museum curator who was stationed in Teheran,[21] while another says the bowl was bought quickly in a local bazaar.[22]

Stalin arrived in a bad mood: he did agree to have his photograph taken under the British legation coat of arms, but turned down one of Roosevelt's infamous cocktails, refused to shake Churchill's hand,[23] and criticised the confusion created for him by the profusion of silverware. One of the British interpreters, Hugh Lunghi, remembers a "complex layout of cutlery", and that it seemed to worry Stalin, who questioned Birse, Churchill's personal interpreter, as to which to use when.[24]

Clearly, Churchill's table was "set with British elegance. The crystal and silver sparkled in the candlelight".[25] The

Ready for the dinner guests at the British legation

dining-room table that Churchill used is now in storage as it was later deemed too wide for the ease of cross-table chat, which might explain why the Prime Minister sat Stalin and Roosevelt next to him rather than across the table. Otherwise, the room itself looks much as it does today, despite all the changes in Iran since then. There are the same side tables – on one of which Churchill's cake would have been waited the lighting of its birthday candles.

In addition to the President's son, Lieutenant Colonel Elliott Roosevelt, Captain Randolph Churchill and his

Make a wish, 69th birthday

sister Sarah; FDR's son-in-law Major Boettiger, and Harry
Hopkins' son, Robert; were all at the birthday dinner. In his
memoirs, Churchill wrote that his two children were invited
in after the dinner for the birthday tributes but contemporary photos clearly show Sarah sitting at the table, between
two American admirals, Leahy and King. And the official
seating chart lists their names.

The photographs show only three glasses at each place,

The Big Three, dining together for the first time, 1943

two for wine and a smaller one for port. Perhaps the champagne glasses were handed round afterwards with the birthday cake. Or maybe this photo was taken before the table was completely set.

Sarah Churchill describes the dinner:

> The three interpreters – one for each of the Big Three – rose I felt, to histrionic heights. It wasn't just a matter of interpreting serious proposals, but of translating the nature of the different senses of humour which flashed between the three. Toasts were proposed and answered all through the long banquet … Between the courses anyone who felt inclined would spring up and propose a toast. Then the toaster would walk around and clink glasses with the toastee.[26]

Details about the foods and wines leaked out from British and American attendees afterwards, most of whom had followed their respective leaders back to Cairo. Cocktails, wrote an American journalist, "looked like tomato juice … probably the famous Middle East Bloody Marys, made by mixing tomato juice and vodka".[27]

The menu was:

Persian soup
Boiled salmon trout from the Caspian
Turkey
"Persian lantern ice"
Cheese soufflé

And champagne and both French and Persian wines with which to accompany the multiple toasts that had become so much a part of the ritual of those war leaders' meetings. They allowed Churchill that night to set aside the multiple irritations inflicted on him by both the President and the Marshal and to praise both the President (toasted by Churchill as President and personally) and Marshal Stalin (as "Stalin the Great"). The Soviet custom that the man proposing the toast clink glasses with the subject of his toast meant that Stalin was up and about throughout the meal, touching glasses all around the room. The small birthday cake would not have served the 34 guests but it did accommodate the 69 candles, in the shape of a V, and made the occasion more festive.

The "Persian lantern" dessert – the source of the most unexpected and perhaps amusing event of the dinner – is best described by General Brooke, who was near Stalin's interpreter Valentin Berezhkov:

When we came to the sweet course, the Chief of Legation

Cuisine had produced his trump card. It consisted of a base of ice 1 foot square and some 4 inches deep. In the centre a round hole of some 3 inches diameter had been bored, and in this hole a religious nightlight had been inserted. Over the lamp and hole a perforated iron tube stood erect some 10 inches over the ice. On top of this tube a large plate had been secured with icing sugar. On the plate rested a vast cream ice, whilst a small frieze of icing sugar decorated the edge of the plate! When lit up and carried in by white gloved hands with long white fingertips the total effect was beyond description. Two such edifices entered and proceeded solemnly around the table whilst each guest dug into the ice. I watched the tower ... and noticed that the heat of the lamp had affected the block of ice that it rested in. The perforated iron tower ... looked more like the Tower of Pisa! The plate ... had now assumed a rakish tilt! An accident was now inevitable ... With the noise of an avalanche the whole wonderful construction slid over our heads and exploded in a clatter of plates between me and Berezhkov. The unfortunate Berezhkov was at that moment standing up translating a speech for Stalin and he came in for the full blast! He was splashed from his head to his feet, but I suppose it was more than his life was worth to stop interpreting! In any case he carried on manfully whilst I sent for towels and with the help of the Persian waiters proceeded to mop him down. To this day I can see lumps of white ice cream sitting on his shoes, and melting over the edges and through the lace holes![28]

Another description of the famous dessert – a highlight of Churchill's birthday dinner – comes from Lieutenant General Sir Hastings Ismay, Churchill's Military Secretary:

... the pudding ... went by the name of "Persian Lantern", and consisted of an enormous ice-cream perched on a large block of ice in which burned a candle. The waiter responsible for passing this chef d'oeuvre paid more attention to the speech which Stalin was making than his own business. As a result, instead of holding the dish straight he allowed it to tilt more and more dangerously, and by the time he reached Pavlov, the Russian interpreter, the laws of gravity could be denied no longer, and the pudding descended like an avalanche on his unfortunate head. In a moment ice-cream was oozing out of his hair, his ears, his shirt and even his shoes. His translation never checked.[29]

Air Chief Marshal Sir Charles Portal was heard to say, *sotto voce*: "Missed the target" – meaning it should have been tipped over Stalin's head.

The sharp-eyed Admiral of the Fleet, Sir John Cunningham, later described the "Persian Lantern" as an "ice pudding". He also identifies the Russian interpreter as Pavlov.[30] (There is some confusion about which Russian interpreter was actually there. Much later, Berezhkov wrote a memoir in which he lets us believe he was present. The official guest list prepared by Harriman says it was Pavlov; the list from the British Embassy in Teheran says it is Berezhkov. Hugh Lunghi says that, after 1942, Pavlov was Stalin's only English interpreter. Oddly, the Soviet leader toasted – not once but twice – Churchill's valet, Sawyers, who was probably standing at the back of the room in the event that his boss might need something.[31] And then the dinner was over. It was successful in easing earlier tensions and may have been the basis for the lunch the following day at which Churchill, Roosevelt and Stalin agreed to a broad strategy for prosecuting the war to a triumphant conclusion, Overlord was to be launched during May 1944, and cooperation between the three nations' military staffs was enhanced.[32]

That evening, the Prime Minister asked Sir Reader Bullard, the British Minister, to commemorate the dinner he had given for Roosevelt and Stalin with a permanent plaque and instructed that it be hung in the legation's dining room. Churchill approved the text, which says, in part:

> These three representatives of allied states were at that moment met in Teheran to concert further measures whereby Nazi tyranny might be most speedily overthrown and mankind set free to enjoy in peace the fruits of its labours and to develop mutual aid for the good of all.
>
> Crescit Sub Pondere Virtus
> (Virtue grows with adversity, translation not on the plaque).

The plaque was engraved on silver and ceremoniously installed, and today frames the hallway just outside the dining room, across from a copy of the seating plan for the dinner. The Soviets later provided their own memento of the dinner but their text was engraved on a two-ton block of granite.[33]

Churchill and Roosevelt left Teheran for Cairo on 2 December. Stalin returned to Moscow.

Twenty years later, on Churchill's birthday, in 1963, Averell Harriman sent him this private note: "All best wishes on your 89th birthday. I vividly recall your 69th birthday twenty years ago when we dined with you in Teheran when plans were laid for victory over Hitler and hopes were high for the development of a peaceful post-war world."[34]

A nice footnote to a memorable evening.

CHAPTER 7

Yalta
February 1945

———— ⟨◈⟩ ————

"Buckets of Caucasian Champagne."[1]

"Our paws are well buttered here."[2]

Yalta was certainly not the easiest of locations for the next meeting of the Big Three. But Stalin would not fly, and refused to leave Soviet-controlled territory. The Soviet dictator, once again, had his way. No matter to Churchill, who believed that this meeting would be what US Secretary of State Edward S. Stettinius, Jr. later called "the most important wartime meeting of the leaders of Great Britain, the Soviet Union and the United States".[3] For Roosevelt, however, the trip to this remote location, crossing parts of Europe still at war, was an arduous undertaking. Hopkins saw the President's willingness to travel to Yalta as a tribute to his "adventurous spirit [which] was forever leading him to go to unusual places".[4] This, at a time when Roosevelt was so seriously ill that his energies would desert him during the meeting. He would die only two months after the Yalta Conference ended.

En route to Yalta, Churchill and Roosevelt met for lunch aboard the cruiser USS *Quincy* at Malta, after which the Prime Minister cabled Clementine: "My friend has arrived in the best of health and spirits."[5] He was alone in that view.

Marian Holmes, one of the Prime Minister's secretaries, noted: "What a change in the President since we saw him in Hyde Park last October. He seems to have lost so much weight, has dark circles under his eyes, looks altogether frail, and hardly as if he is in this world at all"[6] – a description borne out by the photographs of him, which show a very sick man indeed.[7]

After-dinner tête-à-tête

So unwell was the President that the plane to Yalta had to fly very low because of his blood pressure, a problem that would not have seemed serious to Churchill, since his own health during most of the war required the unpressurised planes of that time to fly below 10,000 feet.

Perhaps Churchill saw what he wanted to see on the eve of the Yalta Conference; perhaps he was harking back to his own experience of an almost miraculous return to full health a few years earlier, when he was taken seriously ill with pneumonia but quickly recovered, despite defying his doctors and constantly calling for the forbidden cigars – a defiance repeated when recovering from a broken hip and several strokes

The city of Yalta had become tsarist Russia's leading seaside resort in the nineteenth century, its extravagant villas patronised by the royal family and the aristocracy. After the revolution it became the pre-eminent holiday destination for Soviet workers. But the war had brought severe destruction. The retreating Germans had destroyed much of its infrastructure and vandalised its palaces. For the conference, the Soviets had to bring with them all the furnishings, plumbing, carpeting, windows and even the domestic staff, who were from the prestigious Metropole Hotel in Moscow.[8] Some American delegates who had worked in Moscow recognised familiar faces. Everything had been packed into 1,500 railway coaches[9] which had begun arriving in Yalta just a few days before the start of the meetings.

Yalta's harbour had been so heavily mined, and there were so many sunken ships, that the American and British ships had to anchor at Sebastopol, 90 miles away. Those ships were the "sole link with their home countries, and all messages in and out were transmitted through them".[10] "If we had spent ten years on research we could not have found a worse place," Churchill complained to Harry Hopkins.[11] He was right: Yalta was clearly not the best place for a second meeting of the Big Three, one of whom was obviously failing. Churchill was sufficiently chagrined at the site selection to apologise to Marian Holmes, "What a hole I've brought you to."[12] He described the place as a "Riviera of Hades"[13] and intended to survive "by bringing an adequate supply of whisky good for typhus and deadly on lice".[14] (Churchill had declared "war on lice" in the trenches of the First World War when he discovered that his men were infested with them.) All attendees complained about bedbugs until the US military sprayed DDT everywhere.

After a few days at Yalta, Churchill revised his initial impression, cabling Attlee and the War Cabinet: "This place has turned out very well … It is a sheltered strip of austere Riviera with winding corniche roads …"[15] Perhaps he had found some virtues to the site, or was buoyed by sharing US Secretary of State Edward S. Stettinius, Jr.'s later optimistic assessment of the meetings' importance: "It was not only the longest meeting; it was also the first time that the three leaders reached fundamental agreements on post-war problems"[16] – a bit of an exaggeration since they had earlier agreed on substantial points of war-time strategy at the final lunch at Teheran.

Earlier in the year, Churchill had written to thank the President for two gifts. The first gift was a bound copy of Roosevelt's Prayer for D-Day; the second was three bow ties which Churchill promised he would wear when they got together at Yalta.[17]

Churchill was hoping for a resolution to the problem of Poland, unresolved at previous meetings. Roosevelt had a new item on his agenda: the structure of a post-war institution devoted to maintaining world peace. Roosevelt was determined not to meet the fate of a man he much admired, Woodrow Wilson, who, after the Great War, failed to persuade the American Congress to support membership of the League of Nations.

Not only had Stalin been unprepared to accommodate his allies on where to hold this meeting (just as he would later insist that the next meeting be held in Potsdam, in the Soviet Union's zone of defeated Germany), he also refused to accommodate them on most issues of substance. He was, however, quite prepared to play the gracious host by showering his guests with buckets of champagne and vats of caviar for "breakfast, luncheon and dinner"[18] – much appreciated by Churchill – and "lots of lovely butter",[19] a luxury strictly rationed in Britain (and, although less stringently, at the White House.) When one of the British delegation was heard to complain that there were no lemons for their gin and tonics, and Churchill's daughter, Sarah, commented that caviar tasted better with lemons, the Soviets somehow provided lemon trees with real lemons the next day.[20] When another delegate noticed that a fish tank was empty, the Soviets filled it with water and goldfish the next day.

The Prime Minister had taken off very early from his stop-over at Malta, and landed at a run-down airfield in Saki in the Crimea. After a brief ceremonial meeting with Roosevelt, who had arrived earlier, Churchill was then driven to Yalta – some seven or eight hours away, stopping en route at a rest house. The Prime Minister and his daughter Sarah, plus carloads of trailing staff and press, were greeted there by

Vorontsov Palace: Churchill's villa

Soviet Foreign Minister Molotov and by "a most magnificent luncheon ... prepared for me and the President or anyone else. Champagne, caviare, every luxury. Alas we had eaten a good deal before, but still there was a pleasant hour or two of talk and gourmandizing".[21] Sir John Martin, Churchill's Principal Private Secretary, recalled that "the table groaned with caviare and the pop of champagne bottles went on all the time like machine-gun fire".[22]

Suitably refreshed, the Prime Minister pressed on by car for another three or four hours across rough terrain, and along mostly unpaved road. Saluting Soviet soldiers were stationed at intervals variously reported as at 50, 100 or 200 yards.

The three villas assigned to the national leaders were about half an hour away from each other. The roads between the villas were cleared of all traffic and heavily patrolled by male Soviet troops, whereas the road from the airport had been patrolled by both male and female troops. Quite a show of power for Stalin, a demonstration he would later repeat at Potsdam.

Churchill and his party were billeted at the Vorontsov Palace, designed by a Victorian architect. Joan Bright, a member of the British staff, describes it as a "pseudo-Scottish-castle-cum-Moorish Palace".[23] Cadogan describes it as "a combination of the Moorish and Gothic styles ... a big house of indescribable ugliness – a sort of Gothic Balmoral".[24] It was in fact modelled in part on Windsor Castle, where Count Vorontsov's father, the Tsar's Ambassador to London, had been received by Queen Victoria.

Elizabeth Layton, who was with Churchill at Yalta, later recalled:

> washing facilities seemed to have been neglected. It appeared that the Prince and Princess Vorontsov had concentrated more on eating than on bathing. One bath and three small washbasins served this enormous Palace, and in the morning one queued with impatient Generals and embarrassed Admirals, all carrying their shaving kit, and wishing that their dressing gowns had been long enough to cover their bare ankles.[25]

Unusually, only three of the six nights were booked for formal banquets given by the national leaders. But on all days lavish lunches were served for the leaders and their staffs, both military and political. Cadogan tells us that the Soviets had prepared for arrival day "an enormous luncheon – more caviar and smoked salmon, more vodka, and much food of all sorts, ending with tangerines",[26] not available in Britain and considered a wonderful treat by the Churchills.

Clementine especially appreciated receiving some as a gift via one of the Americans visiting Britain.

Caviar was so often on offer, and in such huge quantities, that it came to be taken for granted. The Prime Minister complained that it was no substitute for news from his private office in Downing Street. In a letter to John Colville, John Martin quotes Colonel Kent (a code name for Churchill) sadly "calling again and again for news and being only offered caviar".[27]

After the midday feast set out on the day of Churchill's arrival, and throughout the conference, there was a general dinner for the entire British contingent, including staff, but the Prime Minister, who had arrived at around dinner time, slipped off to bed early. "He must have dined in his own room," Cadogan writes in his diary.[28]

The absence of formal dinners on the first three nights of the Yalta Conference allowed Churchill to dine privately with his daughter and Anthony Eden, the Foreign Secretary. Sarah, in a letter to her mother, reported her father's daily routine:

> We dine quietly here – generally just Papa and Anthony and me – which of course is heaven … Morning presents a certain problem as he wakes rather late, and there isn't any time for breakfast and lunch and work and a little sleep before the "do" at 4 – so now he has just orange juice when he is called and "brunch" at 11:30 – then nothing until 9 o'clock! This seems a very long time …

And should the Prime Minister feel peckish, or should he still have in mind the advice given long ago by his gastro-enterologist that he could reduce his bothersome

Livadia Palace: Roosevelt's villa and meeting room

indigestion by eating lightly every few hours:[29]

> We are going to send him over some chicken soup in a ther-
> mos – and when they break for a few minutes for tea – he
> could have his chicken soup! If he doesn't have a whisky and
> soda! [30]

The American delegation was assigned to the 50-room
Livadia Palace built by Tsar Nicholas II as a summer retreat,
because the grand rooms on the ground floor would be easily
accessible to the President. Stalin had suggested the plenary
meetings take place there so that the President did not have
to travel between buildings. Today, there is a Churchill Room
at Livadia which commemorates the Big Three's 1945 meeting, furnished with donated volumes about and by Winston
Churchill.

Some in the American delegation were not so lucky with
their room assignments. According to Edward Stettinius, his
"State Department group was small enough to be comfortably housed at the Livadia Palace, but this was not true of
the military staff, five to seven generals were housed in one
room, and ten colonels in another … Some 215 American
staff had access to only a very few bathrooms".[31] Only the
President had his own bathroom, but he had nowhere to hang
his clothes. However, on the second floor of the palace the
American military organised a mess hall where American
and Soviet foods were served to the American delegation.[32]

The first official dinner was given by President Roosevelt
on 4 February for his two honoured guests, the Prime
Minister and the Marshal, plus eleven others. The old
billiard room had been converted to a dining room at the
Livadia Palace, and the billiard table was used for meals. The

fallibility of eyewitnesses' memories is demonstrated by the varying reports of what foods the Americans laid on for their British and Soviet counterparts. Edward Stettinius noted that what he calls "our" dinner was a typical American one. "Although caviar and sturgeon were added as always at every meal, we had chicken salad, meat pie, fried chicken Southern style, and vegetables."[33] But the official State Department log lists vodka as the first item, followed by "five different kinds of wine, fresh caviar, bread, butter, consommé [an agreeable surprise for Churchill], sturgeon with tomatoes, beef and macaroni [very American], sweet cake, tea, coffee and fruit".[34]

The President took to Yalta an assortment of foods including 24 dozen eggs, caviar, oranges, two cases of scotch, one of gin and one of Old Grand-Dad (bourbon) and bottled water.[35]

An unlikely scenario is put out by the website for the Livadia Museum. It says that so wonderful did President Roosevelt consider the "local cuisine that he even sent his two personal chefs away from Livadia as their services were no longer needed".[36] Mike Reilly, the much-respected head of the American presidential security detail, would never have allowed such a potentially dangerous change. Besides, the President was already ill, and unlikely to experiment with local cuisine. Indeed, at one of the dinners he felt unwell and had to leave the table.

There was Russian champagne, and "much good-humoured jesting with the President over the question of whether he had wired Moscow for 500 bottles of champagne, which Stalin said that anyway he would give it to the President on a long-term credit of thirty years".[37]

On 8 February, Stalin was the host at his own conference villa, the Yusupov Palace, built in 1909 by Prince Felix Yusupov who took part in the murder of Rasputin in St. Petersburg in 1916.

Unlike Roosevelt, Stalin included among his 30 guests several of his military chiefs. He also included three daughters who were in Yalta with their fathers: Kathleen Harriman, who proposed a toast in Russian, Anna Roosevelt Boettiger and Sarah Churchill. Stalin's daughter, Svetlana, who had been presented to Churchill in Moscow at an earlier Stalin-Churchill dinner in 1942, was not present.[38]

Cadogan wrote in his diary that he was relieved not to have been included because he was "tired of these silly toasts and speeches".[39] 'Alan Brooke, who had been promoted to the rank of Field Marshal in January 1944, was included and he was "not looking forward to it",[40] after a day touring two of the sites of the Crimean War, Balaclava and Sebastopol – and, as ever, on the look-out for birds. Stettinius notes that alertness was required at all times at the dinners, as elsewhere.[41] He adds that there were "twenty courses, forty-five toasts",[42] confirming Cadogan's prediction of endless toasting. On the day after Stalin's dinner, Cadogan – although not present – recorded in his diary: "The PM seems well, though drinking buckets of Caucasian champagne which would undermine the health of any ordinary man."[43]

Stettinius went on to describe this dinner as "most cordial, and it proved to be the most important dinner of the

Conference. Stalin was in excellent humour and even in high spirits".[44] That night, the President told his fellow guests, he felt "the atmosphere at the dinner was that of a family".[45]

The final glass was raised in a toast by the Prime Minister to the interpreters, one of whom, Hugh Lunghi, told the author that amid all the drinking and toasting, Churchill never overdid it, remaining sober throughout the evening. After all, he was there to work: he wooed Stalin to the best of his considerable abilities, appealing for a post-war world in which the Allies remained united, one in which they could lead both the smaller and larger nations "to the broad sunlight of the victorious peace".[46] Marian Holmes reports that after the dinner given by Stalin, "PM just returned from his dinner, he is next door singing The Glory Song".[47]

> Marian Holmes, travelling with Churchill as one of his two secretaries, sometimes caught the Prime Minister's mood by citing the songs he sang or hummed. On the night of 7 February, after a difficult day arguing about the composition of the proposed United Nations, Churchill was humming "There is a happy land far, far away".[48]

On 10 February 1945, it was Churchill's turn to give the dinner at his own villa. With his usual flair, sense of drama and attention to detail, Churchill arranged for a British regimental guard to line the steps leading up to the villa.

And what a dinner it was. Stettinius called it an "historic evening" and noted that an "excellent dinner was served".[49] The official menu was printed with two addresses: the Vorontsov Villa and 10, Downing Street, Whitehall, with the prime ministerial cypher also shown. The point of including

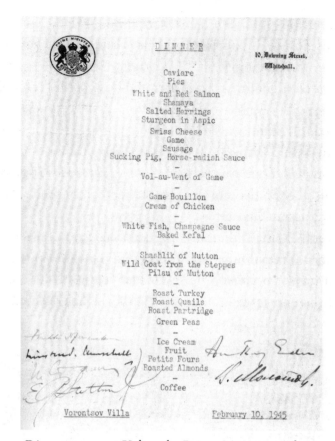

Dinner menu at Yalta, the Prime Minister as host

the cypher and Downing Street was to demonstrate that this was an official government dinner. Charles "Chip" Bohlen carefully preserved his copy of the menu, having had it autographed by the Big Three and their foreign ministers.[50]

Dinner began with caviar, and mixed traditional Western food with typical Russian courses, many of which were similar to what had been served to the Prime Minister in Moscow.

One of the most notable features of all these dinners and of the lunches of the principals and their staffs was the proliferation of toasts, with wine, vodka and champagne, then as now a Russian custom. But drunkenness was not a feature of the dinner on 10 February. Roosevelt took care not to down his drink after each toast. Churchill combined caution with a capacity, developed over a lifetime, to hold his alcohol. Stalin watered down his vodka. Stettinius notes: "Stalin would drink half of his glass of vodka and, when he thought no one was watching, surreptitiously pour water into his glass. I also noticed that he seemed to prefer American to Russian cigarettes."[51]

Several British diarists noticed that the Soviet staff crunched large numbers of apples and pears during and between meals, because, the myth had it, the fruits counteracted the enormous amounts of vodka which seemed to be required drinking.

The Big Three at dinner

Stalin carves up the Nazi bird, Allies looking on

As the presidential staffs prepared to wrap up the meeting on 11 February, the President and his party were given boxed presents by the Soviets. The boxes contained "vodka, several kinds of wine, champagne, caviar, butter, oranges and tangerines".[52]

Oranges were almost unavailable in Great Britain but plentiful in Casablanca where Ian Jacob, attending the Casablanca Conference in January 1943, wrote in his neatly typed diary: "Then the oranges. Large and juicy, with the best flavour of any oranges in the world, they lay about in platefuls everywhere and formed part of every meal."[53]

But gifts can present problems. After the meeting in Moscow between Churchill and Stalin in 1944, the Soviets also gave the British large boxes of food and champagne which the latter assumed were gifts for them. On returning to London, the Soviet embassy asked the British delegation for the "gifts" which had been intended for the embassy staff in connection with the Red Army Day celebrations – only to be told they had all been consumed. It is not clear whether or not Churchill ever found out about the miscommunication between the two departing staffs.

Unhappy with the President's performance at the conference, Churchill told his doctor, Charles Wilson, who had recently been ennobled and was now Lord Moran, that during the meetings "the President is behaving very badly. He won't take any interest in what we are trying to do".[54] This confirms Cadogan's observation that "The President in particular is very woolly and wobbly".[55]

The Prime Minister was glad the Yalta Conference was over. Hugh Lunghi later reflected that he had been particularly "dispirited ... and particularly objected to the overuse of the word 'joint' as in, say, joint agreement. It reminded him, he said, of the 'Sunday family roast of mutton'."[56]

For two days after the end of the meeting, Churchill rested aboard the SS *Franconia* at Sebastopol from the long hours and hard work before flying to Athens. The feasts at Yalta had not dampened post-conference appetites. On board ship, Cadogan wrote in his diary that he had "joined Winston at a terrific lunch – dressed crab, roast beef, apple pie, washed down with excellent Liebfraumilch, and gorgonzola and port!"[57]

For all his persuasive skills, Churchill was unable to achieve one of his principal wartime goals: a free and independent

Poland. Britain's position as a world power was diminishing as American troops flooded into Europe from the west and Soviet troops, outnumbering the Germans by two to one, rolled out across the continent from the east.

Roosevelt did not survive to see these developments: he died on 12 April 1945, just two months after the Yalta Conference ended. It fell to his Vice President, Harry S Truman, to fill his place at Potsdam, the next and final meeting of the Big Three.

CHAPTER 8

Meeting at Potsdam
July 1945

———— ⊰※⊱ ————

*"It fell to me to give the final banquet on the night of the
23rd. I planned this on a larger scale.*[1]

Prime Minister Churchill.

When Churchill arrived in Potsdam, fifteen miles
south-west of ruined Berlin, on 15 July 1945, three
days in advance of the final Big Three meeting (code-named
Terminal), he had several reasons to be happy. The
European war was won, the Pacific war a month from victory. Churchill's two months of telegraph and telephone exchanges with the new American President gave him confidence that he would work well with Harry Truman at the
formal meetings that would start a few days later. To the
Prime Minister, the circumstances of the Potsdam negotiations, if not of Britain's geopolitical position, seemed ideal:

victorious war leaders gathering for meetings at the highest level, with elaborate dinners of the sort that provided a stage on which he could shine and employ his potent personal, table-top diplomacy.

But the horizon was not cloudless. Churchill was aware that his ability to control events had diminished. American troops outnumbered British soldiers in the field, and Soviet troops had rolled out east at a phenomenal rate. He could not quickly duplicate with Truman the easy camaraderie he had developed with Roosevelt. He also knew that Stalin intended to dominate Eastern Europe and beyond, if possible, and had his troops in position to enable him to do just that.

The recent British general election, its results still being tabulated to include late-arriving soldiers' ballots, created uncertainty as to how long he might remain Prime Minister. Some of his advisers, among them his son Randolph, told him he had nothing to fear. Randolph assured his father that when the results were announced on 25 July, he would have a majority of somewhere between seventy and one hundred seats, most likely eighty; and Max Beaverbrook, two days before the election, put the Prime Minister's likely majority at around one hundred. Churchill knew better: he predicted "a hotly contested election".[2] and cabled Truman in advance of the Potsdam summit: "As you know, electioneering is full of surprises."[3] To his colleagues at the Potsdam meeting, he announced: "Some of us will be back."[4]

The Potsdam Conference, the last and longest of the wartime Big Three summits and the only one at which Churchill was joined by Truman, was held from 18 July to 2 August 1945. The meeting was convened largely at Churchill's behest,[5] but the site was selected by Stalin, who claimed to be taking his lead from Roosevelt's toast at Yalta, in which the President proposed that the next meeting be held in Berlin, to celebrate the downfall of Hitler. Churchill toured Berlin and, always magnanimous to fallen enemies, was deeply moved by the devastation. Berlin was "a chaos of ruins", he later wrote, its inhabitants "haggard".[6] Although Berlin had been heavily damaged by Allied bombings and too ruined to accommodate the Big Three conference, Potsdam, just south of the German capital, was relatively unscarred by the war.

Stalin, like Churchill, knew how to set a stage, in his case not by displaying any charm or gift for oratory, but by showing off Soviet power, a method he preferred to Churchillian persuasiveness. Potsdam was controlled by Stalin's armies, which allowed him to secure the roads between the villas housing the delegations and the conference centre with an ostentatious show of military strength. Stalin had even arranged for the courtyard of the meeting hall to be "carpeted with a 24-foot red star of geraniums, pink roses, and hydrangeas",[7] lest any of the conferees forget who controlled the territory on which they were meeting.

Potsdam had several features to recommend it as a site for a Big Three conference. To its south-east was Babelsberg, a former German movie studio and colony which had suffered little war damage and contained a great many elegant villas, with lawns sloping down to the several lakes and canals; enough villas to house all the diplomatic and military attendees and their staffs more comfortably than had been possible at Yalta. The delegations were much larger than at previous summits: the American delegation was four times the size of the group that President Roosevelt had brought to Yalta.[8]

The Prime Minister was assigned Villa Urbig, a pink stucco

Welcome to my villa: Churchill greets Truman and Stalin

house at what was then 23 Ringstrasse in a quiet residential area of Babelsberg, while his party was assigned fifty houses to allocate among more than 250 people. In her memoirs, Joan Bright, a brilliant manager of the arrangements for the British delegations at several conferences, noticed that every single house contained a "beautiful Steinway or Bechstein grand piano".[9] Chief Petty Officer Stewart Pinfield, who had been in charge of catering for the Prime Minister in Newfoundland and at Teheran in 1943, and by some accounts partly responsible for the melting Persian ice pudding, was summoned once again to supervise the Prime Minister's kitchen, a sensitive post given Churchill's view of the importance of dinners in the coming negotiations.

Arrangements for caring for and feeding some thousand people were immensely complex. The Russians could ship supplies overland, but, because each delegation was respon-

On the day of Churchill's arrival in Potsdam, Cadogan reported in his diary that he had dinner with the Prime Minister, Eden and "Archie Kerr only. Best fried filets of real sole I've had for six years. I made the salad myself, which was successful!"[10]

sible for provisions in its own set of villas, everything for the Americans and British attendees had to be flown in. Joan Bright's list of absolute necessities to meet the needs of the British delegation was extensive: food and drink, cooking utensils, cutlery, ashtrays, table linen, glass, china, caterers, cooks and waiters. Even drinking water was to be air-lifted in.[11] Joan Bright also requested "sixty dustpans, brushes and broom pails, scrubbing brushes. Two hundred house flannels. Sixty mops. Twenty four sauce pan brushes ... Two gross dusters, thirty three-tier bunks with palliases [straw-filled mattresses] and pillows. One hundredweight soda and one hundred tin bath and sink cleaner".[12] And new shirts for the Prime Minister's guards.[13] In his notes, Lord Moran recorded with some distaste that the French windows in Churchill's villa were "very dirty".

President Truman was assigned a stucco house at 2 Kaiserstrasse. Although painted yellow, it became known as the Little White House, and is now home to a liberal German political foundation. The Americans also flew in all the supplies needed by the eleven Navy cooks and stewards in the Truman entourage. "Cases of liquor and wine were flown in. A planeload of bottled water from France arrived daily."[14]

Sixty-one years later, when Lady Soames revisited her father's villa to celebrate the placing of a commemorative plaque, she "recalled the difficulties of fulfilling even basic household tasks" in the city of Potsdam, as she arranged a dinner party for Truman and Stalin, at which her father was to play host. "I had to do the flowers for this large party and it was certainly a challenge to even find them."[15]

Control of the Potsdam area made it easier for the Soviets to provide for the feeding and housing of their own military and diplomatic staffs. They set up cattle, poultry and vegetable farms and "two special bakeries, manned by trusted staff and able to produce 850 kg of bread a day",[16] and brought from Moscow by train anything else they needed and could not requisition locally. This access to food supplies simplified the task of catering for the typically lavish Soviet post-session buffets held in the Music Room of the Cecilienhof Palace.

The 176-room Cecilienhof Palace was Stalin's final reason for choosing Potsdam: a mock-English-Tudor mansion built for Crown Prince Wilhelm, the last Hohenzollern, and named after his wife, Crown Princess Cecilie. The palace – which today serves as a museum, restaurant and hotel, and for political meetings of the European and German Federal governments – was ideal for the plenary sessions. Set in 180 acres, it contains a large, double-height central meeting room on the ground floor. Lohengrin would have been at home here.

Stalin had this vast central meeting room, as well as all the villas, remodelled and refurnished, and the electricity system repaired, once again requisitioning everything he needed to furnish the villas and meeting room from the impoverished, war-torn Germans for whom he felt no Churchill-style sympathy.

The separate suites on different sides of the central room served two purposes. First, the national leaders could enter simultaneously from different doors, all the same size,

The Big Three and supporting staffs, at the Cecilienhof

solving a potential protocol problem. At the plenary sessions, the three national leaders – the British Prime Minister, Winston Churchill; the Soviet "man of steel", Generalissimo (no longer the mere "Marshal" he was at Yalta) "Uncle Joe" Stalin; and the newcomer to big power summits, American President Harry S Truman, entered separately and simultaneously, accompanied by what Lord Moran described as their "captains, who had survived the miscalculations of six years of world war".[17]

Second, the separate suites allowed each delegation to confer in private, to compare notes and prepare for the next session. Not unsurprisingly, the rooms claimed by Stalin's party for what today would be called break-out sessions were the largest and brightest: with two doors, and a polygonal bay window with cushioned window seats, overlooking the lake. The Generalissimo's desk straddled the room at an angle, giving him a clear view of everyone entering or leaving it.

The only daylight in the conference chamber comes from an immense many-mullioned window at one end; and for the late-afternoon meetings from a giant brass chandelier hung very high in the ceiling. The meeting room itself would have done little to dissipate the gloom generated by the war leaders' inability to agree on the post-war organisation of the world. In this pseudo-Wagnerian setting, around the special ten-foot round conference table made in Moscow,[18] one era of bloody history ended and another contentious one began. The armchairs assigned to the leaders were larger than the rest, with golden putti heads on the backs. Seated on one side of each leader was his principal foreign adviser: the American Secretary of State, James F. Byrnes, the British Foreign Secretary, Anthony Eden, and the Soviet Foreign Minister, Vyacheslav Molotov. On the other side sat each leader's interpreter. These aides and advisers were assigned armless chairs, which enabled them to lean over more easily for whispered conferences with their chiefs. The seating hierarchy was matched by a vehicular one. Churchill and his staff were chauffeured about in an armoured Humber Pullman. Clement Attlee, now Leader of the Opposition, who had served as Deputy Prime Minister in the coalition government, and Anthony Eden were assigned smaller armoured Humbers; lesser mortals, the military and diplomatic staffers who were assigned conference seats behind the front row, rode in Daimlers.

Churchill was looking forward to meeting Truman.

They had exchanged many important cables and spoken on the phone since Truman had become President but had not met in person. After their first working meeting in Potsdam, Truman noted in his private diary that Churchill "is a most charming and clever person". Perhaps unaware of Churchill's deep admiration for the United States, he added that Churchill "gave me a lot of hooey about how great my country is. I am sure we can get along if he doesn't try to give me too much soft soap".[19] In his memoirs, Truman, knowing that he was writing for publication, recorded, less controversially,: "I had an instant liking for this man who had done so much for his own country and for the Allied cause."[20]

Truman and Stalin reflected their perceptions of the declining importance of Britain and its Prime Minister by meeting without him on the day before the formal meeting opened. On the morning of 17 July, Stalin showed up unexpectedly at Truman's villa, with Molotov in tow. It was the first encounter of the American and Soviet leaders. Protocol was abandoned as they sat down to get acquainted. As time passed, a Truman aide slipped into the room and asked if the President wanted to ask his new friends to stay for lunch. The President asked what was on the menu. "Liver and bacon" was the reply. The President told the aide: "If liver and bacon is good enough for us, it's good enough for them."[21] Stalin at first said he could not stay but was persuaded to do so. After Stalin admired the wines served, Truman sent him "twelve bottles of Niersteiner (1937 vintage) wine, twelve bottles of Port wine and six bottles of Moselle wine as a gift".[22] After lunch, when Stalin and Molotov had left, the President took a nap.

That afternoon Churchill, too, had a busy lunch. This one with Truman's Secretary for War, Henry Stimson, who told him that the Americans had successfully detonated an atomic bomb.

The following day, 18 July, Churchill invited Truman to lunch in his villa, before the next plenary session, due to start late in the afternoon. Churchill proudly noted the President called this lunch "the most enjoyable luncheon he had [had] for many years."[23] From the Prime Minister's point of view, it was also among the more useful: he had an opportunity to discuss with the President the implications of the successful detonation of the atomic bomb.

Attesting to the difficult nature of the issues confronting the leaders is the fact that many of the agenda items were the same as those with which they had wrestled at the Teheran and Yalta conferences: reparations; the borders and divisions of Germany; the future governance of Poland; the continuing war in the Far East; and the structure of a long-anticipated institution to preserve world peace.

There were official banquets at which each of the Big Three were hosts, as well as smaller working staff dinners every night (also breakfasts, lunches and teas). It was in these settings that Churchill hoped that not only he, but also his military and political staffs, would establish the tripartite personal relations that would carry through to broad agreements on the agenda items, and to post-war cooperation. At Truman's official dinner on 20 July, the President again served those wines that Stalin had praised, along with a well-known claret, Mouton d'Armailhacq, and a Pommery champagne 1934.

The celery, lettuce, tomatoes and ice cream were flown into Babelsberg from the USS *Augusta* berthed at Antwerp. Other courses, presumably provided locally were pate de foie gras, caviar on toast, vodka, cream of tomato soup, perch sauté meuniere, filet mignon with mushroom gravy, shoestring potatoes, lettuce and tomato salad, French dressing, Roca cheese, vanilla ice-cream, chocolate sauce, demi-tasse ...[24]

Truman, who loved classical music and played the piano very competently, and as often as possible, asked Stalin to name his favourite composer. Stalin replied, "Chopin" – a Polish freedom-loving émigré who spent most of his adult life in France, and a composer who probably would have been Gulag-bound, or worse, if he had lived in Stalin's time. The President therefore arranged that a classically-trained piano-playing US Army sergeant, Eugene List, would begin the musical entertainment with one of his personal favourites, the Chopin Waltz in A Minor (Opus 42).[25]

Sixteen years later, during the festivities for President Kennedy's inauguration in 1961, President Truman was a guest at the White House and Eugene List played Truman's favourite Chopin waltz again.[26]

Stalin so enjoyed the performance that he shook the sergeant's hand warmly afterwards. Cadogan joked with Molotov that they should hire Sergeant List to play while they discussed the Polish Question.[27] Churchill was less impressed: his taste ran more to the gaiety of Gilbert and Sullivan, and music hall ditties, hummable tunes and martial airs. It would be interesting to know the reaction of Molotov, who it is said, played the violin well enough to busk in the early days before he rose to power with Stalin.[28]

Not to be outdone, Stalin, for his own banquet the following evening, 21 July, rushed in four musicians from Moscow, including two female violinists whom Truman describes as "rather fat,"[29] and, in a letter home to his wife Bess, "a dirty-faced quartet".[30] Churchill undoubtedly would have preferred conversation, but it was not to be. President Truman told the Prime Minister he would be leaving the dinner as soon as "our host indicates the entertainment is over".[31] As did Churchill who once quipped: "I stay until the pub closes."

Not long after Churchill returned to his villa that night, a directive went out for entertainers for the dinner party he planned to give: "He ordered up the whole of the Royal Air Force Band – the String Orchestra".[32] Organising an emergency flight from London was no easy matter for those in charge of logistics, but the Prime Minister was determined to have his dinner party go well. Besides, he had, for some reason, decided to add a ham course to the proposed menu so that, too, had to come by air from London.

The seating plan and programme for Churchill's banquet on 23 July were important enough to him to be pasted into the Churchill family albums – now called the Broadwater Collections – with the following note, in bold capitals, to his then-secretary Elizabeth Layton:

THIS IS THE CARD OF THE "BIG THREE" DINNER
AT POTSDAM 23-7-45 AND MUST BE
CAREFULLY PRESERVED IN MR. CHURCHILL'S
SCRAP BOOK PLEASE

Churchill first had to decide how many guests he could invite. So important did he consider the physical comfort of a dinner to be that he ran a test: he had some of his staff sit around the table and pretend to be Stalin or Truman – to make certain the elbow room was adequate.³³ He calculated that he could fit only 28 at a table that had been hastily constructed by the sappers, so he was required to recall several invitations, including one to the Solicitor General, Sir Walter Monckton. Comfort and space, Churchill felt, would ease the flow of conversation. Churchill himself arranged the seating.

On the morning of 23 July, the Prime Minister began to fret about the dinner plans. Moran tells us that Churchill felt "that he has discharged his duty as host if he provides good plain fare and gives his guests plenty of elbow room to get at it".³⁴ But for whatever reason, the Prime Minister that morning upset the pineapple juice on the table by his bed. He gruffly ordered his valet, Sawyers, out of the room even though the clean-up was not finished. Some of his tension might have come from his anticipation of the upcoming dinner, which he regarded as the most important of the conference. His tension might also have been caused by three additional facts. First, he worried about how and when to tell Stalin of the successful testing of the new atomic weapon. Second, by this stage in the conference, Churchill was aware of the earlier attempts by Stalin and Roosevelt – continued at this conference by Truman – to marginalise him. His dinner was, in a sense, an attempt to regain standing and control of events. Third, the dinners that preceded his had gone reasonably well, setting a standard Churchill felt he had to match or, better still, exceed.

The assembling diners, sipping either the 1937 Krug or the alternative offering of amontillado, must have been surprised to hear the string orchestra of the Royal Air Force strike up Freire's Mexican Serenade, "Ay-ay-ay". Truman later recalled: "I liked to listen to him [Churchill] talk. But

(139)

W.S.C.

Dinner

Cold Clear Soup
Hot Turtle Soup

Fried Sole

Roast Chicken
Boiled New Potatoes
Peas

Cold Ham
Lettuce Salad

Fruit Salad
Ice Cream

Scotch Woodcock

10. Downing Street,
Potsdam.
23rd July, 1945.

(126)

W.S.C.

Amontillado

Hallgartener   Krug   St. Julien
Riesling   1937   1940
1937

Stokes Port

Prunier Brandy

Cointreau

Bénédictine

10. Downing Street,
Potsdam.
23rd. July, 1945.

Churchill's dinner,
Potsdam
Menu, music, wines,
seating chart

General of the Army H. H. Arnold   Sir Edward Bridges

Army General A. J. Antonov   Marshal of Aviation F. Ya. Falalev

Field-Marshal the Honble. Sir Harold Alexander   Field-Marshal Sir Bernard Montgomery

Marshal of the Soviet Union G. K. Zhukov   General of the Army G. C. Marshall

Admiral of the Fleet Sir Andrew Cunningham   Marshal of the Royal Air Force Sir Charles Portal

Andrew Cunningham   Major A. Birse   Mr. V. N. Pavlov

His Excellency Generalissimo J. V. Stalin   His Excellency Mr. V. M. Molotov

Prime Minister   The Rt. Honble. Anthony Eden

The President of the United States of America   The Honble. James F. Byrnes

Mr Charles E. Bohlen   Field-Marshal Sir Alan Brooke

The Rt. Honble. C. R. Attlee   Admiral of the Fleet N. G. Kousnetsov

Fleet Admiral W. D. Leahy   Lord Moran

Field-Marshal Sir Henry Maitland Wilson   Fleet Admiral E. J. King

Commander C. R. Thompson   General Sir Hastings Ismay

Entrance   *Edward Bridges*

PROGRAMME OF MUSIC

by

The String Orchestra of the Royal Air Force

Conductor - Wing-Commander R. P. O'Donnell, M.V.O.

I

"Ay-ay-ay" (Mexican Serenade)	. . . .	Friete
"Carry me back to Green Pastures"	. . .	Pepper
"On Wings of Song"	. . . .	Mendelssohn
"Sons of the Soviet"	. . . .	Curzon

II

"Serenade"	. . . . .	Mozart

III

"Holberg Suite"	. . . . .	Grieg

IV

"Serenade Espagnole"	. . . .	Chaminade
"Deep River"	. . . .	arr. Coleridge-Taylor
"Irish Reels"	. . . .	arr. Hartley
"Skye Boat Song"	. . . .	arr. Moffat

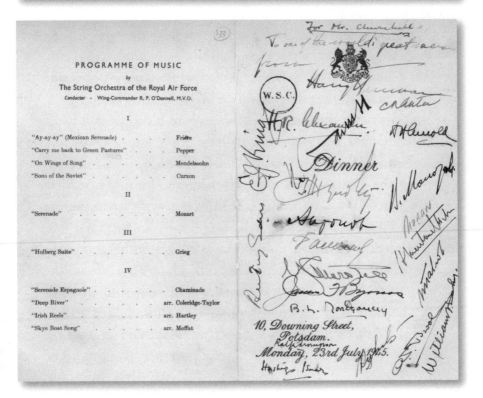

For Mr. Churchill,
To one of the world's great men
from
Harry Truman

Dinner

10, Downing Street,
Potsdam.
Monday, 23rd July 1945.

he wasn't very fond of music – at least my kind of music",[35] which was the classical music the President had played a few nights earlier at his own dinner.

Churchill's decision to match his conference partners' musical offerings was more out of necessity and not to be seen as a spoilsport, than from any love for dinner-time musical entertainment, which Churchill believed interfered with the main purpose of the dinner – conversation. The leaders were there to cement relationships, not to listen in silence to after-dinner music, at least in Churchill's view.

He had very carefully placed the Generalissimo to his left and the President to his right because Stalin, at the opening session, had proposed, with a shrewd eye for flattery, that the American President serve as presiding officer at the conference.

Whereas the principal foreign advisers sat beside their leaders at the plenary sessions at the Cecilienhof, at the dinner Churchill placed Eden, Molotov and Byrnes opposite their chiefs so that they could be brought into the conversation whenever the Big Three chose, or excluded from it when they thought best. In order to have Stalin on one side and Truman on the other, Churchill had to deviate from his usual practice of keeping his interpreter next to him: Major Birse was placed one seat away, on Stalin's left, with Pavlov across from Birse.

The printed menu – like many of his contemporaries, Churchill referred to menus as "bills of fare" – offered the diners, to start, a choice between a cold clear soup and hot turtle soup (a comforting reminder to Churchill of earlier days), neither being the detested cream soup. The soup course was accompanied by a 1937 Hallgartener Riesling. The Riesling carried on through the next course – fried sole.

On the front of the dinner card and on the menu itself is a repeat of the form used at Yalta, with both Downing Street and Potsdam addresses. This address was used because the villa was considered to be the Prime Minister's official residence while in Potsdam, and the Prime Ministerial cypher meant that the dinner was official government business. Memories differ as to where Churchill's dinner actually was held: at his private villa, at the Cecilienhof, or elsewhere. To add to the confusion, there is another menu for this dinner that is headed Schloss Cecilienhof. Perhaps the staff ate in the Cecilienhof dining room, which was larger, sharing the same menu. Admiral Cunningham recalled later that the official dinner was at the Prime Minister's house at Babelsberg,[36] as does the German-language guidebook to the Cecilienhof.

Whatever the location, what is certain is that Churchill served "the good plain fare" that Moran tells us the Prime Minister felt it a host's responsibility to provide, including roast chicken, boiled new potatoes and peas (new peas were one of his favourites). But the quality of the claret was not up to the usual Churchillian standards. The 1940 Saint-Julien vines "suffered wartime neglect", earning the wine only two stars of a possible five, according to wine expert Michael Broadbent.[37]

Churchill's selection of the final course before the dessert – cold ham and lettuce salad – was an afterthought that had been flown in from England at the last moment, perhaps to liven up the dull menu.[38] The dessert consisted of fruit salad and ice-cream (another Churchill favourite). By the time this was served, the orchestra was playing the tuneful *Holberg Suite* by Edvard Grieg, a move up the quality scale from Mexican music, and undoubtedly more pleasing to the presidential ear.

The dinner ended with the sappers, drafted as waiters, bringing in Scotch woodcock, a Victorian/Edwardian savoury served hot at the end of the meal. It consists of scrambled eggs, cayenne pepper, and Gentleman's Relish on buttered toast, with anchovies crossed over the top. A traditional British food of the sort upon which Churchill had been raised. The reactions of the Prime Minister's foreign guests to this offering are not recorded. It was accompanied by Stokes port, Prunier Brandy (an elegant brandy produced since the 1700s), Cointreau and Benedictine – and the inevitable cigars.

This straightforward, uncomplicated meal was a useful bridge over the tensions, stresses and ever-widening differences that had appeared at the meetings throughout the day. The sound of clinking glasses, toasts (brief speeches, really) in both languages, their interpretations and a seating arrangement – the Big Three side by side – that facilitated easy conversation, including frequent changing of places with the President at one point briefly sitting opposite Churchill, all combined to create an atmosphere very different from the formal plenary sessions. Churchill became increasingly jovial, and attentive to Stalin, whom, as at Teheran, he called "Stalin the Great", in recognition of the fact that the Generalissimo's power was far greater than that of the Russian Tsar, Peter the Great. Stalin, no stranger to flattery but too shrewd and wary to be affected by it, was all business. The wines and food notwithstanding, he turned the conversation to the coming showdown with Japan, and the Soviet Union's possible role.

That was not the only serious business transacted at the dinner. Truman, by pre-agreement with Churchill, wisely mentioned, almost casually, to Stalin that the West had a new and more powerful weapon. Stalin did not let on that he had known all along about the existence of the bomb from German-born, British-educated Klaus Fuchs, who operated in Britain, and worked on the Manhattan Project.

After dinner, to Churchill's surprise, Stalin "got up from his seat with the bill-of-fare card in his hand and went around the table collecting the signatures of many of those who were present. "I never thought to see him as an autograph-hunter!", Churchill later wrote.[39] Churchill complained that, if everyone did as Stalin had done, he would have to sign 28 menus, and sent Sawyers (ever-present in rooms when Churchill might need him) around with Churchill's own menu card. Lord Moran wrote of how "all these hardened, sophisticated, wandering men" joined in the milling about, borrowing pens, exchanging information and signing each other's menu cards, adding to the general relaxed conviviality.[40] So successful had Churchill been at cracking the formal ice of the daytime sessions that the usually dour Stalin became, in Moran's words, "smiling and almost amiable".[41]

After formal toasts had been offered, Churchill filled what he describes as one "small-sized claret glass with brandy" for himself and another for Stalin. "We both drained our glasses at a stroke" and, as Churchill recalled, "gazed approvingly at one another".[42] Unfortunately for Churchill, neither the brandy nor the mutual approving gazes kept Stalin from pursuing his post-war agenda. Having shown himself a collector of autographs, Stalin became, in the words of one historian, "a collector of territories" as well.[43]

Churchill's warning not to treat his post-election return to Potsdam as a certainty proved prescient. So that he could be in London for the election results, delayed for three weeks after polling day by the need to receive and count the votes of overseas troops, he left Potsdam on 25 July, only two days after playing host to the American President and the Soviet Premier at his grand dinner. The confident forecasts he had received of a renewed mandate to govern proved to be wishful thinking. The Labour Party received an overwhelming majority; its leader, Clement Attlee, was the new Prime Minister; and Churchill, who did retain his parliamentary seat, was reduced to a new role as Leader of the Opposition. It was Attlee, initially attending the conference as Leader of the Opposition, who returned to Potsdam as Prime Minister to continue the meetings with Truman and Stalin.

July 1945 was thus an important turning point in Churchill's career. Despite regaining the premiership in 1951, Churchill would never again lead with the vigour and effectiveness that characterised his wartime leadership. By the time he returned to Downing Street in 1951, just short of 77 years old, age and ill health had had their inevitable effects, Britain's role and influence in world affairs was diminished, and President Eisenhower and his Secretary of State, John Foster Dulles, proved less susceptible to the Prime Minister's charm and persuasive powers.

Would the course of events have been different at Potsdam had the purposefully convivial Churchill not been replaced, mid-meeting, by the more monosyllabic Clement Attlee? That is unlikely. Churchill's charm, his eloquence, his far-sighted view of the future shape of world events — foreseeing the totalitarian horrors a tyrant like Stalin would impose on those lands his armies had overrun, and the Cold War Churchill would describe only six months later in his "Iron Curtain" speech in Fulton, Missouri — were in the end no match for what today we call "facts on the ground". In 1945 those facts overwhelmingly favoured the Soviet dictator.

CHAPTER 9

From Fulton to Bermuda:
The Limits of Dinner-table Diplomacy

———————⟨≋⟩———————

"This pig has reached the highest state of evolution." [1]

*"I will be host at the banquets and elsewhere but you will
preside at any formal conference."* [2]

To the surprise of most of his close associates, but not to
him, Churchill's short-lived Conservative caretaker government had been voted out of power on 26 July 1945 and he
had to resign as Prime Minister. According to Lord Moran's
published diary, the former Prime Minister, aged seventy, was
weary in body ands mind after five tense and hectic years as
a wartime leader travelling the world to deploy his personal
skills on behalf of the British people. Perhaps. But after a
few months of recuperation at Lake Como and the French
Riviera, he went back to work as Leader of the Opposition,
as a working historian, and as a speaker on the world stage,

full of zeal to help reshape the post-war world and strengthen the Western democracies.

President Truman had personally invited Churchill, the man about whom he noted in his memoirs: "I like to listen to him talk", to give a speech in March 1946 at Westminster College, in Fulton, Missouri, Truman's home state. Churchill accepted. He would spend two nights on the presidential train, play poker late into the night with Truman, and once again use the dinner table – in this instance also a card table – to persuade an American President to share his views on foreign policy, which were realistic but focused hopefully on the "seeds of peace" as the Soviets tightened their grip upon the countries they had liberated from Nazi Germany.

In 1933, Churchill wrote: "Nowhere in the world have I seen such gargantuan meals as are provided upon American trains. I have always been amazed at the immense variety of foodstuffs which are carried in the dining-cars, and the skill and delicacy with which they are cooked, even on the longest journey ..." We have to assume the presidential dining car, some thirteen years later, provided just such meals.[3]

Churchill's arrival in the small Midwestern town was eagerly anticipated. At Fulton, the chef of the Fulton Country Club prepared a typical American, country-style lunch. The "meal was served family-style to the distinguished guests at small tables of four to six people. Churchill and Truman were seated together. The cook ensured that each of her assistants would be able to say that they had served Churchill

En route to Fulton with President Truman

and Truman personally by allowing each of them to offer second helpings of one of the dishes to the two visiting dignitaries".[4]

That day's lunch included the not-yet-world-famous Callaway ham, fried chicken, buttered corn, rolls with cherry preserves (no butter) and angel food cake with strawberry topping – all many cuts above the dishes Churchill had endured from Mrs. Nesbitt's kitchen during his stay at the White House in 1941. And a contrast with the fare in Britain, where rationing remained in force.

Churchill's gallant description of his portion of the Callaway ham – "This pig has reached the highest state of evolution" – was not his typical response to foreign foods, especially those in which one of the courses required the slaughter of one of his favourite animals. The compliment was heart-felt; he spoke fondly about the Callaway hams years later. The company was quick to trade on his comments.

Fifty years later, when Lady Thatcher spoke at Westminster College on the anniversary of her predecessor's "Sinews of Peace" speech, she was served the same lunch, including the Callaway ham.

It has become fashionable to honour Churchill at commemorative events by duplicating the meals he was served. In April 1999, the US Navy, after commissioning a guided-missile destroyer, the USS Winston S. Churchill, invited guests to a lunch including, as far as possible, Churchill's favourite foods, "worthy of Chartwell's Mrs. Landemare".[5] In 2003, at the 50th celebration of the 1953 Bermuda Summit, the main meal served at that conference was duplicated. And the meal served first to Churchill and 50 years later to Lady Thatcher at Fulton was replicated in 2006 as a fund-raiser for Westminster College.

In his Fulton speech Churchill famously warned that an "iron curtain" had fallen across Europe "from Stettin in the Baltic to Trieste in the Adriatic". The interests of the members of the wartime alliance no longer being compatible, he called for the formation of a new Western alliance to oppose Soviet expansion in territory and influence. At the urging of the State Department, which feared that Stalin would be offended if America did as Churchill was pressing it to do, Truman – after encouraging him to toughen it in several places – carefully distanced himself from what has come to be known as Churchill's Iron Curtain speech.

The lack of initial success at Fulton was duplicated some

seven years later in Bermuda, at a conference proposed by Churchill, two years after he became Prime Minister for the second time. By then the effects of age, including increased deafness, and a stroke suffered in June 1953, from which it took him several months to recover (rereading *Phineas Finn* while doing so), were taking their toll. But he was full of enthusiasm to work on setting a course for what would later become détente.

After his stroke, Churchill immediately advised President Eisenhower that the planned Bermuda Conference would have to be postponed, attaching a full medical report to his telegram. The nation's newspaper publishers agreed not to report the nature and extent of the Prime Minister's illness.

By November 1953, a mere five months after his severe stroke, Churchill was very much on the mend. He celebrated his 79th birthday in the Cabinet Room with a party that featured a most unusual cake created by a London baker: a single tall layer with the spines of all the many books he had written replicated around the outside of it, as if it were a small circular library. A ribbon was tied around the cake, which was topped by a single tall candle, while a black confectionery dog, meant to be Rufus, Churchill's beloved poodle, tried to clamber up the candle to reach a tiny cat at the top. This set a pattern for some of Churchill's later birthdays when English bakers competed to bake the most original, even outlandish, cake, hoping for some publicity for themselves in addition to celebrating birthdays.

Immediately after his birthday celebration, Churchill left London for Bermuda. He had suggested this venue for the meeting, in part because in the British Crown colony he could act as host and lay on the pomp and ceremony he felt the arriving President deserved. Churchill went to con-

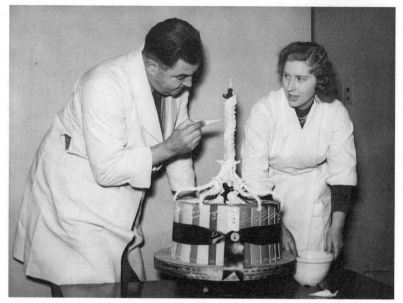

Churchill's 79th birthday cake

siderable lengths to make the conference attractive to the President, including selecting what he called the Mid-Ocean Golf Club as the site.

Churchill thought that adding the word Golf to the name of the Club would be an inducement for the President to accept. But Eisenhower, sensitive to press criticism at home of the amount of time he spent on the links, said he could not agree to meet at a golf club. The Prime Minister was forced to admit his fib: he had inserted the word golf in the club's name to entice the President.

On 8 November, Churchill promised the President warm Caribbean seas, writing:

My dear friend,
    I am so glad that it is all fixed … I will be host at the banquets and elsewhere but you must preside at the confer-

ence. I am bringing my paint box with me as I cannot take you on at golf. [6]

The seventeen-hour flight in the stratocruiser (two refuelling stops were necessary, at Shannon in Ireland and at Gander in Newfoundland) allowed Churchill time to dip into one of his favourite authors. As he had done on his 1941 sea voyage to meet another American president, the Prime Minister read a C.S. Forester novel, this time *Death to the French*, perhaps an ironic reflection of his disappointment that Eisenhower had insisted France be represented by its Prime Minister, Joseph Laniel, ending Churchill's hopes for a one-on-one meeting with him.

Churchill was eager to obtain Eisenhower's approval for a new approach to Moscow, including a summit meeting with the new Soviet leaders, Stalin having died in March. But Eisenhower had warned him earlier that he was not eager for the new multilateral meeting with the Soviets that Churchill

Mid Ocean Club, Bermuda

so desired. He wrote to Churchill:

> ... even now I tend to doubt the wisdom of a formal multi-
> lateral meeting since this would give our opponent the same
> opportunity ... to balk every reasonable effort of ourselves
> ...[7]

The first plenary session at the Bermuda Conference was held in the late afternoon of 4 December, continuing the tradition of late-afternoon meetings established at wartime summits. The Prime Minister officially requested that the President preside and Eisenhower quickly agreed.

A photograph now hanging on the wall of the Mid Ocean Club shows Eisenhower telling the British and French prime ministers where to sit.

Less officially, Churchill requested permission to smoke his cigars. The President quickly agreed, knowing he could then smoke his own cigarettes.

The meetings covered many issues of joint concern, but on the issue that had brought the Prime Minister to Bermuda – restarting negotiations with the Soviets – Churchill, despite the tremendous efforts he made, had to accept failure. He attributed his lack of success to two things: the intransigence of Secretary of State John Foster Dulles, and his own failing health. He told Lord Moran: "Dulles is a terrible handicap ... Even as it is I have not been defeated by the bastard. I have been humiliated by my own decay."[8] There might have been an additional factor: President Eisenhower might have remembered that Churchill had fought to have General George C. Marshall appoint-ed chief of operation for Overlord (the 1944 invasion of Europe), rather than then-General Dwight D. Eisenhower.

On 8 December the summit concluded and the conference room at the Mid Ocean Club was hastily converted into a formal dining room.[9] The Speaker of the Bermuda Assembly gave a dinner to celebrate "The Three Power Talks". But since both the President and the French representatives had left that morning before the official banquet, so only the British delegation was present. As was the custom, the Speaker proposed the first toast to the Queen. After other toasts, Churchill replied "as principal speaker, and did it very well", in John Colville's opinion.[10]

Fifty years later, on 8 November, 2003, the Churchill Centre gave an anniversary lunch at the Mid Ocean Club. The menu for the buffet lunch was contemporary, more varied than the December 1953 original, with lighter foods

The Big Two and the French Premier, Laniel

153

Admiral

Dinner

Given by the Speaker

in honour of

The British Delegation

to

The Three Power Talks

Tuesday
December 8th 1953

Mid-Ocean Club
Bermuda

Toasts

The Queen
Proposed by   THE SPEAKER

The President of the United States
Proposed by   B. C. C. OUTERBRIDGE, ESQ., M.C.P.

His Excellency The Governor
Proposed by   THE SPEAKER

The British Delegation to the 3-Power Talks
Proposed by   HIS EXCELLENCY THE GOVERNOR

Reply by Sir Winston Churchill

TIO PEPE

TRAMINER RESERVE
1947

MOET & CHANDON
1945

CROFTS 1917

HINE 60 YEAR OLD
LIQUEURS

Menu

Le Cocktail de Crevettes

La Vichyssoise en Tasse

Le Poisson des Bermude Bonne Femme

Le Tournedo Grille Maitre d'Hotel

Les Pommes de Terre Sautee

Les Petits Pois a la Francaise

La Salade de Saison

Creme Glacee Tutti-Frutti

Le Cafe Royale

Menu for the Bermudians' dinner honouring the British Delegation

more appropriate to Bermuda's summery weather. The drinks offered were certainly different: hard liquor (only on a "cash basis") and "bottles of wine on tables, mostly white, $30.00". Rather different from the elegant wines served at the 1953 dinner. Flowers were "to be inexpensive".[11] Guests arrived by bus. It is difficult to imagine the Prime Minister and the President, after a hard day of bargaining, queuing up for a self-service meal, although Churchill was no stranger to the trying venues of wartime Europe and willingly consumed sandwiches while on the campaign trail.

It should come as no surprise that Churchill left Bermuda still determined to arrange one more Big Three summit, a dream unrealised.

Churchill alone, Bermuda

SECTION 2

CHAPTER 10

Food

———◁◈▷———

"When I dine after a hard day's work, I like serenity, calm, good food, cold beverages."[1]

"Give me a few well-cooked dishes I can really enjoy."[2]

"It is well to remember that the stomach governs the world," wrote Churchill when planning the feeding of his troops on the north-west Indian frontier at the tail-end of the nineteenth century.[3] His stomach was often on his mind, perhaps because of his intermittent struggle with indigestion, which he called "indy", and about which he consulted the eminent gastroenterologist, Dr. Thomas Hunt.

Dr Thomas Hunt, of 49 Wimpole Street, in addition to certain dietary suggestions, offered Churchill the wise

Churchill at dinner, cartoon by Vicky

advice to exercise "not more than twice a day – and no longer than 15 minutes."[4]

Many years later, in 1954, after a discussion about which scales were in fact accurate in showing his true weight, a tomato diet had been suggested to Churchill. He wrote to his wife that he "had no grievance against the tomato but I think I should eat other things as well."[5]

Over the years, his aides came to understand the imperative of "tummy-time". Flying to Washington in June 1942, Churchill referred to his "tummy-time" as determining when meals should be served in flight, saying that he "didn't go by sun time ... but by 'tummy-time' and I want my dinner."[6] (When he landed, he went on to the British embassy for a second dinner.) In 1943, he left Washington, flying to

Newfoundland, thence to Gibraltar and on to Algiers. He slept in his flying boat but insisted that his meals be served at his "'stomach-time' without regard to changing time zones."[7]

In 1944, Churchill sardonically suggested that there be a "series of Cabinet banquets, a sort of Salute The Stomach Week".[8]

We have many menus covering much of Churchill's long life. They reveal a preference for fine, well-prepared meals, consisting of plain food as that term was understood by his class in his day. Here are two such meals. On 5 May 1914, three months before the outbreak of the First World War, as First Lord of the Admiralty, Churchill dined at the Ritz in Paris, with one guest, and had the bill sent straight back to London to Admiralty House. Alas, the stamped receipt from the Ritz blots out the main courses but we can see that he drank a Paulliac and ate pommes and petit pois.[9] And, a year later, in May 1915, Churchill and one guest dined at the Carlton Hotel on truites, roast beef, *salade*, *pommes* and *compote* (the Carlton Hotel was badly damaged by German bombs in 1940).

Minutes and other chronicles also show Churchill's willingness to make do with less when the circumstances required it. During the "Black Dog" days – as Churchill called his depression – after his resignation as First Lord of the Admiralty in 1915 following the Dardanelles setback, he tried to console himself as he wrote to his brother, Jack, from Hoe Farm where the family was living: "We live very simply – but with all the essentials of life well understood and well

Bill of fare,
Paris Ritz,
1914

provided for – hot baths, cold champagne, new peas and old brandy."[10] New peas were a lifelong favourite and featured three decades later in the menu for the dinner party given by him at the Potsdam Conference.

Of course, Churchill had his own definition of plain food, even under the trying circumstances of life at the front. In November 1915, Churchill wrote to Clementine from the trenches of the Western Front asking her to send him every week "a small box of food to supplement the rations. Sardines, chocolate, potted meats, and other things which may strike your fancy".[11] Two months later, he reminded her to send him "large slabs of corned beef: Stilton cheeses:

cream: hams: sardines – dried fruits: you might almost try a big beef steak pie: but not tinned grouse or fancy tinned things. The simpler the better: & substantial too; for our ration meat is tough and tasteless ..."[12] A month later he reported to Mrs. Churchill that during an attack "we hastily seized our eggs & bacon, bread & marmalade and took refuge".[13]

Not everyone would characterise the foods he asked be sent to the trenches as "the simpler the better" but we should remember the diary entry of Harold Nicolson, a contemporary and fellow member of the upper class, 25 years later, after lunching with the Churchills in their wartime flat, "We have white wine and port and brandy and hors d'oeuvre and mutton. All rather sparse."[14] Not how we would understand the term.

Impatience with badly prepared foods came to the surface when Churchill, by then Prime Minister, was entertaining Molotov and other Soviet officials at Chequers. The Soviets' schedule had been erratic and meals were often late or postponed indefinitely. At one dinner, quail was served but to the Prime Minister's nose, they were not quite "right" and too dry. He was "displeased" and said to the caterer, "These miserable mice should never have been removed from Tutankhamen's tomb."[15]

At more formal dinners, Churchill's taste seems to have diverged even further from the plain food, well prepared, that he told his contemporaries he preferred. Of course, to someone born in Blenheim Palace, plain food would have meant something vastly different from what it means today, or indeed even from what it meant to his contemporaries.

Churchill's likes and dislikes were formed in rarefied late-Victorian and Edwardian society, in which diners of his social class were accustomed to multiple courses, and quite elaborate courses at that. And nothing in his girth or in his consumption of cigars and champagne suggests any late-in-life conversion to moderation. Norman McGowan, who cared for Churchill late in life, said he was "blessed with an excellent digestion and a lively regard for the pleasures and benefits of good food and wine. Not for him is the ascetic regime of so many famous men of advancing years".[16]

Aged 88, Churchill, having recovered sufficiently from a broken leg, attended a dinner of his beloved Other Club at the Savoy, where "the food and wine are remarkable".[17] The chef proudly prepared what is reported to have been Sir Winston's favourite dishes:[18]

PETITE MARMITE SAVOY
FRIED FILET OF SOLE WRAPPED IN SMOKED SALMON AND
GARNISHED WITH SCAMPI
FILET OF ROAST DEER STUFFED WITH PÂTÉ DE FOIE GRAS
AND SERVED WITH TRUFFLE SAUCE

No dessert is mentioned. Few would call this plain food, and the accounts of other witnesses are not completely consistent with this chef's view of what Churchill preferred at this late stage in his life.

With Anthony Eden, a private dinner consisted of "champagne and oysters in his bedroom";[19] and with Field

Marshal Alanbrooke "a tête-à-tête dinner sitting in arm-chairs in the drawing room", dining on "plovers' eggs, chicken broth, chicken pie, chocolate soufflé and with it a bottle of champagne between us, port and brandy!"[20] Even under difficult circumstances, Churchill's fare was very often a cut above the ordinary. When escaping from captivity in South Africa, he hid for two days' living on two simple cold roast chickens, melon and whisky, a diet denied most fugitives.

It may well be that Churchill preferred to say, and perhaps even to believe, that "plain food" was his culinary choice because from at least the eighteenth century "the patriotism of plain cooking was one feature of Englishness", with "the roast beef of old England ... an emblem of solidity, unyielding to Napoleon's batterie de cuisine".[21] Claiming a preference for plain food, in short, was used by Churchill and his contemporaries to wrap themselves in the flag, to assure themselves that no matter how high their station, they had not abandoned their muscular Britishness for the more effete tastes of continental Europe. No drippy French sauces for a true Englishman. "The PM doesn't like his chicken 'messed about'," affirms Lord Moran,[22] referring to Churchill's dislike of devilled chicken.

But Churchill's exposure to the troops in the field and their vastly different culinary backgrounds, together with his experience of wartime rationing, and advancing years did acquaint him with the virtues of simpler English fare. Lady Williams, a credible witness to his preferences during his second premiership, reports that his tastes ran to simple foods, and that among his favourites were jellied consommé, Irish Stew, and plain chicken. Lady Williams also relates that, after a long night, sometimes at two or three a.m., the Prime Minister would suddenly signal that her dictation (or to use

Churchill's words, "take down") chores were over by holler-
ing "soup!" This meant that he wanted his customary late-
night bowl of jellied consommé and that he was ready for
bed. Indeed, Churchill seems to have had a more-than-average
interest in soups, his preference for consommé matched by
his aversion to cream soups.

> Such a Churchill favourite was consommé that, in 1934,
> he formally asked the Ritz in Paris for its recipe and
> paid their invoice of 190 Fr. when it arrived. In 1938 he
> found confirmation for his preference from a doctor who
> suggested a diet that, among other restrictions, allowed
> "no soups except clear consommé".[23]

Colville, Churchill's Assistant Private Secretary during the
war, described a dinner he had with the Prime Minister and
his daughter Mary:

> The tastelessness of the soup so excited his frenzy that he
> rushed out of the room to harangue the cook and returned
> to give a disquisition on the inadequacy of the food at
> Chequers and the fact that the ability to make a good soup
> is the test of a cook.[24]

> Edmund Murray, one of Churchill's bodyguards, provides
> another "soup!" story. Churchill was staying at the
> royal palace in Denmark after receiving an award from
> King Frederick IV of Denmark. Churchill's regular valet
> had the night off so when he required his "soup!" there
> was no one to prepare the consommé. The story goes

that the King himself prepared the soup and served it to Churchill.[25]

Churchill preferred his Irish stew with "plenty of small onions and not much broth".[26] Irish stew was on offer at a lunch with General Eisenhower, and when Ike praised the sauce and crust – mostly potatoes and some meat – Churchill promised that "this would be our main dish for the Tuesday luncheons. It was."[27] Irish stew also became a favourite with Eisenhower's Chief-of-Staff, Walter Bedell Smith, who joined Ike and Churchill for private lunches on Tuesdays in the months before D-Day. We are less sure of why Churchill once complained that someone "forgot to add pineapple chunks" to his Irish Stew".[28]

Mrs. Georgina Landemare knew better than anyone how Churchill defined plain food, and that he liked it perfectly cooked. She was the Churchills' cook throughout much of their lives, at Downing Street, Chartwell, Chequers and elsewhere. Eight years older than Churchill, Georgina Landemare started off as scullery maid in the country houses of Hertfordshire. Somehow, somewhere, she learned to cook and graduated into the kitchen where she met and married a famous French chef, Paul Landemare. They became what are now known as celebrity chefs, famous for the perfection of their Anglo-French cuisine and for catering for special events of the English social scene, like Cowes Week.

"In the 1930s she came for special weekends to Chartwell, but from the outbreak of the war, she became full time. She retired officially in 1953 but still came on occasions to help out during 1954."[29] She was adored by the Churchill family and particularly the Prime Minister who never complained about her cooking as FDR did about Mrs. Nesbitt's. So fond of his cook was Churchill that he left her two paintings in his will. Lady Williams confirms that she was much loved by the entire family.

She received the freshest fruits and vegetables from Chartwell, on Mondays by car and on Thursdays by train in hampers.[30] Colville gives Clementine credit for providing "ambrosial food,"[31] but some credit must also go to Mrs. Landemare.

Lady Churchill, who helped her edit her book and wrote the introduction for *Recipes from No. 10: The Churchill Family Cook*, said she was "enchanted" to have Mrs. Landemare "because I knew she would be able to make the best of rations and that everyone in the household would be happy and contented". Lady Soames said later she was able to "combine the best of French and English cooking".[32] And "One thing tested her a lot ... was when my father, to show it was business as usual, sometimes decided to use the dining room at No. 10, instead of the Annexe. So darling Mrs. Landemare would have to transfer from one kitchen to the other, sometimes at a rather late stage, and be driven round in the duty car, with the covered dishes, wrapped in shawls to keep them warm, clasped tightly on her lap."[33]

Sawyers, Churchill's ever-present valet, once rather "harshly informed an American cook [who had cooked a partridge for one and a half hours] that Mrs. Landemare cooks partridge for only fifteen minutes".[34] She knew the Prime Minister liked his meats underdone, never overcooked, which might have created some problems, given

Churchill's habitual lateness to meals. She was a legend.

A family memoir paints a picture of this indomitable woman. In October 1940, minutes before a bomb fell on No 11 Downing Street, the Prime Minister rushed into the kitchen to warn her. She is reported to have retorted "Sir, the soufflé isn't quite done."[35]

On a gloomy family afternoon in late July 1945, when the voting results had so catastrophically thrown Churchill out as Prime Minister (but not out of his seat in the House of Commons), Lady Soames recollected that the cook was making honey sandwiches and saying: "I don't know what the world is coming to, but I thought I might make some tea."[36]

Years later, Mrs. Landemare told Joan Bakewell (in a TV interview) that the Prime Minister liked Irish stew, and asked that it be reheated the following day "if any were left".

In the same interview, Mrs. Landemare said: "I did my best to look after him – it was my war work." [37]

Churchill's preference for well-cooked plain foods was not rigidly applied. On 25 September 1985, at a commemorative dinner at the Savoy, The International Churchill Societies (as The Churchill Centre was then called) served a dinner that included what were believed to be Churchillian choices. Here is that menu in full:

La Petite Marmite Churchill
Le Contrefilet de boeuf rôti Yorkaise
Les pommes noisettes
Les haricots verts frais en branche

Les quartiers de poires rafraichies au citron la bombe
glacée pralinée
Ou
Les batons de celeri farcis au Roquefort
Pol Roger white foil, extra dry

Richard Langworth reports that Churchill preferred Stilton to sweet desserts, "but he could easily be persuaded to take both".[38]

Another source tells us that Churchill ordered "off the menu when it came to the dessert course. His choice of Roquefort cheese, a peeled pear and mixed ice-cream never varied,"[39] – although we do know that there were times when Stilton was at least equally preferred to Roquefort.

In January 1941, after Alfred Duff Cooper said a press conference was a success, Churchill replied "... starving mice appreciate a Stilton cheese when it is set before them."[40]

I have found very few Churchill comments on dessert. At a lunch in 1941, when a baked jam pudding was served, he said: "This is the sort of thing which helps [Minister of Food] Lord Woolton" and expressed great "satisfaction at seeing it on the table".[41] Note that he did not say anything about the dessert itself or its taste. Lady Williams, who dined frequently with him when serving as his secretary during his second premiership, recalls that he never ate fruits (except at breakfast), puddings or sweets. He did, however, once seem irritated because Mrs. Churchill had apparently "used some of his favourite honey, sent from Queensland, to sweeten the

Churchill scoops caviar, lunch at Yalta

rhubarb".[42] No mention that he actually ate the dessert.

Churchill did, however, have a "passion for cream", Norman McGowan tells us, and "would empty the jug himself and then look around the table. "Does anyone want cream?" he would ask rather pugnaciously."[43]

Menus, of course, are one thing, quantities of food actually consumed are quite another. Although Churchill loved caviar, and can be seen dipping into a large vat of the delicacy at Yalta, Lady Williams notes that he ate only small portions.

Churchill's desire for perfectly prepared and certainly not overcooked foods led to at least one deliciously amusing incident when he was on board a British destroyer on 15 August 1944, on his way to watch from the sea the American landings in the South of France. Lieutenant Derek Hetherington of the Royal Navy was instructed, while the Prime Minister was sleeping, to prepare lamb cutlets for him, to be ready in the way he liked them the moment he woke up. Not knowing when Churchill would wake up, and

171

being instructed not to wake him, Hetherington cooked the first pair of cutlets until they were overdone, then cooked pair after pair so that when Churchill woke up, there would be at least one pair done just as he liked them.[44]

It is obvious that some eye witnesses' reports are at variance with others, at least in details recollected. No matter. In the end what does matter for our purposes is that Churchill never allowed his preferences for food and wine to interfere with the main purpose of his dinner gatherings, or with the conviviality of the occasion. People and conversation were always the indispensable items on his menus.

CHAPTER 11

Champagne, Whisky and Brandy

———————— ⬥ ————————

"You can't make a good speech on iced water."[1]

"I have always practiced temperance."[2]

Churchill consumed what by modern standards are large quantities of alcohol. Among his list of essential provisions when, not yet 25, he set sail for South Africa in 1899 on a journalistic assignment to cover the Boer War, were some forty bottles of wine and "18 bottles of Scotch whiskey (10 years old), 12 Rose's Old Lime Juice …" plus packing cases and the correct labelling.[3] How much of this he was planning to consume personally we cannot be certain. He might have intended some for entertaining his fellow journalists and officers, or for gifts.

Churchill was a lifelong consumer of whisky, insisting that it be served without ice,[4] and very weak indeed.[5] He drank it so weak that close observers described it as "mouthwash". For Churchill, whisky was an acquired taste – a drink he initially "disliked intensely" but for which he overcame his early "repugnance", writing in 1930 that "to this day, although I have always practiced true temperance, I have never shrunk when occasion warranted it from the main basic standing refreshment of the white officer in the East."[6]

That Churchill enjoyed whisky in the diluted form in which he habitually imbibed it there is little doubt. Confined to Lenox Hill Hospital in New York City after being hit by a car in 1931, he asked the attending physician, Dr. Otto C. Pickhardt, to write the following note, which he knew he would need in that era of Prohibition:

> This is to certify that the post-accident convalescence of the Hon. Winston S. Churchill necessitates the use of alcoholic spirits especially at meal times. The quantity is naturally indefinite but the minimum requirements would be 250 cubic centimetres.[7]

A decade later, President Roosevelt's adviser, Rexford Tugwell, reported that during long evening conversations between Churchill and the President, "quantities of spirits disappeared ... although Churchill thrived on them."[8] Another Roosevelt speech writer, Robert Sherwood, noted that "the wine flowed more freely" when Churchill was in the White House.[9]

It is, however, a long way from enjoying whisky – and other alcoholic beverages – to doing so to excess. The evidence on Churchill's alcohol consumption is not straightforward, since many contemporary observers have left us differing accounts, and Churchill himself was no stranger to myth-weaving. Like the late Queen Elizabeth, the Queen Mother, who knew the value of her image as a no-nonsense gin-and-tonic-drinking woman, Churchill saw political profit in portraying himself as a whisky, champagne and brandy lover. Captain Butcher, one of Eisenhower's top aides, wrote after the war: "Ike had the impression that the PM rather relishes his reputation as a heavy smoker and drinker, but actually is much more moderate than rumour would indicate."[10] Unfortunately, there were times when the myth was not useful: before he met Churchill, Roosevelt had heard tales of his later-to-be comrade-in-arms' fondness for alcohol, and felt constrained to ask Wendell Willkie, his Republican presidential rival who later became his emissary, on the latter's return from a visit to Britain in 1941: "Is he a drunk?"[11]

The short answer to that question should have been "No". For one thing, to use the vernacular, Churchill could hold his liquor, Tugwell's comment that he "thrived" on quantities of spirits being only one of several such observations. Robert McCormick, publisher of the *Chicago Tribune* and Churchill's host during his 1932 visit to Chicago, told his own doctor: "The only man I know who can drink more liquor and hold it better than I is Winston Churchill."[12] And after a meeting at Chequers in the summer of 1941, the Canadian Prime Minister, Mackenzie King, wrote in his diary:

> Churchill talked very freely to me at dinner about many topics and also fully with respect to any that I brought up. He took a good deal of wine to drink at dinner. It did not seem

to affect him beyond quickening his intellect and intensifying his facility of expression."[13]

Roosevelt's speech writer, Robert Sherwood, noticed that Churchill's "consumption of alcohol continued at quite regular intervals through most of his waking hours without visible effect".[14] And Michael Reilly, head of presidential security, was "open mouthed in awe" at "the complete sobriety that went hand in hand with his drinking".[15]

One of Churchill's wartime private secretaries, John Peck, writing to Sir Martin Gilbert, reported: "Personally, throughout the time I knew him I *never* saw him the worse for drink."[16]

Another reason for disbelieving reports that Churchill drank to excess is that many come from political opponents or unhappy political allies, or are simply implausible. In the former category we have comments from a diverse group: Adolf Hitler, Lord Reith, supporters of Neville Chamberlain, and Oliver Harvey.

HITLER: A report, cited by A.N. Wilson, states that Hitler referred to Churchill as that "super-annuated drunkard supported by Jewish gold".[17] Whether Hitler was the victim of over-zealous intelligence reports or wishful thinking, or both, we do not know. That it was not based on first-hand evidence we do know: the German Führer and the British Prime Minister never met.

REITH: No fan of Churchill, the ill-humoured Lord Reith, former head of the BBC, wrote in his diary for 14 April 1940, after a lunch with Churchill at the Admiralty, that he "looked as if he had been drinking too much – as he did last Wednesday". Reith's report was undoubtedly coloured by Churchill's barrage of criticisms of the BBC, perhaps best summarised by these remarks to Lord Moran:

> I am against the monopoly enjoyed by the BBC. For eleven years they kept me off the air. They prevented me from expressing views which have proved to be right. Their behaviour has been tyrannical. They are honeycombed with Socialists – probably with Communists.[18]

CHAMBERLAIN: It obviously suited Churchill's political opponents, and he of course accumulated many over his long career in politics, to engage in a bit of character assassination. Andrew Roberts' research reveals one such instance: Chamberlain's supporters played up Churchill's drinking as "part of their general air of moral superiority".[19]

HARVEY: Churchill's relations with the Foreign Secretary, Anthony Eden, were always fraught, in part because of Eden's impatience to move into No. 10. Which might explain why, in December 1944, Oliver Harvey, then Private Secretary to Eden, wrote in his own war diaries, "at 10:30 last night Churchill, Eden and others met in the bowels of the earth. P.M. in his boiler suit and rather sozzled, A.E. in his bottled green smoking coat ... P.M. bellicose and repetitive, repeating snatches from the long speeches to the Poles we heard in Moscow."[20]

Then we have the implausible tales. One such comes to us from Stalin's Marshal of the Air Forces, A.E. Golovanov, who described Churchill's behaviour at a dinner with the Soviet leader on 14 or 15 August 1942:

> Churchill takes up a bottle of Armenian cognac, examines the label and pours Stalin a glass. Toasts follow toasts. Churchill was getting visibly inebriated. Walks out unsteadily. Stalin to

Golovanov after Churchill is gone: "Don't worry. I will not lose Russia in my cups. But Churchill, he'll hit the roof when they tell him what he blabbered out today."[21]

It is quite possible that Stalin was boasting to his colleagues of his ability to out-drink Britain's Prime Minister. Other reports of the same meeting suggest that Churchill avoided excessive consumption of alcohol even on that very liquid occasion. "Every five minutes throughout the dinner," Lord Moran wrote, "we were drinking somebody's health."[22] The "list of toasts appeared interminable",[23] but even after an added round of post-dinner liqueurs with Stalin, Churchill took his leave at such a pace down the Kremlin's long corridors that, according to Sir Archibald Clark Kerr (then British Ambassador to the Soviet Union), Stalin had to "trot, for he had to be brisk in order to keep pace with Mr. Churchill ..."[24] That report is separately confirmed by Lord Moran, and is hardly consistent with the description of Churchill walking out "unsteadily".

It does seem that Churchill meant it when he wrote that excessive drink "causes a comatose insensibility".[25] "Whatever Churchill's consumption of alcohol", writes one Churchill historian, "it was a lifetime habit, not a temporary response to the pressure and tension of wartime leadership. There is no credible evidence that Churchill's drinking persistently affected his policies during the war, or, for that matter, his policies before the war."[26] A careful study of the minutes of the various international meetings he attended, and of diaries of those who dined with him, furnishes no reliable evidence that he ever became what is now called "impaired" in circumstances where that would be dangerous to the interests of his nation or interfere with the performance of his various jobs. My own interviews with people who knew Churchill well confirm historian Robert Rhodes James's conclusion that Churchill's drinking has been "grossly exaggerated",[27] a view borne out by Lord Alanbrooke.

In his diaries, the Field Marshal was quick to condemn some of Churchill's friends and colleagues for drinking more than they should have, but only once suggests that Churchill over-indulged. Alanbrooke writes on 6 July 1944 that the Prime Minister "was very tired ... and had tried to recuperate with drink. As a result he was in a maudlin, bad-tempered, drunken mood, ready to take offense at anything, suspicious of everybody and in a highly vindictive mood against the Americans". If correct, and it is not impossible that such instances occurred, but rarely, it should be remembered that this was only a month after D-Day, on a day during which he had already given a speech in the House on the "flying bombs, and had a meeting that lasted from 10 p.m. until 2 a.m."[28] One can easily imagine that he would have been exhausted. "It is surprising that there are only three or four places where the [Alanbrooke] diary criticizes [Churchill's] practice [of drinking daily] while three other personages are labelled outright drunks: the American Admiral King, Australian Commander in Chief General Blamey, and senior Soviet General Voroshilov."[29]

Despite the weight of the evidence, the myth of Churchill regularly drinking to excess persists. Even the voluntary docents at Roosevelt's Hyde Park residence in New York perpetuate the myth, telling visitors that Churchill used to walk around "all day with a drink in his hand". Not so. When I visited Hyde Park with Lady Williams, she corrected the guide in no uncertain terms. "This tale is false," she said. "The Prime Minister would not have walked around throughout the day with a glass in his hand. It was not his style."

Then there are the anecdotes, as colourful as they are contradictory. Even the most casual student of Churchill is familiar with the never-confirmed tale of Bessie Braddock's charge, "Winston, you are drunk," to which Churchill is alleged to have responded: "Bessie, you are ugly. But tomorrow I shall be sober."[30] The popularity of this anecdote, in which Churchill seems to acknowledge inebriation, adds to the myth of his alcoholic excesses, a myth he did nothing to dispel. Note that even on this occasion – assuming there had been such an occasion – Churchill was quite capable of a lucid and cutting answer to a critic.

Churchill must be considered culpable for contributing to the myth-making, for reasons mentioned earlier. He enjoyed entertaining his guests with comments on his drinking habits. At a dinner given by Roosevelt on his yacht, *Williamsburg*, in 1942, Churchill asked his scientific advisor, Lord Cherwell, whom he called "Prof", to whip out his ever-present slide rule and do a calculation. The Prime Minister estimated that in 62 years he had on average consumed a quart of wine and spirits a day. Question: if all of those drinks were poured into the salon in which they were dining, how deep would they be? The response from the teetotaller Prof was: "Just under two-and-a-half feet." This, the future US Secretary of State, Dean Acheson, reported, was "very disappointing to the Old Man. He had expected that we would all be swimming like goldfish in a bowl, whereas it would hardly come up to our knees".[31]

Set aside self-interested tales of contemporaries, the American tendency to judge Churchill's consumption by the standards of their own country's customs and the rather romantic view Churchill seems to have had of himself as a prodigious consumer of alcohol, and consider the reports of the many people who observed his habits close up. There is agreement on several points:

- He had no use for cocktails, pre-dinner or otherwise. Churchill disliked mixed drinks of the sort that appealed to many Americans. After a meeting with Roosevelt and their military staffs at Quebec in August 1943, Churchill joined Roosevelt and several others at Treasury Secretary Henry Morgenthau's Fishkill Farms estate. Morgenthau's son, Robert, mixed mint juleps. "Knowing of Churchill's intemperance, he was surprised when the Prime Minister had just one."[32] It is likely that any inclination the Prime Minister had for a second round disappeared with the taste of a mint julep, not the sort of drink on which he had been reared. Indeed, years later, when celebrating Christmas with, among others, one of his secretaries, Jo Sturdee, he snatched from her hand a "fiery cocktail which knocked me back at the first gulp", and advised her: "No, no, if you want to get drunk, do get drunk on something decent," and "then got down to champagne".[33]

In spite of this, Joe Gilmour, head barman at the Savoy Hotel from 1940 to 1976, is said to have invented a Blenheim cocktail – also known as the four score and ten – in honour of Churchill's 90th birthday. It consisted of 3 parts brandy, 2 parts yellow Chartreuse, 1 part Lillet, 1 part orange juice, and 1 part Dubonnet.[34]

- He drank Johnnie Walker Black Label – some sources say Red – which, interestingly, is a blend, not a single malt. In 1946, Berry Brothers apologised for the fact that Churchill's requested Johnnie Walker Black Label was unavailable and that the Berry's Best Whisky had proved "not suitable to his palate", recommending instead Cutty Sark. Berry Brothers refunded the payment for the unacceptable six bottles of the shop's brand which were returned.[35]

- The whisky that seemed to some observers to be omnipresent was most often diluted with water or with soda, to the point where "It was really a mouthwash", Jock Colville told Churchill's biographer Martin Gilbert. "He used to get frightfully cross if it was too strong."[36] Colville's observation is shared by John Peck who told Sir Martin, "The glass of weak whisky ... was more a symbol than anything else, and one glass lasted him for hours."[37] Harry Hopkins, and several others whom I interviewed, including Lady Williams, uniformly support the Colville and Peck reports.[38]

- At times, when Churchill was feeling "sorry for himself ... he had a stiff whisky and soda", once at a quarter to nine in the morning during a stopover on his journey to the Teheran Conference.[39] Of course, he had crossed several time zones so his tummy-time would have told him it was late in the day.

- Champagne topped the list of Churchill's favourite drinks, followed by brandy.

Churchill also had a favourite wine merchant, Randolph Payne in Pall Mall, whose telegraphic address was LUSCIOUS, PICCY, LONDON.[40] Some say the favoured merchant was Hatch Mansfield from whom Churchill did buy wines and spirits. As noted earlier, in 1899, Churchill ordered from Randolph Payne:

6 bottles 1889 Vin d'Ay Sec

18 bottles St. Emilion

6 bottles light port

6 bottles French vermouth

18 bottles Scotch whisky (10 year old)

6 bottles Very Old Eau de Vie landed 1866

12 Rose's Cordial Lime Juice

6 x 1 dozen cases for same, packing, marking etc.

All to be shipped aboard the SS *Dunottar Castle* to Churchill in South Africa.[41]

Pop!

In 1947, Churchill told Odette Pol Roger that 44 Avenue de Champagne, Epernay, is the world's most drinkable address"[42]. Dean Acheson recalled Clementine telling him that the Churchill "always had his own bottle of champagne by his place at the table, to be independent of the vagaries of butlers".[43] It is reasonable to assume that the bottle was of the since-discontinued 50 cl size, which Churchill preferred to the 75 cl bottle now commonly sold:[44] "A single glass of champagne," Churchill wrote in 1898, "imparts a feeling of exhilaration. The nerves are braced: the imagination is agreeably stirred; the wits become more nimble." He quickly added, "A bottle produces the opposite effect".[45] Lady Halifax's memoirs describe Churchill at one dinner as "grumpy and remote ... But mellowed by champagne and good food he became a different man, and a delightful and amusing companion".[46]

> In 1898, just before the battle of Omdurman, Churchill was strolling along the banks of the Nile with his fellow officers. British officers hailed him from gunboats afloat on the river, and asked: "How are you for drinks? We have got everything in the world on board here. Can you catch? And almost immediately a bottle of champagne was thrown from the gunboat to the shore. It fell into the waters of the Nile, but happily where a gracious Providence decreed them to be shallow and the bottom soft. I slipped into the waters up to my knees, and reaching down seized the precious gift."[47]

Every celebratory event in Churchill's long life was marked with champagne. On 8 May 1945, standing on balconies

A victory toast with the Soviet Ambassador Gusev, May 1945

both at Buckingham Palace and at the Ministry of Health, he received the appreciative thunderous applause of the British public. Later that night, he told his staff that he would visit the American and Soviet embassies to celebrate VE Day with them. At the Soviet embassy, the champagne did not seem to work its usual magic. The Prime Minister raised a glass of champagne with Ambassador Gusev, Mrs. Gusev and Churchill's daughter Mary. But they were not a happy-looking group, for reasons that were becoming apparent.

Not just any champagne would do. Churchill was "one of the world's most expert connoisseurs of champagne".[48] He sometimes drank older and stronger vintages or varieties such as the Krug 1920, 1926, and the 1937 that he served at Potsdam. But his favourite of favourites was Pol Roger, either the 1921 vintage, a dozen bottles of which Victor Rothschild provided "from his dwindling stock at

Merton Hall" when Churchill's supply was exhausted,[49] or his ultimate favourite, the 1928 vintage, a case of which Odette Pol Roger sent him on each of his birthdays until supplies ran out in 1953. "Thereafter she reserved the choicest vintages for him; by 1965 he had only worked his way through the harvest of 1934."[50]

Odette Pol Roger was a clever businesswoman. Smart Parisian tastes "had run towards Pommery and Clicquot",[51] but she made her brand world famous, helped certainly by Churchill's favouring it so publicly. It is a mystery how he first became such a fan of Pol Roger. We do know he

Odette Pol Roger with Churchill

had ordered a case of the 1895 vintage when a Cabinet Minister and President of the Board of Trade.[52] It was only years later, in 1944, that he met Odette Pol Roger at the Armistice Day party at the British embassy in Paris, introduced by the Ambassador, Duff Cooper. They quickly became life-long friends. In return for Madame Pol Roger sending him regular shipments, Churchill sent her a copy of his memoirs inscribed "Cuvee de Reserve. Mise en bouteille au Chateau Chartwell".[53] He also named one of his racehorses Pol Roger; it won the Black Prince Stakes on 2 June 1953, the very day of Queen Elizabeth II's coronation.

Commemorative bottle

After Churchill's death, Mme. Pol Roger ordered that the labels on all bottles of champagne exported to Britain be given a black mourning band, a practice discontinued only in 1990 when the house switched to a blue border to emphasise Churchill's naval connections and "his loyalties to the Senior Service" as First Lord of the Admiralty.[54]

Today the only champagne served at receptions at Churchill College, Cambridge, is Pol Roger, still generously being donated by the firm.

As with food – Churchill made do and enjoyed spare fare when circumstances demanded – so with drink. When required to live off the land, Churchill would do so with gusto: witness Sir Alexander Cadogan's report that at the Yalta Conference the Prime Minister was seen to be drinking "buckets of Caucasian champagne which would undermine the health of any ordinary man".[55]

As for brandy, Churchill believed that "fine old brandy is something to be treasured". He never added water to it – "That is a great crime," he told his valet, Norman McGowan – and he preferred to pour his own, as he did with the bottle of champagne he kept at his side during meals.[56] After retiring as Prime Minister for the second time in 1955, Churchill enjoyed what his then Private Secretary, Anthony Montague Browne, called his Long Sunset – which included annual journeys to the South of France to his beloved Hôtel de Paris in Monte Carlo. An added bonus was that the management of that hotel, who had walled up the cellars in 1940, decided to destroy these "fortifications" in Churchill's honour – producing a bottle of fine old brandy.[57] This certainly met Churchill's "nothing but the best" standard. Anthony Montague Browne, who accompanied Churchill during many of his travels during the later years, recalled that L'Hertier de Jean Fremicourt was then Churchill's preferred brandy.

The Prime Minister also much enjoyed Château Yquem, which Victor Rothschild served at a dinner party at the Savoy in 1944 to lighten Churchill's "dark" mood when the evening brought news of the grave difficulties being encountered at the Anzio beachhead.[58] Lady Williams told the author that Churchill did not care much for other Sauternes and sweet wines, preferring brandy after dinner.

It is reported that the Savoy provided a bedroom for the famous Churchillian after-lunch naps, taking good care of a treasured guest.[59]

Churchill could be humorous about his drinking. In 1943, after the Casablanca meeting, he wrote to Harry Hopkins

Cornucopia at 86

about a dinner at the "White House", as Roosevelt's villa there was called: "Dinner at the White House (dry, alas!); with the Sultan … After dinner, recovery from the effects of the above".[60] On Churchill's 86th birthday, a wise bakery presented Churchill with a cake in the shape of a cornucopia, with tiny whisky and champagne bottles pouring from its mouth.

Churchill was generous with his wines. He told his lifelong friend, Violet Bonham Carter: "There has never been a day in my life when I could not order a bottle of champagne for myself and offer another to a friend."[61] In the early 1960s, he was engaged in correspondence with Emery and Wendy Reves, his frequent hosts in the South of France, at their villa, La Pausa, concerning the disposition of the "12 bottles of champagne Madame Pol Roger sent you". Reves was forbidden by British customs regulations from shipping them to Churchill, who had already returned to Britain. Churchill advised Reves to hold onto the champagne until his next visit and to "make use of it yourselves in the interim".[62]

> Six rooms from La Pausa are today recreated at the Dallas Museum of Art. The dining room is set as it would have been when Churchill dined there with friends, including, among others, Field Marshal Montgomery, Aristotle Onassis, Lord Cherwell and Noel Coward. The splendid collection of more than 1,400 French impressionist paintings that hung at La Pausa are now in Dallas.

Churchill was also generous with his wines at parties and dinners. Mrs. Churchill was away when he gave a summer cocktail party at Chartwell, but she heard that "32 bottles of champagne were consumed among 32 people. I hope the tasty

A weak whisky and soda at Mansion House

tit-bits made by Mrs. Landemare were also appreciated."[63]

Two things seem clear about Churchill's relationship with alcohol. His use of spirits differed little from that of members of his class: Victor Rothschild, working for the security service MI5 during the Second World War, eased the heavy burdens of long days at the office by dipping into an open bottle of champagne kept on his desk.[64] Second, Churchill enjoyed his various drinks, and felt they added to the conviviality of his dinner parties. But he never allowed drink to impair his judgment. One of Churchill's most famous quips seems to have been true – that he had taken more out of alcohol than it had taken out of him. That, after all, is what matters.

CHAPTER 12

Cigars

———————⟨⟩———————

*"As we got up from the table, his cigar was going like a
steam locomotive on a stiff grade."*[1]

No discussion about Churchill at dinner would be
complete without mention of his ever-present cigar.
Churchill probably would have smoked vast quantities of
them if he had never entered public life: they were one of
his great pleasures. But they served two other purposes: pro-
longing the after-dinner discussions at which he shone, and
serving as his political symbol.

Churchill fell in love with cigars in 1895, when he visited
Cuba as a 21-year-old reporter for the *Daily Graphic*, covering the island's eventually successful war for independence
from Spain. He smoked his first Havanas then, and as Larry

Victory symbol

Arnn, a Churchill scholar, has said: "Thereafter, cigar and Cuban were synonymous for Churchill."[2] He had been a heavy cigarette smoker while at Sandhurst, where his father, Lord Randolph Churchill, provided him with boxes of his own best cigarettes. At the turn of the century, his mother asked J.J. Fox Cigar Shop, St James's, to open an account in her son's name. Thereafter he often ordered her favourite gold-tipped handmade Turkish cigarettes for her when placing an order for himself.

Lord Randolph, who encouraged his son's cigarette smoking, heartily disapproved of his cigar smoking. In response to that disapproval, the young subaltern made what must have been one of the worst predictions of his life: "I don't think I shall often smoke more than one or two a day – and very rarely that."[3] He later took the same line when responding to his gastroenterologist, Dr. Hunt, who had recommended "Cigars – to use a holder and reduce the number." Churchill responded: "… numbers [of cigars] will, I trust, be reduced".[4] No indication of by whom – an odd or purposefully vague sentence structure for so punctilious a writer as Churchill, suggesting the lack of a deep commitment to smoking less.

His father and his doctor notwithstanding, records at Fox of St. James's, his principal supplier from 1900 until his death, show orders often in the hundreds. Even allowing for the consumption of his dinner guests, the quantities ordered indicate massive consumption and made Churchill one of Fox's better customers.

Once he discovered fine Havanas, neither age nor infirmity diminished his enthusiasm for cigars. In early 1943 he was taken seriously ill with pneumonia but, according to his doctors, continued to smoke. Some twenty years later, when recovering from a broken hip and again warned by his doctors against smoking, Churchill continued defiantly to puff away.[5] Neither the broken hip nor the several strokes he suffered (the most serious in 1953, when he was briefly paralysed) deterred him from indulging his habit.

As time passed, and Churchill's fame spread, he realised that his cigar had become a symbol, as important a part of his image as the jaunty Camel cigarette and holder later became for Franklin D. Roosevelt. As early as 1904, one of his wartime biographers wrote: "The cartoonists lent their services, and already the famous lineaments were beginning to take shape, the squat form, the perpetual cigar".[6]

Many wartime cartoons show Churchill as the British bulldog, often puffing on a cigar. He clearly felt that the cigar helped convey his determination to win the war and his confidence that Britain would prevail. Dean Acheson would later sum up Churchill: "Everything felt the touch of his art – his appearance and gestures, the siren suit, the indomitable V sign for victory, the cigar for imperturbability."[7]

Churchill rarely smoked cigars to the end. His valet, Norman McGowan, reported that he never saw him finish a cigar. He habitually left about half in the ashtray, and ordered that all of those half-smoked cigars be turned over to his gardener for use as pipe tobacco.[8] Roy Howells, however, who also cared for Churchill during the last years of his life, noted that he did at times, in those last years, smoke cigars to the end. McGowan calculates that Churchill smoked nine or so cigars a day. Smoked to the end or only partially, that is a lot of fine tobacco, even by the standards of a time in which cigar smoking was not impeded by the restrictions we live with today.[9]

Churchill's love of cigars was so well known that it produced a substantial flow of gifts from admirers all over the world. This flow was not one way: Churchill delighted in sharing his taste with others, although he was careful not to introduce his grandson, Winston, to his own preference for only the best. Churchill directed Robert Lewis (the firm later acquired by J.J. Fox) to send a box of cigars to his grandson on the occasion of his birthday. They were to be "of good quality, but not quite as good as the Romeo & Juliet, and of medium size".[10]

Churchill could sometimes be generous with his cigars as he was with his champagnes, but not overly so. In 1949, when his inventory included a large cache of Jamaican cigars, he

Don't want to spoil the boy

upbraided his butler for offering guests some of his finest Cubans, which he preferred to keep for himself.[11]

Like all devoted cigar smokers, Churchill developed his own quirks and rituals. His pilot during the First World War, Lieutenant Gilbert Hall, described Churchill holding his cigar between his first finger and his thumb while leisurely rolling it across the top of his coffee cup.[12] He invented what he called "bellybandoes". He would light a candle in order to warm the tip of his cigar, "next he lovingly wrapped a piece of gummed brown paper around the other end", so that "it stopped the end from becoming too wet when I chew it'". He was proud of his invention and bragged: "I designed

Firing up

that myself."[13] Whether he realised it or not, his bellybandoes limited direct contact with the tobacco and hence his
intake of nicotine.[14]

Churchill was as fussy about the matches he used as he was

> In 1936, Dr Hunt had recommended that Churchill reduce
> the number of cigars smoked (advice unheeded as we have
> seen) and that he use a cigar holder (advice heeded perhaps
> by inventing the bellybando).[15]

Merci for the light, at Cherbourg, 1944

about his cigars. He preferred long matches, long enough to remain lit after the sulphur had burned off so that the odour could not contaminate the aroma and taste of the cigar. He favoured two-inch long cedar matches specially flown over in large cartons from Canada.[16] These he used not only to light his Havanas, but also to pierce the end, ignoring the piercer on his watch chain and the elaborate cutters that he received among the many cigar-related gifts.[17] Emery Reves, Churchill's literary agent and a generous host, gave him a silver pagoda-shaped ashtray with a trough on top to hold his cigar,[18] a gift that became Churchill's favourite cigar accessory.

Churchill's preferred smoke in the 1930s was the Royal Derby Longfellow, but a 23 January 1949 inventory of his stock at Chartwell, which totalled between 3,000 and 4,000

Some of my favourite things from Fox Cigar Shop

cigars, reveals a range of brands. His favourites were Romeo y Julieta, a box of which survives (barely) in the Fox Churchill Museum that his tobacconist has created in St. James's, and the no-longer-made La Aroma de Cuba.[19]

Churchill preferred these and other large Havanas, as his hosts at the Casablanca Conference learned when he quite surprisingly ran out of cigars. The best that his American hosts could then produce was a box of five-cent White Owls. After removing the price, the Americans presented them to him. That night, FDR's Chief of Staff, General George C. Marshall, commented "that the prime minister must be giving up smoking. He usually smoked three or four cigars at a session, but that day he took one or two puffs on a cigar and put it out".[20]

During the war, Churchill's cigars created problems for his protection unit. Scotland Yard feared that some of those he was receiving as gifts might be poisoned,[21] and that Churchill's habit of chewing his cigars would make coating them with cyanide or botulinus toxins, or inserting a small explosive detonated by the heat of the flame, highly effective ways for enemies to dispose of him.[22] Unfortunately, there was no way of testing the cigars without destroying them: Douglas Hall, a renowned collector of all things Churchillian, notes that "a large cabinet from the Cuban Ambassador" was deemed to be suspect by the Downing Street security staff and, much to Churchill's disgust, [they] ordered it blown up.[23] Churchill was understandably unhappy, and unwilling, to give up the large shipments he received as gifts. The security staff reluctantly agreed that random testing and close examination of cigars received from sources Scotland Yard and MI5 deemed reliable would be sufficient protection.

Churchill's security detail was not alone in confronting problems created by his incessant cigar smoking. His hosts at various dinner parties also had to take account of his smoking. Lord Beaverbrook rolled up his treasured white rugs – the product of fashion designer Captain Molyneux – when Churchill came to dinner so that the cigar ash "should not be spilled on them".[24] Nor would the Prime Minister give up his cigars on his many flights to conferences and meetings during the war.[25] He went so far as to have a huge armchair with an ashtray attached installed on his de Havilland Flamingo, and aircraft designers included venting windows next to the co-pilot seat that Churchill often chose to occupy.

What are we to make of Churchill's massive consumption of cigars? First, it is clear that either by virtue of genetic inheritance or plain luck, he could take the strain his smoking imposed on his health. On 29 August 1944, nearing his 70th birthday, Churchill returned from Rabat in the grip of a high fever – 103°–104°. He reported to Roosevelt[26] that "a small patch on his lung was diagnosed",[27] possibly either caused or exacerbated by his heavy smoking. The Prime Minister made astonishingly rapid progress. According to Colville, by 30 August "The P.M. was better and did a certain amount of work in bed"; by 31 August "a very marked improvement" allowed plans for the Second Quebec Conference to proceed; and the next day "The P.M., with temperature normal, is in tearing form."[28] On 5 September 1944, although his daughter Mary characterises her father as "barely recovered", he left London to board the *Queen Mary* for the voyage to Halifax, Nova Scotia, and the Second Quebec Conference.[29]

Second, his lack of compunction about accepting expensive gifts would, in our later age of tabloid and investigative journalism, have mired him in scandal: fine cigars and cases of champagne, as well as cigar cutters and other trinkets arrived regularly and in profusion. But this was of a piece with Churchill's attitude to gifts and hospitality in general. Clementine Churchill did not like to see him "accepting hospitality from the very rich and, in her opinion, not always very suitable people".[30] Jock Colville observed that Churchill "drank their flowing champagne, and basked in the beautiful surroundings of their villas and yachts, without asking himself if he was accepting what they supplied for the wrong reasons". Whether or not Churchill fully understood Clementine's "scruples, he felt no obligation to be bound by them".[31]

Third, Churchill ultimately played by the rules, as we shall see in the next chapter on rationing. There are many minutes in the Churchill Archives that instruct his staff to check on the prices of cigars before ordering, to fill out the import licences required by the Board of Trade, and to pay the duty required of others.

In one telegram, Churchill wittily asked his New York agent when the "relief column"[32] would arrive. When the agent cabled the arrival date, Churchill cabled back: "Many thanks. No need for vanguard."[33]

Last, as F.E. Smith put it, Churchill was "easily satisfied with the best of everything and the larger the better". Churchill was satisfied that fine, large Havanas added pleasure to his days and evenings, contributed to his image as a defiant war leader, and allowed him to extend dinner parties and the conversations he so relished. As we would say today, the cigar was Churchill's brand, instantly recognised throughout the world. Picture the Prime Minister walking through bomb-shattered areas, cigar in hand, exuding defiance and the confidence that Britain's plight would eventually end, and the war would be won: a more reassuring image would be difficult to imagine.

CHAPTER 13

Rationing

————————⟨◈⟩————————

During both of Churchill's terms as Prime Minister, stringent food rationing was in effect in Britain. And during both those terms, Churchill presided over a number of glamorous and lavish dinner parties, both at home and abroad. How was he able to provide for the dinners at which he entertained important British and overseas visitors? And what was the reaction of a public that was doing without many perceived necessities, much less the luxuries on which Churchill and his guests dined? Finally, how was it that rationing and the Prime Minister, who escaped some of its consequences, and his Minister of Food, Lord Woolton, all remained highly popular?

The answers lie in Churchill's shrewd approach to the problem of food shortages. He had two basic goals: to maximise supplies for all, and to make sure that the public remained broadly supportive of any rationing schemes that had to be put in place.

To maximise supplies, Churchill had to encourage food production at home, and do everything possible to keep up the flow of imports. No easy chore, especially when three-quarters of a million American troops would be arriving in advance of D-Day[1] – these troops are "great addicts of ice cream, which is said to be a rival of alcoholic drinks", minuted the Prime Minister[2]. Churchill also insisted that German prisoners of war receive the same number of calories as British civilians, lest the Germans retaliate against British PoWs by cutting their rations.[3]

An increasingly successful German U-boat campaign in the early days of the war, and the diversion of ships to military purposes and to the transport of supplies to the Soviet Union, meant that food imports were seriously reduced. The Prime Minister coped with this problem in a variety of ingenious ways. He:

- insisted that food – and later tobacco[4] – be included on the list of Lend-Lease goods available from America on favourable financial terms;

- increased the allotments programme that enabled the public to grow more of its own food on communal plots, which eventually included Victory Gardens on any open space, and dug up tennis courts; growing cabbages in Kensington Gardens; and giving Hyde Park its own piggery;

- increased domestic grain allotments to permit individuals to keep chickens "to give [them] ... something to talk about" and to "produce their own eggs and thus save shipping and labour";[5]

- expanded the Women's Land Army, initially established in June 1939 on a volunteer basis in anticipation of the war. It included, by 1943, some 80,000 Land Girls, young women from cities and towns who learned farming skills;

- urged the Ministers of Shipping, Agriculture, Fishing and Food constantly to do all possible to maximise domestic supplies and imports.

Churchill did succeed in maintaining public support for the broad rationing scheme: a support so firm that many British housewives favoured continuing rationing in peace time.[6] (Men, perhaps because their work required more calories, were less keen).[7]

Churchill's plan rested on three strategies. First, the rationing scheme had to be and be seen to be fair. So when the access of upper-income diners to restaurants at which ration coupons were not required threatened to cause a loss of support for the scheme, the government subsidised some two thousand non-profit restaurants established by local authorities to provide lower-income families with an opportunity to dine out. Home Intelligence Reports suggested that the popularity of these restaurants was due to the fact that, by offering a meal for less than a shilling, "they gave poorer folks a chance to do what the rich have always been able to do – have a meal without giving up coupons".[9] On 21 March 1941, the Prime Minister wrote to the Minister of Food, Lord Woolton:

I hope the term "Communal Feeding Centres" is not going to be adopted. It is an odious expression suggestive of Communism and the workhouse. I suggest you call them "British Restaurants". Everybody associates the word restaurant with a good meal, and they might as well have the name if they cannot get anything else.[8]

Churchill's suggestion was adopted and these establishments became the proudly patriotic "British Restaurants".

Second, Churchill knew that in order to maintain support for the rationing programme, he himself had to abide by the scheme's rules. So he subjected his own requirements to the rationing plans, meticulously requesting extra coupons when entertaining official visitors and listing their names. The Churchill Archives are replete with formal requests for extra rations of tea, sugar and other foods, with the prominent visitors indicated. When these requests became so numerous as to be burdensome to the Ministry of Food, the requirement that guests be listed was waived by the Ministry, and extra coupons were issued to Churchill's cook, Mrs. Landemare.

By staying clearly within the rules – even returning unused food coupons to the Ministry of Food,[10] – Churchill reduced the opportunity for critics to claim the rules that existed for them did not apply to him. Adherence to the rationing rules extended beyond foods: witness a letter received by his secretary on 7 March 1945, in response to a request for coupons for items that included five pairs of socks and a Royal Air Force vest:

You asked me the other day if a further 72 coupons could

be supplied to cover the purchase of uniforms, etc., required by the Prime Minister in connection with the Crimea Conference. You will be glad to hear that the Board of Trade have been graciously pleased to approve of the issue of these coupons, which are enclosed herewith.[11]

Mr.Seal.

    Mr.Churchill wishes me to ask you to take steps in a matter which I mentioned to him this morning. Both at Chequers and at No.10 the rationing makes it very difficult to entertain officially to the extent which Mr.Churchill finds necessary.

    He would like you to get in touch with the Ministry of Food and makes an arrangement whereby in both instances extra rations can be supplied to cover official guests - a list of whom will be made each week. So as to be a week in hand Mr.Churchill suggests a list of last week's guests should be provided now and in future at the end of each week a list be produced of those who have been entertained who can come under this category.

        M.S.
        24. 6. 40.

Some more, please

Soap was another item in short supply. When Churchill was living at the White House in January 1942, his secretary meekly requested some soap from the housekeeper for his bath. He was asked: "What kind would you like?" "Oh, any kind, just soap," the Secretary responded, sounding as if he couldn't believe that different kinds could be provided.[12]

None of this means, however, that the Prime Minister led a life anything nearly as austere as the ordinary Briton. One of his biographers wrote: "In reality he suffered less than any other people from the exigencies of war."[13] Like other well-to-do people, he could dine in restaurants and clubs that had access to finer produce and at which coupons were not needed.

Churchill also benefited from gifts from well-wishers around the world and from those in Britain who had access to home-grown foods, such as fish and game from their estates. There were food parcels from Roosevelt and other Americans with whom he worked, and from Stalin, who sent tubs of caviar, and from Lord Beaverbrook, who, when in Moscow after a long meeting, "sent out his secretary to buy twenty-five pounds of caviar for Mr. Churchill".[14] The Soviet Ambassador in London, Ivan Maisky, sent the Prime Minister a gift of onions.

Game came from Sandringham and Balmoral, as personal gifts from King George VI.[15] Labels were used to ensure that the game, freshly shot, arrived in the kitchens at Downing Street. Hare, partridge, grouse and two woodcock arrived from Lord and Lady Davies of Llandinam.[16] Sir Hanson Rowbotham sent a brace of pheasant and hares from the Isle

Labels for game from the King

of Wight – these, killed on 9 December 1942, were shipped to London the following day.[17]

Fish, although never rationed, was sometimes in short supply. One of Churchill's shortest instructions (perhaps his shortest) was to a senior official at the Admiralty, who had asked what fishing policy was to be. Churchill's two-word reply: "Utmost fish". His first concern was for the British people's diet, not himself.

Fish was always a most welcome gift from those close to the Prime Minister, or those who wanted to thank him for his service to the nation. Joan Bright, a well-respected staff member, responsible for many of the complex administrative logistics on his overseas journeys, told the author that really good Dover sole was a Churchill favourite. One piscatory gift, marked "by express train, deliver immediately" to Downing Street, came from the Duke of Westminster's lodge, Loch More, in Sutherland; the nearby Laxford River, its currents described as "merry",[18] is famed still for its superior salmon-fishing. Other gifts came to Downing Street on a regular basis – including oranges from US General "Hap" Arnold,[19] and chocolates from the Prime Minister of Quebec.[20] One parcel of champagne and pheasants, in honour of Churchill's 68th birthday, came from the brick manufacturer, Sir Percy Malcolm Stewart, with thanks to the Prime Minister for his inspiration "to win in the darkest days". He went on: "... may you be spared to lead us to triumphant victory."[21] Clementine Churchill was most grateful for "a small bag of tangerines" that Averell Harriman brought for her from Lisbon,[22] and was also named as the designated recipient of one of the eight uncooked Smithfield hams "wrapped individually" that Harriman sent to Commander Thompson for distribution to her and others, including the First Lord of the Admiralty, A.V. Alexander.[23]

Long after the war, Montgomery would arrive at Chartwell "lugging a case of plum brandy he had brought from Marshal Tito as a gift to Churchill, or a case of port from the Portuguese Prime Minister, Salazar".[24] The Portuguese Ambassador in London gave Churchill six cases of port,[25] a drink the young Churchill had been warned off by Dr Hunt years earlier.

Although Churchill was careful to obey all the rules, there was an occasional assertion of privilege. Historian

Max Hastings, never one to minimise what he believes to be Churchill's failings, notes that at one dinner party at the Savoy the Prime Minister, to the consternation of "the ascetic" Canadian Prime Minister Mackenzie King, contravened rationing regulations by ordering both fish and meat courses.[26] But this must have been a rare event. Hastings also notes that the "Prime Minister's wife often found it no easier than her compatriots to find acceptable food".[27] Which explains Commander Thompson's previously cited recollection that Churchill, when in America, "enjoyed roast beef or steak so much that, with rationing in force at home, he often saved half his portion at dinner-time and had it for breakfast next morning".[28] It also explains why, when entertaining Eleanor Roosevelt and other visiting Americans at the No. 10 Annexe – Churchill's wartime above-ground home and office – Mrs. Churchill apologised for the food: "I'm sorry, dear, I could not buy any fish. You will have to eat macaroni." Secretary of the Treasury Henry Morgenthau, after another dinner, noted without enthusiasm: "They gave us little leftover bits made into meat loaf."[29]

Finally, in his campaign to ensure that rationing was accepted, Churchill focused relentlessly on keeping regulations to the bare minimum necessary to support the war effort. Rationing is inherently intrusive on daily lives, and the Prime Minister knew that regulators had a tendency to make it more intrusive than necessary. In July 1941 he minuted Lord Woolton:

> Though rigid rationing might be easier to administer, some system which left the consumer a reasonable freedom of choice would seem much better. Individual tastes have a wonderful way of cancelling out ...[30]

"Are you getting enough to eat?"

J.J. Llewellin, who replaced Lord Woolton as
Minister of Food in December 1943, received a similar minute urging him to "cut out petty annoyances ... [in] the private lives of ordinary people".[31] As the Cabinet Secretary
Norman Brook (later Lord Normanbrook) noted: "There
was in fact a strong bond between Churchill 'and ordinary
people'. Their interests lay close to his heart, and he was
always concerned to promote their welfare."[32]

As the Prime Minister understood those interests, they included some rather specific dietary requirements. Understanding the British love of beef and his own preferences for it ("personally I am a beef-eater,"[33] he wrote in 1933) might have been among the reasons he pressed his ministers to include in British diets beef, beef and more beef. He advised Lord Woolton:

> Almost all of the food faddists I have ever known, nut-eaters and the like, have died young after a period of senile decay. The British soldier is far more likely to be right than the scientists. All he cares about is beef ... The way to lose the war is to try to force the British public into a diet of milk, oatmeal, potatoes etc., washed down on gala occasions with a little limejuice.[34]

If beef was not to be had, there was always pork:

> The only point in doubt is whether you have asked for sufficient pork. America would find it difficult to provide us with beef or mutton, but pork supplies can be rapidly expanded and, if necessary, imported in non-refrigerated tonnage.[35]

And if neither beef nor pork, there were always rabbits. In June 1941, Churchill minuted Lord Woolton:

> Have you done justice to rabbit production? Although rabbits are not by themselves nourishing, they are a pretty good mitigation of vegetarianism ... what is the harm in encouraging their multiplication in captivity?[36]

There were few aspects of the nation's consumption with which Churchill did not concern himself. He always had time for matters relating to British well-being and morale, finding the time to:

- ask why banana imports had been suspended. (Because, responded Lord Woolton, the Admiralty had requisitioned "a large number of refrigerated boats ... for other war purposes ... without any consultation with me[37]);

- ask whether whisky distilling, to which no grain had been allocated since 1941, could be resumed in 1944. (It could, allowing sufficient time for it to mature for the eight years required by "the U.S.A. market ... which earns us dollars);[38]

- demand a full report to Cabinet on raw material and distribution problems that brewers claimed would produce "a very serious shortage of beer in the near future";[39]

- suggest to the ministers of War and Transport that "we should certainly use some of the shipping space in vessels returning from N. Africa for bringing over oranges and lemons from the Mediterranean area to this country ... "[40]

- remonstrate with Llewellin about press reports of shortages of salt and vinegar;[41]

- ensure that there were adequate supplies of sugar for bee keepers, including his own hives at Chartwell, in the spring when natural food from blossoms might not yet be sufficient, resulting in, as Churchill put it, "starving the bees of private owners".[42]

There are many other celebrated stories illustrating Churchill's remarkable attention to detail when it came to maintaining a rationing scheme. But perhaps the most telling – and most surreal – is the one involving plovers' eggs. Plovers' eggs were another Churchill favourite, a fact sufficiently well known to unleash a supply of these eggs to him from several admirers. When Sir William Rootes, a wealthy car manufacturer, sent some plovers' eggs to the Churchills, Clementine, in her 7 April 1942 note of thanks, wrote: "They are a great delicacy and rarity and Winston is very fond of them."[43] And when, on 20 April 1942, Audrey Pleydell-Bouverie, a friend of Queen Elizabeth, sent him "a few that [she] collected this weekend", the Prime Minister, during a very difficult month and year of the war, asked that she be telephoned with his thanks.[44] In April 1944, his second cousin, the 10th Duke of Marlborough, wrote to the Prime Minister from the Dorchester Hotel: "Please accept these plovers' eggs. There are, I fear, only twelve but I have not the personnel now available to find them."[45] Churchill did once share his treasured eggs, at one of their regular lunches, with General Eisenhower, who remembered later that "they were golden plover … It was the first time I had ever tasted them. I loved them … He was always finding some special thing".[46]

Whether it was the Prime Minister's special love of plovers' eggs, or excessive bureaucratic zeal that set off the following train of events we cannot know.[47] It seems that he had "heard on good authority" that plover, partridge and pheasant eggs were on sale – by "Messrs. Fortnum and Mason", no less – and he asked the Ministry of Food for "a special report on this which he regards as most urgent," undoubtedly a part of his on-going desire to prevent violations of regulations that would generate "class feeling". Both the ministries of Food and Agriculture, and the Metropolitan Police investigated. A plain-clothes officer verified that indeed "eggs" were on sale at Fortnum's but there was some confusion about what kind of eggs they actually were. A sales clerk told the policeman that they were gulls' eggs, not plovers' eggs, which were not allowed to be sold. Having checked several reference books and the Ornithological Department at the Natural History Museum, the serious-minded undercover copper reported that:

> ...the eggs being sold were indeed those of the black-headed gull and not those of the lap-wing [a part of the plover family]. The eggs of the latter bird are of a distinctive shape although of a similar colour and marking to a gull's egg and of approximately the same size. In my view therefore a genuine mistake has been made by the informant ...

This full and detailed correspondence, which eventually involved not only the Prime Minister reporting what he had "heard" but also the ministries of Food and Agriculture, the Home Office, the West End Central Station of the Metropolitan Police and the London Area Egg Officer (an expert on pheasant eggs), took place during the month in which Hitler attacked the Soviet Union.

This tale tells as much about the problems of maintaining a rationing scheme as it does about Churchill's preferences for these eggs. By insisting that the scheme be applied fairly, by adhering to the rules himself (with their impact ameliorated to some degree by his special circumstances and the kindness and appreciation of friends), by pressing the bureaucracy to do what it could to maximise food production and imports,

Churchill shored up Britain's willingness to endure the hardships of shortages of food and most civilian goods in order to win the war. If at times his inquiries triggered an overreaction from the bureaucracy, so be it. His management of the rationing scheme was one of his least remarked and most important contributions. No small achievement.

Between premierships, South of France, 1948

EPILOGUE

I was never fortunate enough to have had dinner with Winston Churchill. But during the five years I have spent working on this book, I have come to see aspects of his character and personality – humanity, humour, curiosity, zest and resilience – that were revealed at the dinner table to an extent not explicitly noted in many of the biographies that rightly concentrate on his enormous impact on world affairs. Churchill was capable of a toughness of the sort displayed in his decision to tell Stalin, face to face, that there would be no second front in 1942. But that necessary toughness should not obscure his basic humanity. He cared deeply for the people of Britain, admired their morale and steadfastness in the face of almost unimaginable adversity, and understood their daily lives in ways that most politicians only profess to comprehend. The historian Gertrude Himmelfarb points out that Churchill's support of free trade, which early in his career caused a break with the Conservatives, was "a social rather than an economic issue".[1] Protectionism, he said, meant "dear food for the million, cheap labour for the millionaire".[2] That lifelong concern for the welfare of the British people was again manifested in his development of the rationing plan instituted during the Second World War, with its emphasis on ensuring that the less-wealthy were as much as possible treated as well as the better-off, and that vital shipping was diverted to maintaining adequate food supplies. Indeed, Churchill's humanity extended to fallen enemies, as the now-famous statement that precedes each volume of his history of the Second World War – "In victory, magnanimity" – shows. As we have seen, he was overcome with compassion for the plight of the "haggard" bombed-out Berliners he saw during his tour of the German capital during the Potsdam Conference.

This consideration infused not only his policies, but his personal treatment of people. Yes, he could be impatient at times, and at times less than sensitive to the needs of his dinner companions to call the evening to a close. But he also saw to it that his gardener received the unused tobacco from his cigars to use as pipe tobacco, that Bernard Baruch's desire for privacy when attending a dinner party was respected, and that an old friend and comrade-in-arms, General Jan Christiaan Smuts, would not be demoted to the second spot at his wartime dinner table, even though Churchill had good strategic reasons to put General Eisenhower, also attending, on his right.

221

The Churchillian humanity extended, as I discovered, to animals. I am encouraged in applying that word to his concern for cats, dogs, pigs, bees, geese and turtles – creatures that reappear throughout this book – by the fact that the Oxford English Dictionary defines the word as "disposition to treat human beings and animals with consideration and compassion, and to relieve their distresses". Churchill could not bring himself to carve a goose ("You'll have to carve it, Clemmie. He was my friend.") at one of his dinner parties, diligently fed the fish at Chartwell; and paused to do the same for the fish at his Moscow dacha en route to an important meeting with Stalin. That did not stop him from enjoying the goose once carved, and beef properly cooked, of course, but those were instances in which his compassion was trumped by his zest for life.

So deeply did he enjoy food, champagne and cigars that I had to prepare separate chapters on these items. It is true that he was "easily satisfied with the best", but it is also true that he heartily enjoyed a humble shepherd's pie when visiting the front, and picnic fare in the company of his generals. If Pol Roger was not available, Caucasian champagne would do – no complaints. Only when it came to his cigars did his ability to do with less than the best fail him: witness his rejection – a quiet rejection, no tantrum – of the cheap cigars offered to him by the Americans when his own supply inexplicably ran out at the Casablanca meeting.

That zest was not confined to food, champagne and cigars. It extended to the baths he so enjoyed, to battles as far away as Cuba and India, and to the challenge of debates in the House, where his enthusiasm for combat enlivened the proceedings. "When he gets up to go," noted Woodrow Wyatt, a Labour Member and opponent whose service partially overlapped Churchill's, "the vitality of the House goes with him. It subsides like a reception after the champagne is finished."[3]

One cannot spend years with Churchill without also coming away with an admiration for his humour, his playfulness. He most often seemed to find a way to wrap a devastating riposte in humour to remove some of its sting, and used humour as one of the weapons with which to dominate a dinner table, whether in the presence of friends and admirers, or of the glowering Joseph Stalin. Invited to drinks by a very angry dictator after a particularly tense meeting, Churchill reports: "I said I was in principle always in favour of such a policy." I hope that jest survived its translation.

Even a reader only casually acquainted with the life of Churchill will have been exposed to the retelling of his bons mots, retorts, quips and jokes. The House of Commons cheered when, accused of sleeping during a members speech, Churchill quickly shot back: "I wish I were." Such comebacks diffused criticism and cheered his supporters, and quickly spread through Whitehall. His staff, at the Admiralty, Downing Street, Chequers and elsewhere benefited from the tension-diffusing effect of his touches of playfulness amid serious events.

He never played the clown or buffoon, or told jokes as we generally use the term. His humour always had a point. When he nicknamed Harry Hopkins "Lord Root of the Matter", he did so to convey Hopkins' importance and his inclusion on Britain's side in the war effort. And when confronted in Adana by the Turkish Foreign Minister's recitation of how difficult life was in Britain, part of the Minister's effort to demonstrate that Britain might well lose the war, Churchill countered tales of rationing by taking out the largest cigar anyone had ever seen, and remarking with a pixie-like grin: "And we are down to the tiniest cigars", with the stress on the word "tiniest".[4]

Often his humour, not unexpectedly, was based on language and wordplay. And not always in English – occasionally in French, albeit fractured French. Whatever the language, Churchill's humour "lightened the burdens of the dispirited and were quoted as the words of a champion", writes a late editor of *The Washington Post*.[5]

His dinner table companions relished and repeated Churchill's witticisms. That is one reason why we have records of so many of his conversations and quips today. Some of these tales are verifiable, others are plausible, still others fabricated, with Richard Langworth regarded as an expert on what Churchill said or did not say.

I also came to realise that the dinner table was the perfect venue for the display of another Churchill characteristic: a boundless curiosity. Every aspect of life attracted his interest, which extended from floating harbours to bath taps, from dining-room chairs to plovers' eggs, from sugar for bees to maritime rights. Dinner companions were often chosen for their ability to satisfy his wide-ranging curiosity as to how things worked, how people lived, what opponents were planning.

Churchill also satisfied his curiosity by using his many wartime travels to visit places and people not necessarily essential to the war effort. When in Teheran en route to Moscow, he lunched with the Shah. When in Washington in 1941 to meet with Roosevelt, he found time for a visit with a cousin and dinner with leading administration figures. When in Cairo, he visited the sphinx, and made arrangements to conduct a tour of the pyramids for President Roosevelt, and to arrange for the wheelchair-bound President to be brought to a vantage point to view the Atlas Mountains, still another example of his consideration for the circumstances of others and a desire to share a good thing with a friend.

Finally, the sheer resilience of the man is a wonder. He could maintain his composure at a dinner at the White House after being informed of a series of devastating military setbacks, and doggedly return to his wooing of the President. He could recover quickly from pneumonia and set off on an arduous trip across the Atlantic to meet and dine with Franklin Roosevelt. He could recover from a stroke and immediately head to a meeting with President Eisenhower in Bermuda, hoping his dinner-table talents would outweigh the intransigence of John Foster Dulles. And, in the end, he could leave a failed meeting in Bermuda, rebuffed in his desire for a summit meeting with the Russians, and almost immediately resume planning for just such a meeting.

I do not mean to be so besotted with the subject of this book as to suggest Churchill was a paragon. He was not. But he was humane, funny, curious and resilient – not inconsiderable virtues. As one historian put it, Churchill was "quiet simply, a great man".[6]

Diners

Dean Acheson
US Secretary of State, 1949–53. As Roosevelt's Assistant Secretary of State during the Second World War, Acheson played a key role in framing policies ranging from Lend Lease to plans for the post-war financial order at the Bretton Woods conference. First as Truman's Under-Secretary and then as his Secretary of State, he proved a forceful advocate of containing the further spread of Soviet power and was instrumental in establishing NATO. He strongly encouraged Truman to intervene in the Korean War and to support French efforts in Indochina. He died aged 78 in 1971.

A. V. Alexander
Labour politician who succeeded Churchill as First Lord of the Admiralty. Born in 1885, the son of a blacksmith, he left school at 13 and served in the Artists' Rifles in the First World War. In the post-war Labour government he served as Minister of Defence and Labour leader in the House of Lords. He died in 1965.

Clement Attlee
Leader of the Labour Party, 1935–55 and Prime Minister, 1945–51. Attlee served as Churchill's Deputy Prime Minister in the War Cabinet, putting aside political differences in a successful

partnership. He enjoyed Churchill's respect and also endured his occasional jibes. He was a former public schoolboy who fought in the First World War and whose social conscience was shaped by witnessing poverty in the East End of London where he was a local mayor and MP. His wife was a closet Tory. He died in 1967, two years after Churchill.

Bernard Baruch

Amassed a fortune on Wall Street. Baruch (1870–1965) was a financial adviser to various US presidents, including Roosevelt during the war. He was also a long-standing friend of Churchill, offering personal financial advice and generous hospitality.

Lord Beaverbrook

Press magnate and Minister of Aircraft production, 1941, Minister of Supply 1941 and Lord Privy Seal, 1943–5. Born Max Aitken in Canada in 1879, he was the son of a Scottish minister. He bought the *Daily Express* in 1916, turning it by the 1930s into Britain's best-selling newspaper. Beaverbrook supported appeasement but was also considered a crony of Churchill. During the war he built a popular reputation because of his perceived energy in improving armament production. He contrived to combine a firm belief in the British Empire with repeated calls for more help for the Soviet Union and the early opening of a Second Front in Europe.

Valentin Berezhkov

Stalin's interpreter at the Tehran, Yalta and Potsdam conferences. In retirement he remained loyal to Stalin's memory though when the Soviet Union broke up in 1991 he moved to California, where he died in 1998. One of his sons wrote to Ronald Reagan asking if he could defect; another became interpreter to Boris Yeltsin.

Arthur H. Birse

Born in Russia and trained as an international banker, Birse was fluent in Russian and an expert in Russian affairs. During the war, he served in the Intelligence Corps in Cairo, achieving the rank of major in the British Army. He was later appointed to the British embassy in Moscow. He was asked to translate for Churchill at Teheran, Moscow in 1944 and at Yalta. In 1945, he acted at Churchill's interpreter. He also interpreted for Eden, Attlee and Bevin

Charles E. Bohlen

The diplomat "Chip" Bohlen (1904–74) was working at the US embassy in Tokyo when Pearl Harbor was attacked and thereafter endured six months in a Japanese internment camp. After his repatriation to Washington he advised Harry Hopkins and President Roosevelt on Soviet affairs. He travelled with Roosevelt to the Teheran and Yalta Conferences, where he served as an interpreter, a role he revived at Potsdam for Truman. Alongside his friend George Kennan, Bohlen helped shape the policy of Soviet containment, and he succeeded Kennan as Ambassador in Moscow in 1953. Rethinking some of his earlier conciliatory overtures, Bohlen concluded that "anyone who started with too many illusions about the Soviets came out disillusioned".

Violet Bonham Carter

Daughter of the Liberal Prime Minister, H.H. Asquith and stepdaughter of Margot Asquith, Violet Bonham Carter lived in Downing Street between the ages of 21 and 27 and knew many of her father's contemporaries, marrying his Principal Private Secretary. She was a close friend of both Winston and Clementine Churchill. Created Baroness Asquith of Yarnbury, she remained active in Liberal politics in the House of Lords. She wrote *Winston Churchill as I Knew Him* in 1965, and died in 1969. Her diaries containing many revealing anecdotes were published in 1996.

Brendan Bracken

Churchill's most loyal supporter in the House of Commons. Born in 1901, the son of an Irish Fenian activist and partly educated in Australia, Bracken arrived in England in 1919 and began a rapid social and political advancement by impressing the editor of *The Observer*, J.L. Garvin. Elected a Conservative MP, aged 28, he became a press magnate of financial newspapers and helped Churchill to survive his own money problems on the eve of the Second World War. He was Churchill's parliamentary Private Secretary from 1939–41 and a successful Minister for Information from 1941 to 1945. During the war, he lent his Swedish cook to the Downing Street Private Office mess in the Annexe. His last years were spent actively in establishing Churchill College, Cambridge. Died 1958.

Bessie Braddock

Labour MP for Liverpool Exchange, 1945–70. A firebrand socialist, campaigner for women and family issues and member of Labour's National Executive. She was known by admirers and opponents alike as "Battling Bessie".

Joan Bright (later Astley)

Personal assistant to Sir Hastings "Pug" Ismay, the Deputy Secretary to the War Office. She handled the British administrative arrangements of six foreign wartime conferences from Quebec to Potsdam. Before the war she had turned down a job offer to go to Germany to teach English to Rudolf Hess's family.

Norman Brook
Prominent Civil servant. Deputy Secretary to the War Cabinet, Permanent Secretary, Ministry of Reconstruction, 1943–5. He took the title Lord Normanbrook in 1963 and died four years later, aged 65.

Alan Brooke
Alongside Churchill, the primary architect of Britain's wartime strategy. Born in 1883, Brooke fought on the Western Front during the First World War and again in France in 1940. Appointed Chief of Imperial General Staff in 1941 and chairman of the Chiefs of Staff Committee. Brooke admired Churchill but was frequently exasperated by his meddling. Promoted to Field Marshal, 1944. On elevation to the House of Lords in 1945, he took the title Lord Alanbrooke. Away from the killing fields, he was a keen ornithologist. Died 1963.

Anthony Montague Browne
Churchill's Private Secretary from 1952 until Churchill's death in 1965.

Reader Bullard
British Minister in Teheran 1939–1946, later Ambassador.

R.A. "Rab" Butler
Senior Conservative politician. Supported appeasement and adopted a defeatist attitude to Britain's chances of survival in 1940. Butler's Education Act of 1944 – introduced when he was President of the Board of Education – was widely acclaimed for improving the scholastic opportunities for the post-war generation. Despite holding high office in the Conservative cabinets of the 1950s and

early 60s, he twice failed in his bid to become Prime Minister in 1957 and 1963. He believed in Bismarck's dictum that politics was "the art of the possible." Died 1982.

James F. Byrnes

US Secretary of State, 1945–47. A South Carolina senator prior to serving as a judge in the US Supreme Court, he was a close associate of Roosevelt during the war and accompanied the ailing President to Yalta and, as Secretary of State, went with Truman to Potsdam. As Secretary of State, he reversed his previous appeasement of the Soviet Union and argued for the reintegration of West Germany into a Western power bloc. Personal differences with Truman led to his resignation in 1947.

Alexander Cadogan

British diplomat. Permanent Under-Secretary at the Foreign Office, 1938–46. In 1971, two years after his death, his diaries were published, providing an illuminating insight into wartime diplomacy.

Neville Chamberlain

Prime Minister, 1937–40. A determined driver of Britain's policy of appeasing Hitler, he nevertheless declared war on Germany when it invaded Poland. He appointed Churchill First Lord of the Admiralty. He was accused of lacking a coherent and determined plan to pursue the war. When Churchill succeeded him as Prime Minister in May 1940, Chamberlain continued as leader of the Conservative Party and used his position to offer Churchill vital support in resisting pressure for peace talks. He remained in Churchill's cabinet as Lord President of the Council until he was overcome by ill-health and died in November 1940.

Clementine Churchill

Churchill's wife. Born Clementine Hozier in 1885, she was eleven years Churchill's junior. She married him in 1908. Thereafter, she stood steadfast throughout his tumultuous life, despite a strong temperament and a determinedly independent streak of her own. She enjoyed outdoor pursuits and travel. She served as President of the YWCA Wartime Fund and Chairman of Red Cross Aid to the Soviet Union Fund. Died, aged 91, in 1977.

Mary Churchill

Churchill's youngest daughter. Born in 1922, she served with the Auxiliary Territorial Service during the Second World War and accompanied her father on many of his journeys. In 1947, she married the future Conservative politician, Christopher Soames and wrote a biography of her mother. Now Lady Soames.

Lady Randolph Churchill

Churchill's mother. Born Jennie Jerome in New York State in 1854, she married Lord Randolph Churchill in 1874. She was noted for her beauty and her attraction to a variety of men. She was unresponsive to Churchill's pleas for attention while he attended boarding schools but later used her charm and wide-ranging social skills and contacts to advance his career. She died in 1921, aged 67, when Churchill was Colonial Secretary.

Lord Randolph Churchill

Churchill's father. Ambitious politician and exponent of populist "Tory democracy" before destroying his career by an opportunistic resignation as Chancellor of the Exchequer in 1886. Died, disappointed, in 1895 when he was 45 and his son 21.

An indifferent parent, who did little to justify his son's lifetime affection and regard.

Randolph Churchill

Churchill's only son. Born in 1911, he left Oxford without taking his degree and became a journalist. Fought and lost six election campaigns, but took advantage of the "wartime truce" to serve as Conservative MP for Preston during the war. He served in the army in North Africa and Italy and was part of the British mission to Tito's forces in Yugoslavia. He wrote the first two volumes of the official biography of his father, but his career was blighted by the burden of high expectations, drink and an irascible temper. He died in 1968, only three years after his father.

Sarah Churchill

Churchill's second daughter. She was born two months into the First World War. She became a dancer – performing with, among others, Fred Astaire – and an actress. In 1936 she married the popular entertainer, Vic Oliver, who divorced her in 1945. She died in 1982.

John Colville

Churchill's Assistant Private Secretary 1940–45 and his Joint Principal Private Secretary 1951–55. Churchill inherited "Jock" Colville as his prime ministerial Assistant Private Secretary from Neville Chamberlain, whom Colville had loyally served. Churchill and Colville enjoyed a warm rapport and Colville's diaries are a major source for the period and are held at Churchill College, Cambridge – an institution he helped endow. He died in 1987.

Alfred Duff Cooper

Conservative politician, diplomat, socialite and historian. An opponent of appeasement, Duff Cooper resigned as First Lord of the Admiralty over the Munich Agreement in 1938. During the war he was Minister of Information from 1940–1, British Representative in Singapore in 1941 (prior to its surrender) and back in the Cabinet as Chancellor of the Duchy of Lancaster, 1941–43. He was Ambassador to France from 1944 to 1947 and wrote an admired biography of Talleyrand.

Diana Cooper

Born Lady Diana Manners, widely rumoured not to be the daughter of the Duke of Rutland, she was considered a great beauty. In 1919, she married Duff Cooper, who subsequently became a Conservative politician. Lady Diana Cooper (as she preferred to be known) was a friend of Churchill's for many years. The Prime Minister appointed Duff Cooper British Ambassador to France in 1944, where she shone as an outstanding and gracious and, sometimes provocative, Ambassador's wife. She died in 1986.

Eric Crankshaw

Head of the Government Hospitality Fund, to which all requests are made for food and wines for foreign guests visitors to Chequers etc.

Andrew Cunningham

Commander-in-Chief of the Royal Navy in the Mediterranean, 1939–42, during which time he oversaw crushing victories against the Italians at Taranto and Cape Matapan. First Sea Lord and Chief of the Naval Staff from 1943 until 1946.

John Cunningham

Having served in the 1940 Norwegian campaign, Cunningham was joint naval commander of the unsuccessful Dakar expedition against Vichy French West Africa. Thereafter he succeeded Sir Andrew Cunningham first as commander of the Mediterranean fleet and then as First Sea Lord from 1946 to 1948.

Archbishop Damaskinos

Damaskinos was the Greek Orthodox Archbishop of Athens and All Greece from 1941 until his death in 1949. During the German occupation of Greece, he had risked death by publicly condemning the persecution of the Jews. He was installed by the Allies to rule Greece as regent on behalf of the exiled King George II and endeavoured to hold the country together as it splintered into civil war between royalist and communist insurgents, prior to the monarchy's return.

Marion Davies

Mistress of William Randolph Hearst. Born in 1900, she was a dancer and Hollywood actress whose films included *Cain and Mabel* and *Ever Since Eve*. She died in 1961.

Joseph E. Davies

US Ambassador to the Soviet Union, 1937–38, whose attempts to improve relations with Stalin led him into many gullible actions – including excusing the Purges – while at his post. His book, *Mission to Moscow*, adapted into a film, provided pro-Soviet propaganda for America's wartime ally.

Louis G. Dreyfus

American diplomat. He held various consular posts, served as

Ambassador to Afghanistan between 1941–42 and 1949–51 and was also Minister to Iran 1939–44. He was Ambassador to Iceland, 1944–46, and to Sweden 1946–47.

Pierson Dixon

British diplomat who was Principal Private Secretary to Anthony Eden from 1943 to 1945 and then to his successor at the Foreign Office, Ernest Bevin until 1948. He was later Ambassador to Czechoslovakia and to France. He was the UK's Permanent Representative at the UN from 1954 to 1960 during which time he had to represent British interests over the Suez Crisis.

Blanche Dugdale

Niece and biographer of the Edwardian British Prime Minister and First World War Foreign Secretary, Arthur Balfour, whose 1917 Declaration promised support for a Jewish homeland in Palestine. Dugdale (1880–1948) was herself a passionate Zionist.

John Foster Dulles

US Secretary of State, 1953–59. Dulles intensified the Communist containment policies of his Democrat predecessor, Dean Acheson, threatening massive nuclear retaliation in the event of a Soviet strike, a policy sometimes described as "brinkmanship". He constructed the South East Asia Treaty Organisation (SEATO) for mutual defence. Although he connived in the overthrow of the Mossadegh government in Iran, he strongly opposed Anglo-French-Israeli action against Nasser's Egypt during the 1956 Suez Crisis. Ill health forced him to retire as Secretary of State in April 1959 and he died the following month. His famous dictums included "the United States of America does not have friends, it has interests".

Anthony Eden

British Foreign Secretary and Prime Minister. He resigned as Foreign Secretary in 1938 because of Neville Chamberlain's meddling and offered measured criticism of appeasement. Secretary of State for War in 1940, he succeeded Lord Halifax as Foreign Secretary later that year. Long seen as Churchill's natural successor, he was repeatedly frustrated by Churchill's failure to step aside in his favour until 1955 by which time Eden's own judgment and health were under strain, resulting in the fiasco of the Suez Crisis in 1956 and his resignation as Prime Minister in 1957. He married Churchill's niece, Clarissa in 1952. Died, 1977.

Dwight D. Eisenhower

US President, 1953–61. As Supreme Commander of the Allied Forces in Europe, 1944–5, Eisenhower had ultimate responsibility for planning the invasion of Western Europe and with the war's conclusion was also initially in charge of the defeated Germany in America's occupied zone. He was Chief of Staff of the US Army from 1945 to 1948 and Supreme Commander of NATO from 1950 to 1952 before focusing on politics.

Alonzo Fields

White House chief butler, 1931–53. A black man from Indiana, he hoped to be a musician, but a temporary job at the White House diverted him to his career in the domestic service of four US presidents. After retirement, he published his memoirs in 1960 and died aged 94.

C.S. Forester

Novelist. Born Cecil Smith in 1899. Churchill was a particular admirer of his Napoleonic War novels about a fictitious Royal

Navy captain, Horatio Hornblower, which began to be published from 1937. Moved to the United States and died in 1966.

King George VI

British King, 1936–52. He was born in 1895 and unexpectedly succeeded his brother when Edward VIII abdicated in 1936. Shy and suffering a stammer, he soon overcame initial doubts about Churchill's suitability when he became Prime Minister in 1940. Churchill reacted to the news of the King's death in 1952 with the solemn response: "Bad news? The worst!"

Alexander Golovanov

Soviet Marshal of Aviation, 1943, and the following year, Chief Marshal of Aviation.

P.J. Grigg

British public servant and friend of Churchill. He was Private Secretary to Churchill when he was Chancellor of the Exchequer, from 1924 to 1929, and Secretary of State for War from 1942 to 1945. Died in 1964, aged 74.

Lord Halifax

Born Edward Wood, he was Viceroy of India from 1926 to 1931 and succeeded his father as Lord Halifax in 1934. As Foreign Secretary from 1938 to 1940, he was not uncritical of Neville Chamberlain's Munich diplomacy but went along with it. He probably enjoyed greater support among Conservative MPs than did Churchill in May 1940 but accepted Churchill as Prime Minister. At the time of the Dunkirk evacuation, he argued in the War Cabinet for a negotiated peace to be brokered through Mussolini. In December 1940, Churchill removed him from the Foreign Office by making him Ambassador in Washington DC. Halifax was a devout Anglican and a keen fox-hunter, hence his nickname, the "Holy Fox".

Averell Harriman

US Ambassador to the Soviet Union, 1943–46, and to Britain, 1946. Harriman was Roosevelt's special envoy to Europe and, as such, was greatly engaged in Anglo-American diplomacy prior to his appointment to Moscow. Late in life, in 1971, he took Anglo-American partnership further by marrying Pamela, the ex-wife of Winston Churchill's son, Randolph.

Pamela Harriman

The daughter of a peer who held the Military Cross and bar, Pamela Digby met Randolph Churchill in 1939 while she was a translator in the Foreign Office. They married in 1939 but their relationship deteriorated after Randolph was posted to Egypt, and they divorced in 1946. Among her many male consorts during this time was the broadcasting pioneer William S. Paley, who described her admiringly as "the greatest courtesan of the century". Another of her wartime conquests, Averell Harriman, eventually became her third husband in 1971. She was appointed by Bill Clinton as US Ambassador to France in 1993 until her death in 1997.

Oliver Harvey

British diplomat. Born 1893. Private Secretary to the Foreign Secretary, Anthony Eden, 1941–43. Assistant Under-Secretary at the Foreign Office, 1943–46 and Deputy Under-Secretary there, 1946–48. Ambassador to France, 1948–54. Ennobled, 1954. His diaries, edited by his son, were published in two volumes after his death in 1968.

William Randolph Hearst

American press magnate. Born in 1863, the son of a senator, he stood unsuccessfully for Mayor of New York in 1905, subsequently becoming a Congressman. His business methods and seclusion at his private mansion at San Simeon made him a model for Orson Welles's Citizen Kane. He died in 1951.

Kathleen Hill

Churchill's secretary. Born in 1900, she was a talented violinist who helped organise the Girl Guide movement in India. When she returned to Britain in 1937, she became Churchill's secretary at Chartwell, and was his personal private secretary during the war. She was the curator at Chequers from 1946 to 1969.

Leslie Hollis

Assistant Secretary to the War Cabinet and the Chiefs of Staff Committee whose memoir, *War at the Top*, provides a fascinating insight especially into the state of British military unpreparedness in the early stages of the war.

Marian Holmes

Churchill's secretary. She joined the Downing Street secretariat in 1938 while Neville Chamberlain was Prime Minister and from 1943 was part of Churchill's pool of secretaries, accompanying him on tours abroad. She continued working as a Downing Street secretary after Clement Attlee became Prime Minister, which she described "as the difference between champagne and water".

Harry Hopkins

The President's principal diplomatic adviser during the Second

World War, and, because he lived almost permanently at the White House, was sometimes seen as even more influential than the Secretary of State. Hopkins worked with Roosevelt to develop the New Deal relief programmes in the 1930s. With war in Europe, the US President sent Hopkins to assess Britain's chances and – after Churchill himself – nobody did more than Hopkins to convince Roosevelt that Churchill was a strong leader of a country that needed American backing and Lend-Lease assistance. Hopkins was also present at the major wartime conferences at Teheran, Casablanca and Yalta. He died in 1946, aged 55.

Roy Howells

Churchill's nurse and personal attendant from 1958 until Churchill's death in 1965.

Cordell Hull

US Secretary of State, 1933–44. Prior to the attack on Pearl Harbor, he had called for stepping-up American rearmament and supporting Britain, albeit while keeping America out of the European war. Much of his work during the war was spent drawing-up plans for the post-war world, including the role of the UN. He retired from the State Department because of ill health, dying in 1955.

Thomas Cecil Hunt

Churchill's gastro-enterologist. He often wrote to Churchill with sensible recommendations on dieting, exercise, smoking and the drinking of brandy rather than port. He saw active service in North Africa and at the age of 70 he founded the British Digestive Foundation. Died in 1981.

Ismet Inönü

President of Turkey, 1938–50 and Prime Minister of the country,

1923–27 and 1960–65. He maintained Turkey's neutrality during the Second World War despite endeavours by Hitler and Churchill to enlist Turkey's support.

Hastings Ismay

British general, known as "Pug". He served with the Camel Corps in the First World War and became Secretary of the Committee of Imperial Defence in 1938. During the Second World War he provided an essential link between Churchill and the military Chiefs of Staff. First Secretary-General of NATO, 1951–7. Died 1965.

Ruth Ive

Worked as a censor for the transatlantic telephone link during the Second World War and recently wrote a lively memoir of her work listening into the conversations between, among others, Churchill and Roosevelt.

Ian Jacob

Military Assistant Secretary to the War Cabinet. After the war he went into broadcasting and was Director-General of the BBC from 1952 to 1960.

Joseph Kennedy

US Ambassador to London, 1937–41. Prominent leader of Boston's Irish-American community. He did not disguise his belief that Britain would be defeated. His sons included John F. and Robert Kennedy, both of whom he outlived.

Archibald Clark Kerr

Experienced British diplomat. As Ambassador to the Soviet Union, 1942–46, he worked hard to build good relations with

Stalin. He attended key conferences at Teheran, Yalta and Potsdam. Ambassador to the United States, 1946–48. Created Lord Inverchapel in 1946 and died in 1951.

John Maynard Keynes

Economist. He was a critic both of demanding war reparations from Germany after the First World War and of Churchill's economic policy in 1925. Keynes argued that mass unemployment could be cured by the government's management of demand. He was a Treasury civil servant during the Second World War and led British negotiations with the United States over Lend-Lease and the post-war international economic order at the Bretton Woods Conference, 1944. Died 1946.

Ernest King

US Chief of Naval Operations during the Second World War. Despite the requirements of working with America's allies, he never hid a deep-seated mistrust of the British. At the Casablanca Conference he almost hit General Alan Brooke. He was not greatly impressed by democratic politicians of any stripe.

William Lyon Mackenzie King

Canadian Prime Minister, 1921–30 and 1935–48. Leader of the Liberal Party from 1919, Mackenzie King was the dominant figure in the first half of Canada's twentieth century. During the 1930s he had made clear Canada's reluctance to join a European war unless Britain was directly attacked, but in 1939 he mobilised his country for a full-hearted commitment, which included not only a massive deployment of Canada's armed forces but also generous financial aid to Britain, while always retaining his dominion's right to independent action. He died in 1950, aged 75.

Hughe Knatchbull-Hugessen

British diplomat. He served as Minister to the Baltic States from 1930–34, Minister in Teheran from 1934–36, Ambassador in China from 1936–38, Ambassador in Turkey from 1939–44 and as Ambassador in Brussels and Minister to Luxembourg from 1944 until his retirement in 1947.

Elizabeth Layton (later Nel)

Churchill's secretary during most of the war years who accompanied him to meetings in the US, Canada, Athens, Casablanca and Yalta. Her book on these years, *Mr. Churchill's Secretary*, is wonderful.

Harold Laski

British Socialist theorist. Academic at the London School of Economics, 1920–50. Chairman of the Labour Party, 1945. Frequent target of Churchill's invective. Died, age 57, in 1950.

William D. Leahy

Fleet admiral of the US Navy.

Professor Frederick Lindemann, Lord Cherwell

Churchill's scientific adviser. German-born and educated physicist, whose mother was American and father a British naturalised Frenchman. He helped transform the Clarendon Laboratory at Oxford University into a world-class scientific research institution. He was Churchill's personal assistant during the Second World War and Paymaster-General from 1942 to 1945 and from 1951 to 1953. A keen pianist and tennis player. His vegetarianism, teetotallism and abstention from tobacco made him an unlikely favourite of Churchill, who nonetheless admired his mental dexterity and love of argument. Created Lord Cherwell in 1941 and died in 1957.

John Jestyn Llewellin

Conservative politician. After working in the Department of Supply, he succeeded Lord Woolton as Minister of Food from 1943 to 1945. He was created Lord Llewellin in 1945 and served as Governor-General of the Rhodesian Federation from 1953 to 1957. Died 1958.

David Lloyd George

Prime Minister, 1916–22. Dynamic Liberal politician who led a coalition government in the latter stages of the First World War. Churchill admired his energy but was disappointed first by Lloyd George's admiration for Hitler's economic policies and then, in 1940, by his defeatist attitude and reluctance to join Churchill's government or accept the post of Ambassador to Washington. Died in 1945, aged 82.

Hugh Lunghi

British diplomat. Born in the British legation in Teheran where his father served as economic advisor to the Shah. After Oxford, he became a Major in the British Army. A Russian speaker since childhood, he was appointed ADC to the Head of the British Military Mission in Moscow in 1943. Served as interpreter for the British Chiefs of Staff and for Churchill at the Big Three conferences as well as at Churchill's meeting with Stalin in 1944 (and later for Khrushchev). After the war served in the British embassy in Moscow and at the Foreign Office. Later joined the BBC World Service.

Oliver Lyttelton

Conservative politician and member of the War Cabinet. In 1941 he was appointed Minister of State in Cairo and liaison officer with the Free French. From 1942 to 1945 he was Minister of Production. Colonial Secretary from 1951 until 1954, when he was made Viscount Chandos. Chairman of the National Theatre from 1962–71 – the Lyttelton Theatre is named after him.

Ramsay MacDonald

Prime Minister, 1924, and 1929–37. Labour politician who split his party by forming a coalition with the Conservative and Liberal parties to fight the economic crisis in 1931. He pressed, unsuccessfully, for world disarmament.

Norman McGowan

One of Churchill's valets, late in Churchill's life.

Harold Macmillan

Prime Minister, 1957–63. Conservative politician who combined progressive social views with opposition to appeasement. During the war he was successively Parliamentary Secretary to the Minister of Supply and Minister Resident, Allied Headquarters in North-West Africa. His period as prime minister was marked by growing consumerism and higher living standards in Britain, accelerated decolonisation in Africa and his failed attempt to join the nascent European Union, the EEC, was vetoed by De Gaulle.

George C. Marshall

As Roosevelt's Chief of Staff, Marshall transformed the relatively under-resourced peacetime US armed forces into a massive power capable of winning a global war. He was both an excellent organiser and picker of capable commanders. His plan for an invasion of Europe in 1943 met opposition from Churchill and was not enacted until June 1944. Although he failed in his post-war mission to bring peace to China, he had more success as Truman's Secretary of State between 1947 and 1949, proposing and driving through the Marshall Plan of aid that fuelled Western Europe's economic – and perhaps political – recovery. Briefly Defense Secretary for a year between 1950 and 51, he then retired from public life, accepted the 1953 Nobel Peace Prize and died in 1959.

John Martin

A civil servant, Martin was Private Secretary to Churchill when he was appointed Prime Minister in 1940, becoming his Principal Private Secretary the following year and serving him closely both in Downing Street and on his trips around the world during the war. After the war, he served in the Colonial Office and was High Commissioner in Malta from 1965 to 1967. He died in 1991.

Robert P. Meiklejohn

Personal assistant to Averell Harriman. Kept a diary of his service with Ambassador Harriman.

Vyacheslav Molotov

Soviet Foreign Minister, 1939–49 and 1953–56. Stalin assigned him to drive through rapprochement with Hitler, agreeing the notorious Molotov-Ribbentrop non-aggression pact in August 1939, enabling the Soviet Union to invade eastern Poland and subsequently the Baltic States and, less successfully, Finland. Once Germany attacked the Soviet Union, he proved a tough negotiator with his new British and American allies. He lived to the age of 96, dying in 1986. Churchill considered him "a man of outstanding ability and cold-blooded ruthlessness".

Walter Monckton

Lawyer, who advised King Edward VIII during the abdication crisis of 1936 and served as Director-General of the Ministry of Information in 1940. He was Solicitor-General in 1945 and subsequently a Conservative MP, serving in Churchill's second administration as Minister for Labour. He gained a peerage in 1957 and died in 1965.

Venetia Montagu

Born Venetia Stanley. Overly close personal confidante – despite considerable age difference – of the Liberal Prime Minister, H.H. Asquith, during the First World War. Married his former Private Secretary, Edwin Montagu. Clementine Churchill's first cousin.

Bernard Montgomery

British soldier. He commanded the British Eighth Army in North Africa in 1942, masterminding its decisive victory over Rommel at the battle of El Alamein and proceeding to sweep German forces out of North Africa and then take the fight into Sicily and Italy. He was Supreme Allied Commander until disagreement with Eisenhower led to the latter assuming the role. "Monty" led ground forces on D-Day and commanded the British advance through Western Europe. He was created Field Marshal in 1944 and Viscount Montgomery of Alamein in 1946 when he succeeded Lord Alanbrooke as Chief of the Imperial General Staff, and served as Eisenhower's deputy as Supreme Commander of NATO in Europe from 1951 to 1958. He was popular with his troops despite his personal asceticism and disciplinarian attitude, but his American colleagues found his manner overbearing, verging on insufferable.

Henry Morgenthau

US Treasury Secretary, 1934–45. Before the war, he had fought with Roosevelt to try and balance the budget. In 1944 he proposed breaking Germany up into its constituent states after the war. Even more controversially, he called for it to be economically disabled and returned to a primarily agrarian society. The plan was adopted in September but Truman backed away from it and, believing his advice was being ignored, Morgenthau resigned in 1945, and published a book propagating his ideas on a Carthaginian peace.

H.V. Morton

Henry Vollam Morton (1892–1972) was a British journalist and travel writer whose *In Search of England* was a best-selling book, first published in 1927 and frequently reprinted. Present at the Newfoundland meeting in the Atlantic. After the war he emigrated to South Africa.

Edmund Murray

Detective and Churchill's personal bodyguard from 1950 until his death in 1965. He shared Churchill's love of painting.

Henrietta Nesbitt

White House principal housekeeper, 1933–46. Born in 1874, her *White House Diary* was published in 1947. Famous for her substandard cuisine.

Harold Nicolson

British diplomat and politician. He opposed appeasement before the war and was elected a National Labour MP in coalition with the Conservatives. During the war he served as Parliamentary Secretary and Governor of the BBC. He was knighted in 1953. A historian and biographer, his diaries provide an illuminating narrative of the events and personalities of his political and social circle from 1930 until 1962.

Vladimir Pavlov

Stalin's principal interpreter at the Big Three meetings.

John Peck

One of Churchill's wartime Assistant Private Secretaries. He was appointed to work for Churchill at the Admiralty and then at Downing Street. He was with Churchill at Potsdam and accompanied him on his tour of the troops in Berlin. Then he transferred to the Foreign Service and became Ambassador to the Republic of Ireland. Knighted in 1971.

Richard Pim

Developed Churchill's Map Room which went everywhere with the Prime Minister including to the White House in 1941 and all foreign conferences. Captain Pim was a trusted staff member throughout the Second World War

Stewart Pinfield

Chief Petty Officer and a Churchill favourite. He was in charge of catering for the Prime Minister at Carthage, Teheran and Potsdam.

Henry Page Croft

Brigadier-General in the First World War and Conservative MP from 1910 to 1940 whereupon he became Lord Croft. He joined Churchill in opposing granting greater sovereignty to India in 1935 and was Parliamentary Under-Secretary of State for War from 1940 to 1945.

Odette Pol Roger

Wife of Jacques Pol Roger, co-director of Churchill's favourite champagne house. Churchill was entranced by her when they first met in 1945 and their friendship continued, fortified by the produce of the family firm, until his death. She died in 2009, aged 89.

Charles Portal

Air Chief Marshal of the RAF, 1940–45. He served in the Royal Flying Corps in the First World War and helped oversee the RAF's rapid expansion in 1939. Despite disagreements, he worked closely and successfully with Churchill and advocated the strategic bombing offensive on Germany. He also won the esteem of Eisenhower. He retired from the RAF in 1945, was given a peerage and directed the British atomic energy programme until 1951. Died 1971.

Jane Portal, (subsequently Lady Williams of Elvel)

Churchill's personal secretary during his second premiership, 1949–55.

Emery Reves

Churchill's literary agent. He was born in Hungary in 1904 but naturalised British in 1940. In later life, Churchill greatly enjoyed staying with Reves and his glamorous partner, Wendy Russell, at their home, the Villa La Pausa on the French Riviera.

John Reith

Creator of the BBC, serving as its first General Manager in 1922 and its Director-General from 1928 to 1938, shaping its public service ethos. A dour Scot, he was made Lord Reith in 1940 and held office successively as Minister of Information,

Transport, Works and Planning. His relations with Churchill were fraught and Churchill sacked him in 1942. He subsequently channelled his energies into the development of new towns and harbouring grudges. Died, 1971.

Eleanor Roosevelt

Wife of President Roosevelt. Born into a wealthy New York family in 1884, she married the future President in 1905. The marriage held together through mutual affection and shared political activism rather than love and exclusive devotion. She outlived her husband by eighteen years and, as a US delegate to the UN General Assembly, chaired the UN Human Rights Commission.

Franklin D. Roosevelt

US President, 1933–45. A wealthy New Yorker whose distant cousin, Theodore, was also President. Confined to a wheelchair by polio in 1921, Roosevelt became Governor of New York in 1928 and was elected to the White House in the midst of the Great Depression. The extent to which his New Deal policies were successful remains contentious, although they did have positive effects on morale. His policy of neutrality – while sending supplies to Britain – ended with the Japanese attack on Pearl Harbor. He died of a cerebral haemorrhage two months after the Yalta Conference and a month before the war's end in Europe.

Victor Rothschild

A member of the banking family, Rothschild became a Labour peer in 1937 and served in the British Security Service, MI5, during the war, winning the George Medal. However, his earlier friendship at Cambridge with those subsequently unmasked as Soviet spies brought him – unfairly – under suspicion. After the war he was a prominent zoologist and advised the Tory prime ministers, Edward Heath and Margaret Thatcher. He died in 1990, aged 79.

Leslie Rowan

Civil servant. Captained the English hockey team both before and after the Second World War. Churchill's Private Secretary 1941, and Principal Private Secretary in 1945, continued to serve and advise the subsequent Labour government on economic policy. Knighted in 1949 and died, aged 64, in 1972.

François Rysavy

Czech-born White House chef, famed for his mastery of international cuisine. In 1957 he published an account of his time in the kitchens, complete with the favourite recipes of President Eisenhower and his wife.

Frank Sawyers

Churchill's valet during most of the war years, accompanied Churchill on most of his overseas trips.

Walter Bedell Smith

Chief of Staff to General Eisenhower during the lead up to D-Day. He later served as American Ambassador to the Soviet Union and Director of the CIA.

Jan Christiaan Smuts

Despite having led a guerrilla campaign against British forces in the second Boer War, Jan Christiaan Smuts (1870–1950) was not only a political champion of South African involvement on the British side in both world wars, but served in the British Army in the First World War and was raised to the rank of British Field Marshal in the Second World War. He was a member of the

Imperial War Cabinet. A scholar as well as a soldier and friend of Churchill, he was a driving influence in the creation of the League of Nations after the first conflict and the United Nations after the second conflict. He was Prime Minister of South Africa from 1919 to 1924 and from 1939 until 1948, when he lost power to the National Party which campaigned against Smuts' increasingly liberal attitude to racial segregation, which it replaced with apartheid.

Edward S. Stettinius
US Secretary of State, 1944–45. One of the architects of the UN, he stepped down as President Truman's Secretary of State in order to become the first US Ambassador to the UN, but resigned in 1946, unhappy at Truman's attitude towards the assembly. Died in 1949, aged only 49.

Henry L. Stimson
US Secretary of State, 1929–33, and Secretary for War, 1911–13 and 1940–45. Already aged 73 when in 1940 Roosevelt asked him to return to the post of Secretary for War which he had last held before the First World War, Stimson was a noted "hawk" in Washington against both the German and Japanese regimes.

Walter Thompson
Churchill's bodyguard. He had been Lloyd George's bodyguard from 1917 to 1920, when he took over Churchill's security. He retired in 1936 to become a grocer, but returned to be Churchill's bodyguard throughout the Second World War.

Commander C. R. (Tommy) Thompson
A Flag Lieutenant at the Admiralty, he was responsible for organising Churchill's wartime travels both in Britain and overseas,

accompanying him throughout and journeying over 40,000 miles in doing so.

Harry S Truman

US President, 1945–53. A Missouri haberdasher by trade who assumed the highest office on Roosevelt's death, although widely discounted as greatly inferior in stature and ability to Roosevelt, whom he had served as Vice-President. Despite winning re-election in 1948, he suffered low popularity during his presidency, although subsequent analysis of his handling of foreign affairs, in particular his decision to use nuclear weapons on Japan, contain communism, sanction the Marshall Plan programme to rebuild Western Europe and engage in the Korean War has led to his being adjudged one of the most underrated presidents in American history.

Sumner Welles

US Under-Secretary of State, 1937–43. Roosevelt described him as "the only man in the State Department who really knew what was going on". Born into a wealthy and influential New York family, Welles had been a page boy at the wedding of Franklin and Eleanor Roosevelt. The two men had a strong rapport and Welles wielded more personal influence on foreign policy matters with the President than the Secretary of State, Cordell Hull. Hull was among Welles's political enemies who forced his retirement by threatening to reveal his homosexual importuning. Thereafter, he attempted suicide and retreated into alcoholism and the manipulative care of his manservant, Gustave.

Wendell Willkie

Unsuccessful Republican contender in the 1940 presidential election. Initially a Democrat, Willkie had come to prominence campaigning against aspects of Roosevelt's New Deal and was the surprise "outsider" choice on the Republicans' 1940 ticket. Despite some tactical backflips during the election campaign, he was mostly a vocal supporter of sending aid to Britain, in contrast to some isolationists in his party. After his defeat, he divided his party by backing Roosevelt's lend lease policy and was sent by the President as a personal wartime emissary to Britain, the Soviet Union and China. Having failed to be re-adopted as the Republican contender and toying with establishing his own Liberal Party, he died in 1944, age 52.

Charles Wilson, (Lord Moran)

Churchill's doctor from 1939. Awarded the Military Cross for his valour on the front line in the Medical Corps during the First World War. As President of the Royal College of Physicians, 1941–50, he was active in the establishment of the National Health Service. Knighted in 1938, he became Lord Moran in 1943. His decision to publish his account of life with Churchill, including details of his physical decline, the year after Churchill's death, was widely condemned for its questionable ethics, although it provided much informative detail for the historian. He died in 1977.

John Winant

US Ambassador to Britain from 1941 to 1946, much respected and admired there. He was dining with Churchill when news of the attack on Pearl Harbor was received. Despite the high regard in which he was held, he suffered depression and committed suicide in 1947.

Lord Woolton

Born Frederick Marquis in 1893, he was Chairman of the John Lewis department store chain from 1936 to 1951. Created Lord

Woolton in 1939, he proved a successful and popular Minister of Food, overseeing rationing, and was Minister of Reconstruction from 1943 to 1945. He was subsequently a successful Chairman of the Conservative Party, helping to revive its post-war fortunes and modernise its organisation, thus contributing to his re-election. He died in 1964.

Woodrow Wyatt

A journalist, author and a Labour MP, he served as Personal Assistant to Sir Stafford Cripps in India. He was knighted in 1983 and became Baron Wyatt of Weeford in 1987. He wrote three volumes of scandalously delicious diaries.

ENDNOTES

*NB: Full details of all publications referred to in these notes
can be found in the bibliography, following*

Prologue

1. Churchill to the House of Commons, 3 November 1953, Hansard HC Deb 5s., vol. 520, col. 29
2. D'Este, Carlo, *Warlord*, p. 386
3. CHAR 2/240B/70, and CHAR 2/240B/152
4. Gilbert, *Winston S. Churchill*, Volume V, p. 617
5. Gilbert (ed.), *The Churchill War Papers, The Ever-Widening War,* Volume 3, p. 320
6. Bradford, Sarah, *George VI*, p. 450
7. Soames, *Mary Clementine Churchill*, p. 445
8. Gilbert, *Churchill, Finest Hour, 1939-1941*, Volume VI, p. 160
9. Gilbert, *Winston S. Churchill, 1917-1922*, Volume IV, p 35
10. Gilbert, *Winston S. Churchill, Road to Victory, 1941-1945*, Volume VII, p. 664
11. Gilbert, *Winston S. Churchill*, Volume VII, p. 802
12. Pawle, *The War and Colonel Warden*, p. 69
13. Pawle, p. 190
14. CHUR 1/285
15. Kass, *The Hungry Soul, Eating and the Perfecting of our Nature,* p. 182

SECTION 1

Chapter 1 The Importance of Dinners

1. Wilson, "World of Books," commenting on Roy Jenkins' life of Churchill, *Daily Telegraph*, 7 June, 2004

2. Sir Christopher Meyer to the author
3. Soames, *Mary Clementine Churchill*, p. 260
4. "In Honour Bound: My Father, Lord Mountbatten", talk by The Countess Mountbatten of Burma, in *Proceedings of the International Churchill Societies*, p. 5
5. Bonham Carter, *Winston Churchill as I Knew Him*, p. 16
6. Skidelsky, *John Maynard Keynes: Fighting for Britain, 1937-1946*, p. 80
7. Coote, *The Other Club*. Endpapers
8. www.bbm.org.uk/Savoyhotel.htm
9. Macmillan, *The Past Masters 1906-1939*, p. 150
10. Gilbert (ed.), *War Papers*, Volume 3, p. 421
11. Martin, *Lady Randolph Churchill, The Dramatic Years, 1895-1921*, p. 295
12. Gilbert, *Winston S. Churchill, Prophet of Truth*, Volume V, *1922-1939*, p. 265
13. Manchester, William, *The Last Lion*, Volume 2, p. 27
14. Roberts, Andrew, *Masters and Commanders*, p. 80
15. *The Washington Post*, 27 December, 1941
16. Gilbert, *Winston S. Churchill, The Stricken World, 1917-1922*, Volume IV, p. 138
17. Gilbert, *Winston S. Churchill*, Volume IV, pp. 138-9
18. Kramnick, Isaac and Sherman, Barry, *Harold Laski: A Life on the Left*, p. 1
19. DeWolfe, Mark (ed.), *Holmes-Laski Letters: The Correspondence of Mr. Justice Holmes and Harold Laski, 1916-1953*, p. 1136
20. Henderson, Nicholas *The Private Office Revisited*, p. 83
21. Davies, Joseph E., *Mission to Moscow*, p. 150
22. Letter from the 4th Lord Dufferin and Ava. Lord Dufferin added, "I shall ever remember the evening throughout my life". CHAR 1/232/11
23. CHAR 1/232/ 7
24. CHAR 1/242/21
25. Nasaw, David, *The Chief: The Life of William Randolph Hearst*, p. 418
26. CHAR 1/254/39
27. Wyatt, *To The Point*, p. 32
28. CHAR 1/244/81
29. Gilbert, email to the author, 19 April 2011
30. Buchan-Hepburn, Patrick, to Sir Martin Gilbert, *In Search of Churchill: A Historian's Journey*, p. 304
31. James Scrymgeour-Wedderburn, quoted in Gilbert, *In Search of Churchill, A Historian's Journey*, p. 231
32. Montague Browne, Anthony, *The Long Sunset*, p. 116
33. Montague Browne, p. 118
34. In conversation with the author
35. Soames (ed.), *Speaking for Themselves*, p. 344
36. Edward Rothstein, "Contemplating Churchill," *Smithsonian*, March 2005, p. 91
37. Soames (ed.), p. 259
38. CHAR 1/386/16
39. CHAR 1/386/17
40. CHAR 7/15/103

41. CHAR 7/15/99
42. Martin, Ralph G., *Lady Randolph Churchill*, Volume I, p. 149, from George W. Smalley, *Anglo-American Memories*, 1911
43. Churchill, *My Early Life*, p. 150
44. Cooke, Alistair, *General Eisenhower and the Military Churchill*, p. 52
45. CHAR 1/315/121 and CHAR 1/268/98
46. CHAR 1/254/40 and CHAR 1/282/66
47. CHAR 1/315/125
48. CHAR 1/315/122
49. CHAR 1/315/123
50. Cooper, *Trumpets from the Steep*, p. 180
51. Norwich, John Julius (ed.), *The Duff Cooper Diaries*, 11 January 1944
52. Letter from Jo Sturdee, later Countess of Onslow, to her family from Hotel de la Mamounia, Marrakesh, Morocco, 7 January 1948. CHUR/ONSL 2
53. Graebner, *My Dear Mr. Churchill*, p. 78
54. Gilbert, *Winston S. Churchill, Road to Victory, 1941-1945*, Volume VII, p. 979
55. Moran, *Winston S. Churchill, The Struggle for Survival*, p. 213
56. Pawle, p. 344
57. Colville, *The Fringes of Power*, p. 639
58. Reported by Elizabeth Olson, "Churchill's Lifelong Romance With a Feisty Former Colony," *The New York Times*, 7 February 2004
59. Cohen, *Supreme Command*, p. 118

Chapter 2: Meeting off Newfoundland

1. FDR to WSC on the occasion of FDR's 60th birthday, in response to the Prime Minister's birthday wishes, Moran, p. 25
2. Larson, Philip P., "Encounters with Chicago", *Finest Hour* 118, p. 30.
3. McJimsey, *The Presidency of Franklin Delano Roosevelt*, p. 138
4. Churchill, *The Second World War, The Grand Alliance*, Volume III, p. 427
5. Colville, p. 415
6. Colville, p. 368
7. Colville, p. 369
8. Dilks, David (ed.), *Cadogan*, p. 395
9. Morton, H., *Atlantic Meeting*, p. 74
10. Dilks (ed.), p. 396
11. Joan Bright in conversation with the author
12. Lash, *Roosevelt and Churchill, 1939-1941*, p. 391
13. Gilbert (ed.), *The Churchill War Papers*, Volume 3, p. 1036
14. Lash, *Roosevelt and Churchill*, p. 391
15. Wilson, Theodore, *The First Summit*, p. 92
16. Morton, p. 104
17. Wilson, p. 104
18. Although the press was barred, Morton and Howard Spring, a novelist, were invited to go along to describe what they saw. They were not told where they were going and were sworn to secrecy by Brendan Bracken. Morton asked

an important question: "Should I pack a dinner jacket?" Bracken said, "yes".

19. Morton, p. 105
20. Montague Browne, *The Long Sunset*, p. 230
21. Langworth, Richard, "On Turtles and Turtle Soup", *Finest Hour* 146, p. 25
22. CHUR 2/96B/224
23. Morton, p. 95
24. Wilson, p. 106
25. Richardson, *From Churchill's Secret Circle to the BBC: The Biography of Lt. Gen. Sir Ian Jacob*, p. 67
26. Martin, *Downing Street: The War Years*, p. 59
27. *Ibid.*, photo insert following p. 56
28. Gilbert, *Churchill: A Life*, p. 889
29. Gilbert, Volume VI, p. 1168

Chapter 3 Christmas at the White House

1. Kimball (ed.), *Churchill & Roosevelt, The Complete Correspondence,* Volume I, p. 286
2. Smith, Jean Edward, *FDR*, p. 542
3. Meiklejohn, Diaries, Reel 52. Harriman had also brought over the gift of an electric shaver which the Prime Minister wanted to use constantly. Voltages were of course a problem.
4. Churchill, Volume III, p. 538
5. Harvey (ed.), p. 70
6. Kimball (ed.), p. 286
7. Ive, p. 72
8. Richardson, pp. 84-85. Jacob joined Churchill on the *Duke of York*.
9. Soames (ed.), *Speaking For Themselves*, p. 461
10. Pawle, *The War and Colonel Warden*, p.145
11. Martin, John, *Downing Street; The War Years*, p. 69
12. Gilbert, *Churchill*, Road to Victory, 1941-1945, Volume VII, p. 18
13. Pawle, London 1963, p. 146
14. Gilbert, *Churchill*, Volume VII, p. 18
15. Gilbert, *Churchill*, Volume VII, p. 9
16. Richardson, *Diary*, p. 88
17. Leasor (ed.), *War at the Top, The Experiences of Sir Leslie Hollis*, p. 29
18. Goodwin, *No Ordinary Time*, p. 301
19. *Time* magazine, 5 January, 1942
20. Roberts, *Masters and Commanders*, p. 84
21. Fields, *My 21 Years in the White House*, p. 81
22. Goodwin, p. 302
23. Stiegler, Sam, interviews. From Medford Afro-American Remembrance Project, p. 7
24. Fields, p. 51
25. François Rysavy as told to Frances Spatz Leighton, *A Treasury of White House Cooking*, p. 79
26. Lady Williams, In conversation with the author, April 2010
27. Macmillan, *Tides of Fortune*, p. 322

28. Graebner, *My Dear Mr. Churchill*, p. 53
29. Harriman papers, Box 446, Folder 2
30. Nesbitt, Henrietta, *White House Diary*, p. 30
31. Nesbitt, p. 273
32. Jenkins, *Churchill: A Biography*, p. 672
33. Bohlen, *Witness to History*, 1929-1969, p. 143
34. Burns, *Roosevelt, The Soldier of Freedom, 1940-1945*, p. 178
35. Nesbitt papers, Library of Congress
36. Whitcomb, John and Claire, *Real Life at the White House*, p. 306
37. McGowan, Norman, *My Years With Churchill*, 1958, p. 70
38. Roberts p. 68
39. Roberts, p. 69
40. Jenkins, p. 672
41. *New York Times*, 11 January 1942
42. Bercuson and Herwig, *One Christmas in Washington*, p. 154
43. Goodwin, p. 302
44. Gilbert, Volume VII, p. 27
45. *Ibid.*
46. Gilbert, Volume VII, p. 28
47. Richardson, p. 91
48. Bercuson and Herwig, p. 164
49. Moran, p. 12
50. Roberts, Masters, p. 84
51. Pawle, p 155
52. Roberts p. 77

Chapter 4 Moscow

1. Moran, p. 60
2. Telegram from Churchill to the Cabinet, copied to Roosevelt, August 15, 1942. CHAR 20/79A/36-38
3. Blake and Louis, *Churchill*, p. 314
4. JACB 1/16 p. 56
5. Pawle, p. 193
6. Mander, Danny, *Winston Churchill's Bodyguard, The Teheran conference 1943*, p. 19
7. Mander, Danny, p. 16
8. Churchill, *The Second World War, The Hinge of Fate*, Volume IV, p. 477
9. Colville, p. 404
10. Churchill, Volume IV, p. 409
11. Gilbert, Volume VII, p. 1
12. JACB 1/16 p. 84
13. Churchill, Volume IV, p. 425
14. Churchill, Volume IV, p. 429
15. Moran, p. 55
16. Moran, p. 56
17. Leon Aron, Russian Scholar at the American Enterprise Institute

in Washington, consulted Sir Rodric Braithwaite, the last UK ambassador to the USSR and the first ambassador to post-Soviet Russia, who confirmed a report from Director of the Federal Archival Service, Professor Vladimir Kozlov and Molotov's grandson, Vyacheslav Nikonov, that the Ninth Directorate "periodically destroys everything in their archives after a decade or so." Memo to the author from Leon Aron, 6 September 2005.

18. Thompson, W.H., *I Was Churchill's Shadow*, p. 98
19. Moran, p. 59
20. Churchill, Volume IV p. 442
21. Gilbert, Volume VII, p. 200
22. Moran, p. 63
23. Gilbert, Volume VII, p. 205
24. CHAR 20/79A/36.
25. Moran, p. 64
26. Gilbert, Volume VII, p. 191
27. Gilbert, Volume VII, p. 181
28. Harriman and Abel, *Special Envoy*, p. 152
29. Sandys, Celia, "Around the World with Winston", *Daily Mail*, 6 September 2008

Chapter 5 Adana

1 FO 195/2478 Press Conference, given by British ambassador Sir H. Knatchbull Hugessen on 2 February 1943
2. Churchill, *The Second World War,* Volume IV, p. 625
3. Gilbert, *Churchill, Road to Victory, 1941-1945*, Volume VII, p. 301
4. Chandler, Graham, "Travels with Churchill", *Air & Space Magazine*, July 2009
5. Gilbert, *Churchill: A Photographic Portrait,* picture caption, p. 289
6. FO 195/2478 Press Conference
7. Moran, p. 84
8. *Ibid.*
9. http//www.*turim*.net/turkey
10. Behrend, George, *Luxury Trains*, p. 119.
11. Danchev and Todman (eds.), *Field Marshal Lord Alanbrooke*, p. 374
12. Gilbert, Volume VII, p. 325

Chapter 6 Teheran

1. Moran, p. 148
2. *Ibid.*
3. Gilbert, p. 555
4. Gilbert, Volume VII, p. 564
5. Harriman Papers, Notes on the Teheran Conference, 27 November - 5 December 1943, Box 110, Folder 10
6. Gilbert, Volume VII, p. 569

7. Churchill, Sarah, *A Thread in the Tapestry*, p. 65
8. Dilks (ed.), *Cadogan*, p. 578
9. Lavery, Brian, *Churchill Goes to War*, p. 245
10. Eubank, Keith, *Summit at Teheran*, p. 177
11. Bullard, Sir Reader, *The Camels Must Go*, p. 256
12. Mayle, *Eureka Summit*, p. 51
13. Ismay, General Lord, *Memoirs*, p. 337
14. Birse, *Memoirs of an Interpreter*, p. 153
15. Harriman and Abel, p. 263
16. Eisenhower, John, *Allies*, p. 410
17. Sherwood, *Roosevelt and Hopkins*, p. 776
18. Churchill, Sarah, p. 65
19. Cunningham, *A Sailor's Odyssey*, p. 588
20. Eubank, p. 342
21. Harriman Papers, Notes on the Teheran Conference, Box 110, Folder 10
22. Mayle, p. 114
23. *Ibid*.
24. Rees, Laurence, *WWII Behind Closed Doors*, p. 233
25. Bohlen, UK Edition, p. 149
26. Churchill, Sarah, p. 66
27. Thompson, John, *Chicago Tribune*, 7 December 1943
28. Danchev and Todman (eds.), p. 488
29. Ismay, p. 341
30. Cunningham, p. 588
31. Pawle, p. 271
32. Gilbert, Volume VII, p. 593
33. Bullard, p. 259
34. Letter from Harriman, State Dept., S8330

Chapter 7 Yalta

1. Dilks (ed.), p. 707
2. Gilbert, Volume VII, p. 1182
3. Stettinius, *Roosevelt and the Russians: The Yalta Conference*, p. 3
4. Sherwood, p. 845.
5. Gilbert, Volume VII, p. 1167
6. *Ibid*.
7. An astute political observer noted at the time "We've just elected a dead man".
8. Leasor, James, *War At The Top*, based on the experiences of General Sir Leslie Hollis, p. 280
9. *Ibid*.
10. Leasor, p. 281
11. Harriman, p. 390
12. Gilbert, Volume VII, p. 1172
13. Gilbert, Volume VII, p. 1187
14. Harriman, p. 390

15. Gilbert, Volume VII, p. 1195
16. Stettinius, p. 3
17. CHAR 20/210/90
18. MART 2 from unpublished John Martin Diary, p. 175
19. Martin, p. 180
20. Ismay, p. 387
21. Gilbert, Volume VII, p. 1172
22. Martin, p. 179
23. Bright, *The Inner Circle, A View of War at the Top*, p. 182
24. Dilks (ed.), *Cadogan*, p. 703
25. Layton, Elizabeth (later Nel), *Mr. Churchill's Secretary*, p. 176
26. Dilks (ed.), *Cadogan*, p. 703
27. Gilbert, Volume VII, p. 1182
28. Dilks (ed.), p 703
29. CHUR 1/285
30. *Ibid.*
31. Clemens, *Yalta*, p. 114
32. Stettinius, p. 82
33. *Ibid.*
34. US Dept of State, Foreign Relations of the US. Conferences at Malta and Yalta, 1945. Washington 1955. Galley 491
35. Nesbitt, p 305
36. www.ukraineplaces.com
37. Stettinius, p. 114
38. Stettinius, p. 218
39. Dilks (ed.), *Cadogan*, p. 707
40. ed., Danchev and Todman, *Alanbrooke*, p. 659
41. Stettinius, p. 83
42. *Ibid*. p. 218
43. Dilks (ed.), *Cadogan*, p. 707
44. Stettinius, p. 219
45. *Ibid*. p. 220.
46. Gilbert, Volume VII, p. 1195
47. *Ibid.*
48. Gilbert, Volume VII, p. 1190
49. Stettinius, p. 272
50. The menu is reproduced in the American edition of Bohlen's memoir, *Witness to History,* but not in the British edition.
51. Stettinius, p. 111
52. U S Department of State, Foreign Relations of the US (FRUS), Conferences at Malta and Yalta, 1945. Galley 496
53. JACB 1/20, p. 53
54. Moran, p. 230
55. Dilks (ed.), *Cadogan*, p. 709
56. Lunghi, Hugh, *A Tribute to Sir Winston Churchill*, Blenheim Palace, transcript of talk, 1 March 1997, p. 8
57. Dilks (ed.), *Cadogan*, p. 710

Chapter 8 Potsdam

1. Churchill, *The Second World War, Triumph and Tragedy,* Volume VI, p. 578
2. Beschloss, *The Conquerors: Roosevelt, Truman and the Destruction of Hitler's Germany, 1941-1945,* p. 239
3. Truman, Harry, *Memoirs: Year of Decisions,* Volume 1, p. 337
4. Truman, p. 381
5. Bohlen, Charles, p. 226. Bohlen was quartered with President Truman in the President's villa.
6. Churchill, Volume VI, p. 545
7. Truman, *Memoirs,* Vol.1, p. 342
8. David McCullough, *Truman,* p. 406
9. Bright, *The Inner Circle,* p. 210
10. Cadogan, *Diary,* p. 763
11. Bright, *Circle,* p. 214
12. Mee, *Meeting at Potsdam,* p. 43. Also in Bright, p. 214
13. Moran, p. 267
14. McCullough, *Truman,* pp. 406-7
15. *Telegraph,* 5 May 2006
16. Montefiore, Simon Sebag, *Stalin,* p. 507
17. Moran, p. 281
18. Garrison, Gary, "Berlin 1945-2006: Historical Epilogue", *Finest Hour,* No.132, p. 18
19. Ferrell (ed.), Robert H., *Off The Record: The Private Papers of Harry S Truman,* p. 51. Bohlen notes, "Where Roosevelt was warmly friendly with Churchill and Stalin, Truman was pleasantly distant." Bohlen, p. 228
20. Truman, *Memoirs,* Vol. 1, p. 340
21. Donovan, Robert J. *Conflict and Crisis,* p. 75
22. Bohlen, Charles, *Log of the President's trip to the Berlin Conference",* Box 30, p. 24
23. Gilbert, *Winston S. Churchill, Never Despair, 1945-1965,* Volume VIII, p. 70
24. Bohlen, Charles, *Log of the President's Trip to the Berlin Conference,* p. 25
25. McCullough, *Truman,* p. 427
26. *Ibid.*
27. Dilks (ed.), p. 767
28. Rayfield, Donald, Times Literary Supplement Review of *Molotov's Magic Lantern,* 23 April 2010
29. Mee p. 166
30. ed., Ferrell, *Dear Bess: The Letters from Harry to Bess Truman,* p. 521
31. Mee p. 166
32. *Ibid.* But the official Programme of Music lists it as The String Orchestra of the Royal Air Force.
33. Moran, p. 281
34. *Ibid.*
35. Truman, *Memoirs,* Vol.1, pp. 340 and 361
36. Cunningham, *A Sailor's Odyssey,* p. 647
37. Broadbent, Michael, *Wine Vintages,* p. 28
38. Pawle, p. 396
39. Churchill, Volume VI, p. 579

40. Moran, p. 282
41. Moran p. 283
42. Churchill, Volume VI, p. 579
43. Ulam, Adam B., *Stalin: The Man And His Era*, p. 626

Chapter 9 Fulton to Bermuda

1. Westminster College Archives Press Release, 14 February 2006
2. PREM 11/418. Full text of telegram in Churchill and Bermuda 20th International Conference November 2003.
3. Churchill, "Land of Corn and Lobsters", *Colliers* magazine, August 1933, p.133
4. Westminster College, Fulton. Missouri, Press Release 14 February 2006
5. Richards, Michael, "Commissioning Day", *Finest Hour* 110, p.15
6. PREM 11/418
7. Gilbert, Volume VIII, p. 807
8. *Ibid.*, p.936
9. Colville, *Fringes*, p. 688
10. *Ibid.*
11. Mid-Ocean Club, 8 November 2003

SECTION 2

Chapter 10 Food

1. Halle, Kay (ed.), *Winston Churchill On America and Britain*, p. 256
2. Moir, Phyllis, *I Was Winston Churchill's Private Secretary*, p. 132
3. Winston S. Churchill, *The Story of the Malakand Field Force*, p. 201 (Originally published by Longmans, Green & Co. in 1898.)
4. CHAR 1/351/50-52
5. Soames (ed.), *Speaking for Themselves*, p. 582
6. Gilbert, *Winston S. Churchill*, Volume VII, p. 127
7. Jenkins, p. 711
8. Addison, *The Road to 1945*, p. 245
9. CHAR 1/116/60
10. Gilbert, *1914-1916*, Volume III, p. 502
11. Soames (ed.), *Speaking for Themselves*, p. 117
12. *Ibid.*, p.164
13. *Ibid.*, p. 178
14. Nicolson. Nigel (ed.), *Harold Nicolson, The War Years, 1939-1945*, p. 166
15. Pawle, p. 171
16. McGowan, p. 87
17. Montague Browne, *Long Sunset: Memoirs of Winston Churchill's Last Private Secretary*, p. 314
18. Howells, *Churchill's Last Years*, pp. 111-112

19. Eden, Anthony, *Memoirs, The Reckoning*, p. 202
20. Danchev and Todman (eds.), p. 390
21. Felipe Fernández-Armesto, *Near a Thousand Tables: A History of Food*, p. 133
22. Moran, p. 283, referring to Churchill's distaste for devilled chicken.
23. CHAR 1/391/1
24. Colville, p. 309
25. Murray, *I Was Churchill's Bodyguard*, p. 90
26. Coote, p. 40
27. Cooke, Alistair, *General Eisenhower on the Military Churchill*, p. 54
28. Martin, John, MART 2, unpublished diaries for 30 November 1944, p. 168
29. Soames (ed.), *Speaking for Themselves*, p. 581
30. Buczacki, Stefan, *Churchill and Chartwell*, p. 258
31. Colville, John, *The Churchillians*, p. 112
32. Soames, Mary, *Finest Hour*, 115, p. 42
33. *Ibid.*
34. Soames, Mary, *Clementine Churchill*, p. 344
35. Brocklesby, Eddie, "Nan's Kitchen at No. 10" from the Serpentine running Club Newsletter, Autumn, 2003, p. 3
36. Brocklesby, p. 3
37. BBC TV Archives, Joan Bakewell Interview, 1973
38. Langworth, Richard, *Finest Hour, Frequently Asked Questions*
39. Nicolson, Juliet, *The Perfect Summer*, p. 47
40. *Finest Hour 144*, Churchill Quiz, p. 63
41. Gilbert (ed.), *Churchill War Papers, The Ever-Widening War 1941*, Volume 3, p. 1470
42. Colville, p. 454 (paperback version)
43. McGowan, p. 89
44. Gilbert, Sir Martin, in conversation with Admiral Hetherington, 1965. Sir Martin Gilbert email to the author 19 April 2011

Chapter 11 Champagne

1. Moir, p 138
2. Churchill, Winston S., *My Early Life: A Roving Commission*, p. 125
3. Churchill, Randolph S., *Winston S. Churchill, Youth, 1874-1900*, Volume I, p. 453
4. Philip and Susan Larson, "Winston S. Churchill and Robert R. McCormick," *Finest Hour*, 131, p. 33
5. McJimsey, George, *Harry Hopkins: Ally of the Poor and Defender of Democracy*. P. 140 refers to the "prodigious quantities of weak whiskey" that Churchill consumed during Hopkins' 1941 visit to Britain.
6. Churchill, Winston S., *My Early Life: A Roving Commission*, p. 125
7. CHAR 1/400A/46
8. Tugwell, Rexford G., *The Democratic Roosevelt*, p. 593
9. Sherwood, Robert E., p. 442
10. Butcher, Captain Harry C., *My Three Years With Eisenhower*, p. 75

11. Skidelsky, Vol. 3, p. 92
12. *Finest Hour*, 131, p. 35
13. King, Mackenzie, Diary, 23 August 1941, from *www.collectionscanada. gc.ca*, p. 879
14. Kimball, Warren F., *Forged in War: Roosevelt Churchill and the Second World War*, p. 22
15. Reilly, Michael F., as told to William J. Slocum, *Reilly of the White House*, p. 125
16. Gilbert, Martin, *In Search of Churchill*, p. 209
17. Wilson, A.N., *After The Victorians*, p. 390
18. Moran, p. 390
19. Roberts, Andrew, *Eminent Churchillians*, p. 170
20. Harvey, John (ed.), *The War Diaries of Oliver Harvey, 1941-1945*, p. 369
21. Nevezhin, Vladimir A., in a collection of "Stalin's Table Speeches", Moscow: AIRO-XX, 2003
22. Gilbert, Volume VII p. 191
23. Moran, p. 59
24. Gilbert, Volume VII, p. 193
25. Churchill, *The Malakand Field Force*, p. 16
26. Kimball, Warren F., "Like Goldfish in a Bowl: The Alcohol Quotient", *Finest Hour*, 134, p. 32
27. James, Robert Rhodes, *Churchill: A Study in Failure*, p. 389
28. Danchev and Todman (eds.), p. 566
29. Harmon, Christopher C., "Alanbrooke and Churchill", a review of the Alanbrooke Diaries, in *Finest Hour* 112, p. 34
30. Langworth, Richard M. (ed.), *Churchill by Himself*, p. 550. (Langworth says that Churchill was paraphrasing a W.C. Fields retort.)
31. Acheson, Dean, *Sketches From Life Of Men I have Known*, p. 66. John Martin tells this same story taking place on 3 August 1941 on the train north when Churchill was on the way to meet with President Roosevelt in Newfoundland. Martin p. 56
32. Beschloss, p. 135
33. Letter from Jo Sturdee, later, Countess of Onslow, to her family from La Mamounia Hotel, Marrakesh, Morocco, 7 January 7 1948, to her family. ONSL 1
34. Louanne Cox, www.helium.com, February 2011.
35. CHUR 1/15/32 and 33
36. Gilbert, Volume VI, p. 336 note 1
37. Gilbert, Martin, *In Search of Churchill*, p. 209
38. Williams, Jane, conversations with author
39. Eden, *The Reckoning*, p. 494
40. *Finest Hour* 144, "The Churchill Quiz", p. 63
41. Churchill, Randolph S., p .453
42. Langworth (ed.), *Churchill by Himself*, p. 37
43. Acheson, p. 64
44. Ray, Jonathan, "Winston Churchill drank Pol Roger by the Pint", *Telegraph*, 30 September 2006
45. *Telegraph*, Odette Pol Roger, 30 December 2000
46. Roberts, Andrew, *The Holy Fox: A Life of Lord Halifax*, p. 186

47. Churchill, *My Early Life*, p. 178
48. McGowan, p. 90
49. Rose, Kenneth, *The Elusive Rothschild, The Life of Victor, Third Baron*, p. 58
50. *Telegraph*, Odette Pol Roger, 30 December 2000
51. *Independent*, Odette Pol Roger, 30 January 2001
52. www.polroger.co.uk
53. *Ibid.*
54. *Ibid.*
55. Dilks (ed.), *Cadogan*, p. 707
56. McGowan, p. 104
57. Kersaudy, Francois, *Churchill et Monaco*, p. 46
58. Rose, p. 73
59. McGowan, p. 55
60. Kimball, Warren, *Finest Hour* 134, p. 31
61. Bonham Carter, p. 135
62. Gilbert (ed.), *Winston Churchill and Emery Reves: Correspondence, 1937-1964*, pp. 376-377
63. Gilbert, Volume VIII, p 630
64. Rose, p. 53

Chapter 12 Cigars

1. Acheson, Dean, *Sketches From Life Of Men I Have Known*, p. 63, after a working lunch with Churchill at the British Embassy in Washington in 1946
2. Welsh, Peter, "A Gentleman of History", *Cigar Aficionado*, Autumn, 1995, p. 1
3. Hough, Richard, *Winston & Clementine*, p. 69
4. CHUR 1/351/50-52
5. Howells, p. 94
6. Wingfield-Stratford, Esmé, *Churchill: The Making of a Hero*, p. 95
7. Acheson, Dean, *Present at the Creation*, p. 596
8. McGowan, Norman, *My Years With Churchill*, p. 93. Howells contends that Churchill did indeed smoke his cigars to the very end. p.35
9. That is the estimate of his valet, who precedes the "nine a day" estimate with the word "only". McGowan, p. 92
10. Photo of letter, preserved at J.J. Fox
11. Golding, Ronald E., "Did You Fly? Hmph!", *Finest Hour* 34, p. 4
12. Gilbert, *Churchill*, Vol. IV, 1916-1922, p. 139
13. McGowan, p. 93
14. Welsh, p. 2
15. CHUR 1/351/50-52
16. Howells, p.37; McGowan, p. 92, reports that the matches were "specially imported from America", not Canada
17. Howells, p. 36
18. Howells, p. 35. This ashtray traveled with Churchill.
19. Welsh, p. 1
20. Hirshson, Stanley P., *General Patton: A Soldier's Life*, pp. 299-300

21. Packwood, Allen, "Cigars: Protecting the Premier," *Finest Hour* 106, p. 1
22. Rose, Kenneth, London, 2003, p. 73
23. Hall, Douglas, *The Book of Churchilliana*, p. 50
24. Vines, C. M., *A Little Nut Brown Man, My Three Years with Beaverbrook*, p. 28
25. West, Bruce, *The Man Who Flew Churchill*, p. 105
26. Gilbert, Volume VII, p. 921
27. Soames (ed.), *Speaking for Themselves*, p. 504. Clementine Churchill described it in a letter to her daughter as "a small shadow on one lung, but he himself is well …" Soames, *Clementine Churchill*, p. 357
28. Colville, p. 507
29. Soames, *Speaking For Themselves*, p. 504
30. Soames, *Clementine Churchill*, Revised Edition, p. 502
31. Colville, John, pp. 215-216
32. CHUR 1/15/169
33. CHUR 1/15/167

Chapter 13 Rationing

1. CAB 120/854
2. CAB 123/74
3. CAB 120/854
4. Gardiner, Juliet, *Wartime London*, 2004, p. 147
5. CAB 123/74
6. Gilbert, Volume VII, pp. 161 and Calder, Angus, *The People's War*, p. 71
7. Calder, p. 405
8. NF 1/292 Home Intelligence Weekly Report, No. 90, 16-23 June 1942
9. Gilbert, *Churchill War Papers*, Volume III, p. 376
10. CHAR 1/379/40 and 1/379/39
11. CHAR 1/389/5
12. Nesbitt, p. 274
13. Hastings, Max, *Finest Years: Churchill as War Lord 1940-1945*, p. 202
14. *News Chronicle*, 30 September 1941
15. CHAR 1/380/25 and CHAR 1/368/85
16. CHAR 2/441/61
17. CHAR 2/446A
18. Profumo, David, The Laxford Shows its True Colours, *Country Life*, 6 October 2010, p. 104
19. CHAR 20/53C/256
20. Char 2/442/51
21. Char 2/446 B
22. Gilbert, *Churchill War Papers*, Volume 3, p. 357
23. Meiklejohn to Thompson, "Subject: Hams", 3 January 1942. Library of Congress, Harriman Papers, Box 161, Folder 6
24. Colville, *The Churchillians*, p. 156
25. CHAR 20/138A/11
26. Hastings, p. 203

27. Ibid.
28. Pawle, p. 155
29. Hastings, p. 203
30. Gilbert, *The Churchill War Papers*, Volume 3, p. 990
31. MAF, 286/8
32. Wheeler-Bennett, Sir John (ed.), *Action This Day: Working With Churchill*, p. 30
33. Halle, Kay (ed.), *Winston Churchill on America and Britain*, p. 259
34. Gilbert, *The Churchill War Papers, Never Surrender*, Volume 2, p. 514
35. MAF 286/6
36. MAF 286/6
37. MAF 286/3
38. CAB 123/74
39. CAB 123/74
40. CAB 123/74
41. MAF 286/8
42. CHAR 1/394/22
43. CHAR 2/446/A
44. CHAR 2/445/72
45. CHAR 1/380/34
46. Nelson, James (ed.), *General Eisenhower on the Military Churchill: A Conversation With Alistair Cooke*, p.54
47. Unless otherwise indicated, correspondence relating to the affair of the plovers' eggs can be found in MAF 286/1

Epilogue

1. Himmelfarb, Gertrude, *The Moral Imagination: From Edmund Burke to Lionel Trilling*, p. 207
2. Jenkins, p. 95, cited by Himmelfarb, *ibid.*
3. Halle, Kay (ed.), *The Irrepressible Churchill*, p. 10
4. Martin Gilbert, email, 19 April 2011, to the author. The cigar may just be seen in the ash tray in the photograph on page 83 of Martin Gilbert's book *Churchill At War 1940-1945: His "Finest Hour" In Photographs*
5. Halle, p.10.
6. G. R. Elton, *Political History: Principles and Practice*, p. 71. Cited in Himmelfarb, *Moral Imagination*, p. 197

~⭑ BIBLIOGRAPHY ⭑~

Primary Sources

Cabinet Papers, National Archives, Kew, CAB
Chartwell Papers, Churchill College, Cambridge, CHAR
Churchill Papers, Churchill College, Cambridge, CHUR
Foreign Office, National Archives, Kew
Harriman Papers, Library of Congress, Washington DC
Jacob Papers, Churchill, College, Cambridge, JACB
Martin Papers, Churchill College, Cambridge, MART
Meiklejohn Papers, Library of Congress
Ministry of Agriculture and Fisheries Papers, National Archives, Kew,
    MAF
Ministry of Information Papers, National Archives, Kew NA
ONSL, Papers of Jo Sturdee, later Countess of Onslow, at Churchill
    College, Cambridge
Premier Papers, National Archives, Kew, PREM

Journals

Air & Space Magazine   *The Independent*
Cigar Aficionado   *New York Times*
Daily Telegraph   *News Chronicle*
Finest Hour   *Time Magazine*
The Guardian   *Times Literary Supplement*
Country Life

Secondary Sources

Acheson, Dean, *Present at the Creation: My Years in the State Department*, New York, 1969

Acheson, Dean, *Sketches From Life Of Men I Have Known*, New York: Harper & Brothers, 1959

Addison, Paul, *The Road to 1945: British Politics And The Second World War*, London: Pimlico, 1994

Bercuson, David J. And Herwig, Holger H., *One Christmas In Washington, The Secret Meeting Between Roosevelt and Churchill That Changed the World*, New York: Overlook, 2005

Behrend, George, *Luxury Trains: From the Orient Express to the TGV*, New York 1982

Beschloss, Michael, *The Conquerors: Roosevelt, Truman And The Destruction of Hitler's Germany 1941-1945*, New York: Simon & Schuster, 2002

Birse, A. H., *Memoirs of an Interpreter*, London: Michael Joseph, 1967

Blake, Robert and Louis, *Wm. Roger Louis, Churchill*, Oxford: Oxford University Press, 1993

Bohlen, Charles E., *Witness to History 1929-1969*, London: Weidenfeld & Nicolson, 1973

Bonham Carter, Violet, *Winston Churchill as I Knew Him*, London: Weidenfeld & Nicolson, 1955

Bradford, Sarah, George VI, London: Weidenfeld & Nicolson, 1989

Bright, Joan (later Astley), *The Inner Circle: A View Of War At The Top*, Stanhope: The Memoir Club, 2007 edition

Brocklesby, Eddie, "Nan's Kitchen at No. 10", the Serpentine Running Club Newsletter, London: 2003

Buczacki, Stefan, *Churchill and Chartwell: the Untold Story of Churchill's Houses and Gardens*, London: Frances Lincoln, 2007

Buhite, Russell D., *Decisions At Yalta: An Appraisal of Summit Diplomacy*, Delaware: Scholarly Resources Inc., 1984

Bullard, Sir Reader, *The Camels Must Go: An Autobiography*, London: Faber & Faber, 1961

Burns, James MacGregor, *Roosevelt: The Soldier of Freedom, 1940-1945*, New York: Harcourt Brace Jovanovich, 1973

Butcher, Captain Harry C., *My Three Years With Eisenhower*, New York: Simon & Schuster, 1946

Calder, Angus, *The People's War: Britain 1939-1945*, London: Jonathan Cape, 1969

Churchill, Randolph S., *Winston S. Churchill, Volume I, Youth 1874-1900*, London: Heinemann, 1966.

Churchill, Sarah, *A Thread In The Tapestry*, New York: Dodd, Mead & Company, 1967

Churchill, Sarah, *Keep On Dancing*, New York: Coward, McCann & Geoghegan, 1981

Churchill, Winston S., *My Early Life: A Roving Commission*, London: Thornton Butterworth, 1930

Churchill, Winston S., *The Malakand Field Force*, USA: Seven Treasures Publications, 2009

Churchill, Winston S., *The Second World War, volume III, The Grand Alliance*, London: Cassell, 1950

Churchill, Winston S., *The Second World War, volume IV, The Hinge of Fate*, London: Cassell, 1951

Churchill, Winston S., *The Second World War, Volume V, Closing the Ring*, London: Cassell, 1952

Churchill, Winston S., *The Second World War, volume VI, Triumph and Tragedy*, London: Cassell, 1954

Churchill, Winston S., *The Story of the Malakand Field Force: An Episode of Frontier War*, New York: W.W. Norton, 1990 edition

Churchill, Winston S. (jnr.) (ed.), *Never Give In! The Best of Winston Churchill's Speeches*, London: Pimlico, 2003

Clemens, Diane Shaver, *Yalta*, New York: Oxford University Press, 1970

Cohen, Eliot A., *Supreme Command: Soldiers, Statesmen and Leadership in Wartime*, New York: Simon & Schuster, 2002

Colville, John, *The Fringes of Power: Downing Street Diaries 1939-1955*, London: Hodder & Stoughton, 1985

Colville, John, *The Churchillians*, London: Weidenfeld & Nicolson, 1981

Cooke, Alistair, *General Eisenhower and the Military Churchill*, New York: Norton 1970

Cooper, Diana, *Trumpets from the Steep*, London: Rupert Hart-Davis, Soho Square, 1960

Coote, Colin R., *The Other Club*, London, 1971

Cunningham, Lord Admiral of the Fleet, *A Sailor's Odyssey*, New York:

E.P. Dutton, 1951

Danchev, Alex and Todman, Daniel (eds.), *Field Marshal Lord Alanbrooke: War Diaries 1939-1945*, London: Weidenfeld & Nicolson, 2001

Davies, Joseph E., *Mission to Moscow*, New York: Simon & Schuster, 1941

DeWolfe, Mark, (ed.), *Holmes-Laski Letters: The Correspondence of Mr. Justice Holmes and Harold Laski, 1916-1953*, Harvard University Press, 1953

D'Este, Carlo, *Warlord: A Life of Winston Churchill at War, 1874-1945*, New York: Harper, 2008

Dilks, David (ed.), *The Diaries of Sir Alexander Cadogan, OM 1938-1945*, New York: G.P. Putnam's Sons, 1972

Donovan, Robert J., *Conflict and Crisis: The Presidency of Harry S Truman*, New York: W.W. Norton, 1977

Eden, Anthony, Earl of Avon, *Memoirs: The Reckoning*, Boston: Houghton, Mifflin, 1965

Eisenhower, John S. D., *Allies: Pearl Harbor to D-Day*, Cambridge Mass: Da Capo Press, 1982

Elton, G.R., *Political History: Principles and Practice*, New York; Basic Books, 1970

Eubank, Keith, *Summit At Teheran*, New York: William Morrow, 1985

Fernandez-Armesto, Felipe, *Near A Thousand Tables: A History of Food*, New York: 2002

Ferrell, Robert H. (ed.), *Off The Record: The Private Papers of Harry S Truman*, New York: Harper & Row, 1980

Fenby, Jonathan, *Alliance: The Inside Story of How Roosevelt, Stalin and Churchill Won One War and Began Another*, London: Simon & Schuster, 2006

Ferrell, Robert H. (ed.), *Dear Bess: The Letters From Harry To Bess Truman, 1910-1959*, New York: W.W. Norton, 1983

Fields, Alonzo, *My 21 Years in the White House*, New York: Coward-McCann, 1961 edition

Fishman, Jack, *My Darling Clementine: The Story of Lady Churchill*, London: W.H. Allen, 1963

Gardiner, Juliet, *Wartime: Britain 1939-1945*, London: Headline, 2004

Gilbert, Martin, *Churchill and America*, London: The Free Press, 2005

Gilbert, Martin, *Churchill At War: 194-1945, His Finest Hour in*

Photographs, London: Carlton Books Limited, 2003

Gilbert, Martin, *Churchill: A Photographic Portrait*, London: Pimlico, 1999 edition

Gilbert, Martin, *Winston S. Churchill, volume III, 1914-1915*, London: Heinemann, 1971

Gilbert, Martin, *Winston S. Churchill, volume IV, The Stricken World, 1917-1922*, London: Heinemann, 1975

Gilbert, Martin, *Winston S. Churchill, volume V, Prophet of Truth, 1922-1939*, London: Heinemann, 1976

Gilbert, Martin, *Winston S. Churchill, volume VI, Finest Hour 1939-1941*, London: Heinemann, 1983

Gilbert, Martin, *Winston S. Churchill, volume VII, Road to Victory 1941-1945*, London: Heinemann, 1986

Gilbert, Martin, *Winston S. Churchill, volume VIII, Never Despair 1945-1965*, London: Heinemann, 1988

Gilbert, Martin (ed.), *The Churchill War Papers, volume 1, At The Admiralty*, London: Heinemann, 1993

Gilbert, Martin, (ed.), *The Churchill War Papers, volume 2, Never Surrender*, London: Heinemann, 1994

Gilbert, Martin (ed.), *The Churchill War Papers, volume 3, The Ever-Widening War*, London: Heinemann, 2000

Gilbert, Martin, *In Search of Churchill: A Historian's Journey*, London: HarperCollins, 1995

Gilbert, Martin, *Churchill: A Life*, London: Heinemann, 1992

Gilbert, Martin (ed.), *Winston Churchill and Emery Reves: Correspondence, 1937-1964*, Austin, Texas: University of Texas Press, 1977

Goodwin, Doris Kearns, *No Ordinary Time: Franklin and Eleanor Roosevelt – The Home Front in World War II*, New York: Simon & Schuster, 1995

Graebner, Walter, *My Dear Mr. Churchill*, London, Michael Joseph, 1965

Hall, Douglas, *The Book of Churchilliana*, London: New Cavendish Books, 2002

Halle, Kay, ed., *The Irrepressible Churchill*, London: Robson Books, 1985

Halle, Kay, ed., *Winston Churchill On America and Britain*, New York: Walker Publishers, 1970

Harriman, W. Averell and Abel, Elie, *Special Envoy to Churchill and Stalin 1941-1946*, London: Hutchinson 1976

Harvey, John (ed.), *The War Diaries of Oliver Harvey, 1941-1945*, London: Collins, 1978

Hastings, Max, *Finest Years: Churchill as War Lord 1940-1945*, London: Harper Press, 2009

Henderson, Nicholas, *The Private Office Revisited*, London: Profile Books, 2001

Hickman, Tom, *Churchill's Bodyguard: The Authorised Biography of Walter H. Thompson*, London: Headline, 2005

Himmelfarb, Gertrude, *The Moral Imagination: From Edmund Burke to Lionel Trilling*, Chicago: Ivan R. Dee, 2006

Hirshson, Stanley P., *General Patton: A Soldier's Life*, New York: HarperCollins, 2002

Holmes, Richard, *Churchill's Bunker: The Secret Headquarters at the Heart of Britain's Victory*, London: Profile Books, 2009

Hough, Richard, *Winston & Clementine, The Triumph and Tragedies of the Churchills*, New York, Bantam Books, 1990

Howells, Roy, *Churchill's Last Years*, New York: David McKay, 1966

Ismay, General Lord, *Memoirs*, London: Heinemann, 1960

Ive, Ruth, *The Woman Who Censored Churchill*, Stroud: The History Press, 2008

James, Robert Rhodes, *Churchill: A Study in Failure, 1900-1939*, Pelican Books, London, 1973

James, Robert Rhodes, *Anthony Eden*, London: Weidenfeld & Nicolson, 1986

Jenkins, Roy, *Churchill: A Biography*, Basingstoke: Macmillan, 2001

Kass, Leon, M.D., *The Hungry Soul: Eating and the Perfecting of our Nature*, New York: Macmillan, 1994

Kersaudy, Francois, *Churchill et Monaco*, Paris: Editions du Rocher, 2002

Kimball, Warren F., *Forged in War: Roosevelt Churchill and the Second World War*, New York: HarperCollins, 1997

Kimball, Warren F., *Churchill and Roosevelt, The Complete Correspondence*, Princeton: Princeton University Press, 1984

Kramnick, Isaac and Sherman, Barry, *Harold Laski: A Life on the Left*, London: Hamish Hamilton, 1993

Kirkpatrick, Ivone, *The Inner Circle, Memoirs of Ivone Kirkpatrick*, London, Macmillan, 1959

Landermare, Georgina, *Recipes From No. 10: Some Recipes for Discerning Cooks*, London: Collins, 1958

Langworth, Richard M. (ed), *Churchill by Himself: The Life, Times and Opinions of Winston Churchill in his Own Words*, London: Ebury Press 2008

Lash, Joseph P., *Roosevelt and Churchill, 1939-1941*, New York: Norton, 1976

Lavery, Brian, *Churchill Goes To War: Winston's Wartime Journeys*, Annapolis: Naval Institute Press, 2007

Layton, Elizabeth (later Nel), *Mr. Churchill's Secretary*, New York: Coward McCann, 1958

Leasor, James, *War At The Top: based on the experiences of General Sir Leslie Hollis*, London: Michael Joseph, 1959

Loewenheim, Francis L., Langley, Harold D., and Jonas, Manfred, (eds.) *Roosevelt and Churchill: Their Secret Wartime Correspondence*, London, 1975

Lunghi, Hugh, "A Tribute to Sir Winston Churchill", Blenheim Palace, transcript of talk, 1 March 1997

Mander, Danny, *Winston Churchill's Bodyguard, The Teheran conference 1943, A multimedia autobiographical story*, California: MMPublishing, 2003

McCullough, David, *Truman*, New York: Simon & Schuster, 1992

McGowan, Norman, *My Years With Churchill*, New York: British Book Centre, 1958

McJimsey, George, *Harry Hopkins: Ally of the Poor and Defender of Democracy*, Cambridge, Mass.: Harvard University Press, 1987

Macmillan, Harold, *The Past Masters: Politics and Politicians 1906-1939*, London: Macmillan, 1975

Macmillan, *Tides of Fortune*, London: Macmillan, 1969

Manchester, William, *The Last Lion: Winston Spencer Churchill, Alone 1932-1940*, Boston: Little, Brown, 1988

Manchester, William, *The Last Lion: Winston Spencer Churchill, Visions of Glory 1874-1932*, Boston: Little, Brown, 1983

Martin, John, *Downing Street: The War Years*, London: Trafalgar Square, 1992

Martin, Ralph G., *Lady Randolph Churchill, 1854-1895*, London: Cassell, 1969

Mayle, Paul D., *Eureka Summit: Agreement in Principle and the Big

Three at Tehran, 1943, Newark, New Jersey: University of Delaware Press, 1987

Mee, Charles, Jr., *Meeting at Potsdam*, New York, 1975

Moir, Phyllis, *I Was Churchill's Private Secretary*, New York: Wilfred Funk, 1941

Morton, H.V., *Atlantic Meeting*, London: Methuen, 1946 ed.

Murray, Edmund, *I Was Churchill's Bodyguard*, London: W.H. Allen, 1987

Montague Browne, Anthony, *Long Sunset, Memoirs of Winston Churchill's Last Private Secretary*, London: Cassell, 1995

Moran, Lord, *Winston Churchill: The Struggle for Survival, 1940-1965*, London: Heron Books, 1966

Nasaw, David, *The Chief: The Life of William Randolph Hearst*, Boston: Houghton Mifflin Company, 2000

Nelson, James (ed.), *General Eisenhower on the Military Churchill: a conversation with Alistair Cooke*, New York: Norton, 1970

Nesbitt, Henrietta, *White House Diary*, New York: Doubleday, 1948

Nicolson, Nigel (ed.), *Diaries & Letters of Harold Nicolson, volume II, The War Years 1939-1945*, New York: Atheneum 1967

Nicolson, Juliet, *The Perfect Summer, Dancing Into Shadow in 1911*, London: John Murray, 2006

Norwich, John Julius (ed.), *The Duff Cooper Diaries 1915-1951*, London: Weidenfeld & Nicolson, 2005

Pawle, Gerald, *The War and Colonel Warden*, New York: Alfred A. Knopf, 1964

Pollock, John, *Kitchener: Architect of Victory, Artisan of Peace*, New York: Carroll & Graf, 2001

Reilly, Michael F. and Slocum, *William J., Reilly of the White House*, New York: Simon & Schuster, 1947

Rees, Laurence, *WW II, Behind Closed Doors: Stalin, the Nazis and the West*, New York, Pantheon Books, 2008

Reilly, Michael F., (as told to William J. Slocum), *Reilly of the White House*, New York 1947

Reynolds, David, *Summits: Six Meetings that Shaped the Twentieth Century*, Allen Lane: London, 2007

Richardson, Charles, *From Churchill's Secret Circle to the BBC: A Biography of Lieutenant General Sir Ian Jacob*, London: Brassey's, 1991

Roberts, Andrew, *Eminent Churchillians*, London: Weidenfeld & Nicolson, 1994

Roberts, Andrew, *The Holy Fox: A Life of Lord Halifax*, Basingstoke: Macmillan 1992 edition

Roberts, Andrew, *Masters and Commanders: How Roosevelt, Churchill, Marshall and Alanbrooke Won the War in the West*, London: Allen Lane, 2008

Rose, Kenneth, Elusive Rothschild: *The Life of Victor, Third Baron*, London, Weidenfeld & Nicolson, 2003

Rose, Norman (ed.), *Baffy: The Diaries of Blanche Dugdale, 1936-47*, London: Vallentine Mitchell, 1973

Rysavy, François, *A Treasury of White House Cooking*, New York: J.P. Putnam's Sons, 1972 edition.

Sebag Montefiore, Simon, *Stalin: The Court of the Red Tsar*, London, Weidenfeld & Nicolson

Sherwood, Robert E., *Roosevelt and Hopkins: An Intimate History*, New York: Harper & Sons, 1948

Skidelsky, Robert, *John Maynard Keynes, volume two, The Economist as Saviour, 1920-1937*, London: Macmillan, 1992

Skidelsky, Robert, *John Maynard Keynes, volume three, Fighting for Britain 1937-1946*, London: Macmillan, 2000

Smith, Jean Edward, *FDR*, New York: Random House, 2007

Soames, Mary, *Clementine Churchill*, London: Doubleday, 2002

Soames, Mary (ed.), *Speaking for Themselves: The Personal Letters of Winston and Clementine Churchill*, London: Black Swan Books, 1999

Stettinius, Edward R., *Roosevelt and the Russians: The Yalta Conference*, New York: Doubleday, 1949

Truman, Harry S, *Memoirs, volume one, Year of Decisions*, New York: Doubleday 1955

Tugwell, Rexford G., *The Democratic Roosevelt*, Baltimore: Penguin Press, 1969

Ulam, Adam B., *Stalin: The Man And His Era*, New York: Viking Press, 1973

Vines, C.M., *A Little Nut-Brown Man, My Three Years with Lord Beaverbrook*, London: Leslie Frewin, 1968

West, Bruce, *The Man Who Flew Churchill*, Toronto: McGraw-Hill, 1975

Wheeler-Bennett, Sir John (ed.), *Action This Day: Working With Churchill*, London: Macmillan, 1968

Wilson, A. N., *After The Victorians*, London: Arrow, 2006

Wilson, Theodore, *The First Summit: Roosevelt and Churchill at Placentia Bay 1941*, Kansas: University of Kansas Press, 1991 revised edition.

Whitcomb, John and Claire, *Real Life at the White House: Two Hundred Years of Daily Life at America's Most Famous Residence*, New York: Routledge, 2002

Wingfield-Stratford, Esmé, *Churchill: The Making of a Hero*, London: Victor Gollancz, 1942

Wyatt, Woodrow, *To The Point*, London: Weidenfeld & Nicolson, 1981

~ꝗ● PICTURE CREDITS ●ꝗ~

p2. *Downing Street dining room*
  Photo by Fox Photos/Hulton Archive/Getty Images
p6. *Digesting the India bill*
  Reproduced with kind permission of Claridges, London and of Curtis
  Brown, London on behalf of the Estate of Sir Winston Churchill, and
  the Master, Fellows and Scholars of Churchill College, Cambridge.
  Copyright © Winston S. Churchill.
p8. *A reinforced dining room fit for the king*
  Courtesy of Downing Street
p10. *Strategy al fresco*
  Courtesy of the Trustees of the Imperial War Museum.
p18. *The Pinafore Room: home of the Other Club*
  © English Heritage NMR
p23. *Randolph's 21st birthday, 1932*
  Reproduced with permission of Curtis Brown, London on behalf
  of the Estate of Sir Winston Churchill, and the Master, Fellows and
  Scholars of Churchill College, Cambridge. Copyright © Winston S.
  Churchill.
p26. *Churchill's favourite stage: the dining room at Chartwell*
  © NTPL/Andreas von Einsiedel
p26. *Dining at Chartwell, 1928*
  © NTPL
p29. *Chartwell garden party and Mrs. Churchill's prudence*
  Reproduced with permission of Curtis Brown, London on behalf
  of the Estate of Sir Winston Churchill, and the Master, Fellows and
  Scholars of Churchill College, Cambridge. Copyright © Winston S.
  Churchill.
p31. *Best to look over the bills*
  Reproduced with permission of Curtis Brown, London on behalf
  of the Estate of Sir Winston Churchill, and the Master, Fellows and

Scholars of Churchill College, Cambridge. Copyright © Winston S. Churchill.

p33. *Churchill and British generals, Alan Brooke, Montgomery and Ismay, plus Randolph, picnic in the desert, Tripoli, 1943*
Courtesy of the Trustees of the Imperial War Museum.

p33. *Churchill and American generals Eisenhower and Patton, picnic lunch in northwestern Europe*
Courtesy of the Trustees of the Imperial War Museum.

p34. *Tea with RAF pilots, September 1941*
Courtesy of the Trustees of the Imperial War Museum.

p34. *Picnic on the hustings, Churchill's daughter, Sarah, pouring tea, 1945*
NI Syndication

p35. *Picnic at Marrakesh 1944*
Estate of John Colville

p42. *The Prime Minister's railway dining car*
© NMSI/Science Museum

p46. *President's dinner for the Prime Minister aboard the* Augusta, *August 1941; and guests*
Courtesy of the Franklin D. Roosevelt Presidential Library, Hyde Park.

p.50 *Churchill reciprocates, 10 August 1941*
www.nationalarchives.gov.uk/doc/open-government-licence/.Crown copyright.

p52. *Churchill and the Presidential gift boxes for every British seaman*
Courtesy of the Trustees of the Imperial War Museum.

p54. *Celebrating the Alliance*
Courtesy of Library of Congress

p55. *Churchill and Soviet Ambassador Maisky's tête-à-tête: lunch at the Soviet embassy, London, August 1941*
Getty Images

p57. *Chequers dining room*
Mark Fiennes photograph

p67. *BOAC menu, on flight to Washington, June 1954*
Courtesy of Mullock's Auctioneers, Shropshire

p68. *The Churchills and Tango at Chartwell, 1933*
© NTPL/Derrick E. Witty

p87. *New Allies. With Stalin, Moscow, 14 August 1942*
© Mirrorpix

p92. *Menu for the Prime Minsiter, Turkey, January 1943*

Reproduced with permission of Curtis Brown, London on behalf of the Broadwater Collection.

p93. *Dining with Turkish President Inonu in his private railway carriage, January 1943*
© British Pathé

p100. *Ready for the dinner guests at the British legation*
Churchill Archive Centre: from an original held by the British embassy in Teheran. Crown copyright.

p101. *Make a wish, 69th birthday*
Churchill Archive Centre: from an original held by the British embassy in Teheran. Crown copyright.

p102. *The Big Three, dining together for the first time, 1943*
© Mirrorpix

p108. *After dinner tête-à-tête*
© Bettmann/CORBI

p112. *Vorontsov Palace: Churchill's villa*
Courtesy of the Trustees of the Imperial War Museum.

p115. *Livadia Palace: Roosevelt's villa and meeting room*
Courtesy of the Trustees of the Imperial War Museum.

p120. *Dinner menu at Yalta, the Prime Minister as host*
Courtesy of the estate of Charles E. Bohlen.

p121. *The Big Three at dinner*
© Bettmann/CORBIS

p122. *Stalin carves up the Nazi bird, Allies looking on*

p128. *Welcome to my villa: Churchill greets Truman and Stalin*
© ullstein bild

p131. *The Big Three and supporting staffs, at the Cecilienhof*
© Bettmann/CORBIS

p138. *Churchill dinner, Potsdam. Menu, music, wines, seating chart*
Reproduced with permission of Curtis Brown, London on behalf of the Estate of Sir Winston Churchill, and the Master, Fellows and Scholars of Churchill College, Cambridge. Copyright © Winston S. Churchill.

p147. *En route to Fulton with President Truman*
Getty Images

p150. *Churchill's 79th birthday cake*
Popperfoto/Getty Images

p151. *Mid-Ocean Club, Bermuda*
Gamma-Keystone/Getty Images

p153. *The Big Two and the French Premier, Laniel*

Time & Life Pictures/Getty Images

p154. *Menu for the Bermudians' dinner honouring the British Delegation*
©Bermuda Archives

p155. *Churchill alone, Bermuda*
Time & Life Pictures/Getty Images

p160. *Churchill at dinner, cartoon by Vicky*
Reproduced with permission of Curtis Brown, London on behalf of the Estate of Sir Winston Churchill, and the Master, Fellows and Scholars of Churchill College, Cambridge. Copyright © Winston S. Churchill.

p162. *Bill of fare, Paris Ritz 1914*
Reproduced with permission of Curtis Brown, London on behalf of the Estate of Sir Winston Churchill, and the Master, Fellows and Scholars of Churchill College, Cambridge. Copyright © Winston S. Churchill.

p171. *Churchill scoops caviar, lunch at Yalta*
Courtesy of the estate of Charles E. Bohlen.

p183. *Pop!*
©Daily Mail/Solo Syndication. John Musgrave-Wood, Daily Mail, 30 November 1957, courtesy of the British Cartoon Archive, University of Kent, www.cartoons.ac.uk

p185. *A victory toast with the Soviet Ambassador Gusev, May 1945*
Courtesy of the Trustees of the Imperial War Museum.

pp186 & 187. *Odette Pol Roger with Churchill & Commemorative bottle*
© Champagne Pol Roger

p189. *Cornucopia at 86*
Getty Images

p191. *A weak whisky and soda at Mansion House*
Courtesy of the Trustees of the Imperial War Museum.

p193. *Victory symbol*
©Topham Picturepoint/TopFoto.co.uk

p196. *Don't want to spoil the boy*
Courtesy of Fox Tobacconists, St James's, London. Reproduced with permission of Curtis Brown, London on behalf of the Estate of Sir Winston Churchill, and the Master, Fellows and Scholars of Churchill College, Cambridge. Copyright © Winston S. Churchill.

p197. *Firing up*
© ullstein bild

p198. *Merci for the light, at Cherbourg, 1944*

© Hulton-Deutsch Collection/CORBIS

p199. *Some of my favourite things from Fox Cigar Shop*
  Courtesy of Fox Tobacconists, St James's, London.

p208. *Some more please*!
  Reproduced with permission of Curtis Brown, London, on behalf of
  the Estate of Winston Churchill, and the Master, Fellows and Scholars
  of Churchill College, Cambridge. Copyright © Winston S. Churchill

p210. *Labels for game from the King*
  Reproduced with permission of Curtis Brown, London, on behalf of
  the Estate of Winston Churchill, and the Master, Fellows and Scholars
  of Churchill College, Cambridge. Copyright © Winston S. Churchill.

p213. *"Are you getting enough to eat?"*
  Courtesy of the Trustees of the Imperial War Museum.

P219. *Between premierships, South of France, 1948*
  Reproduced with permission of Curtis Brown, London, on behalf of
  the Estate of Winston Churchill, and the Master, Fellows and Scholars
  of Churchill College, Cambridge. Copyright © Winston S. Churchill.

~ೞಿ ACKNOWLEDGEMENTS ೞಿ~

Like all students of Churchill, I am deeply indebted to the scholarship of Sir Martin Gilbert. Sir Martin's plate was already overflowing, so I am doubly grateful to him for the patience with which he offered suggestions to a fledgling author of whom many academics as distinguished as Sir Martin, if such there be, would have taken little notice.

Lady Williams, née Jane Portal, who worked with Churchill from 1949 to 1955, has shared some of her memories of the Prime Minister. Her friendship has become one of my most treasured results of writing this book. Andrew Roberts endorsed the idea for this book from the beginning and has been a staunch friend throughout the research and writing, providing encouragement that only a star historian can provide a neophyte writer. And he introduced me to my agent, Georgina Capel.

Without the encouragement and on-going guidance of Gertrude Himmelfarb and Stuart Proffitt I would not have undertaken this project. Without the help of many people I would not have been able to complete it. Alan

Packwood and the staff at the Churchill Archives, to whom Churchill scholars across the world owe so much, were obliging in the extreme. Phil Reed, Director of the Churchill Museum and Cabinet War Rooms during most of the writing of this book, made many useful suggestions and provided wonderfully wide-ranging conversations. Hugh Lunghi, one of Churchill's Russian-language interpreters during the war, shared many of his recollections with me in his most charming manner.

Graham Stewart contributed important suggestions for improving the text. Roger Moorhouse, an historian in his own right, was a most creative seeker of images, and helped with much-needed moral support and humour. Ray Wells of *The Sunday Times* paved the way for original photography while Francesco Guidicini shot the cigar photos at the Fox Churchill Museum, which kindly granted access to its hoard of Churchill memorabilia. Leon Aron, a Russian Scholar, was encouraging and most helpful with his Russian contacts and his translation of the Russian menus.

Andrew Porter of the *Telegraph* provided an important document at a key moment. David Bell was generous with his introductions in Bermuda. Neil Crompton, then in the British Embassy in Washington, put me in touch with Sir Geoffrey Adams. Sir Geoffrey, then the British Ambassador in Teheran, arranged access to the Embassy's treasure trove of photographs of the Teheran Conference and Lady Adams was kind enough to photograph for me the British Embassy dining room as it is today.

Sue Sutton's research skills uncovered many treasures in the Churchill Archives. Leyre Gonzalez deployed her considerable organisational skills to keep the daily flow of information in accessible order, and Rebecca Driscoll helped to solve the inevitable headaches that computers willfully choose to create. Shan Vahidy calmly stepped in at a critical moment to foil a computer attack on the endnotes. The Hudson Institute provided important support.

They have all done their best but I am of course responsible for any remaining errors.

~୬ INDEX ୬~

INDEX

In case of difficulty in purchasing any Short Books
title through normal channels, please contact
BOOKPOST Tel: 01624 836000
Fax: 01624 837033
email: bookshop@enterprise.net
www.bookpost.co.uk
Please quote ref. 'Short Books'